An Astrological Guide
to Understanding Your Child

There are so many different approaches to educating and rearing children. We now seem to have more choices than ever in guiding their future. Knowing whether they will feel confident learning at their own pace or will need a more structured learning environment can make the difference in how successful they feel in school. Each child also has special talents—but how do we know which talents to support? Where can we find insights into the shy, retiring child that will tell us which talents would be more beneficially developed?

With astrology, we can more easily identify these talents. We can also intelligently choose the best type of learning system for a child. By looking at a child's natal chart we are able to discover their natural approach to learning and communication.

By using astrology to understand children we have a tremendous opportunity to help them learn about living in harmony with the Self and with others. This opens them to their optimum potentials. And what better time is there to begin than at the beginning?

About the Author

An internationally renowned astrologer, author, and teacher, Gloria Star has been a professional astrologer for over two decades. She has written the *Sun Sign Book* for Llewellyn since 1990, and has been a contributing author of the *Moon Sign Book* since 1995. She is the author of *Astrology: Woman to Woman* (Llewellyn, 1999). She also edited and coauthored the book *Astrology for Women: Roles and Relationships* (Llewellyn, 1997). Her astrological computer software, *Woman to Woman*, was released by Matrix software in 1997. She has contributed to two anthologies: *Houses: Power Places in the Horoscope* (Llewellyn, 1990) and *How to Manage the Astrology of Crisis* (Llewellyn, 1993). Ms. Star is also a regular columnist for *The Mountain Astrologer* magazine.

Listed in *Who's Who of American Women* and *Who's Who in the East*, Ms. Star is active within the astrological community where she has been honored as a nominee for the prestigious Regulus Award. She has served on the faculty of the United Astrology Congress (UAC) since its inception in 1986, and has lectured for groups and conferences throughout the United States and abroad. Ms. Star is a member of the Advisory Board for the National Council for Geocosmic Research (NCGR), and also served on the Steering Committee for the Association for Astrological Networking (AFAN).

To Write to the Author

If you wish to contact the author or would like more information about this book, please write to the author in care of Llewellyn Worldwide and we will forward your request. Both the author and publisher appreciate hearing from you and learning of your enjoyment of this book and how it has helped you. Llewellyn Worldwide cannot guarantee that every letter written to the author can be answered, but all will be forwarded. Please write to:

Gloria Star
℅ Llewellyn Worldwide
P.O. Box 64383, Dept. 1-56718-649-1
St. Paul, MN 55164-0383, U.S.A.
Please enclose a self-addressed stamped envelope for reply,
or $1.00 to cover costs. If outside U.S.A., enclose
international postal reply coupon.

Many of Llewellyn's authors have websites with additional information and resources. For more information, please visit our website at http://www.llewellyn.com.

A Handbook for Parents

Astrology & Your Child

Gloria Star

2000
Llewellyn Publications
St. Paul, Minnesota 55164-0383, U.S.A.

First Edition
First Printing, 2000

Book design and editing by Joanna Willis
Cover design by Lisa Novak
Art and astrological glyphs designed by Richard Roess

All horoscope charts used in this book were generated using WinStar © Matrix Software.

Library of Congress Cataloging-in-Publication Data
Star, Gloria, 1948–
   Astrology & your child: a handbook for parents / Gloria Star.
      p. cm.
   Includes bibliographical references.
   ISBN 1-56718-649-1
   1. Astrology and child development. I. Title: Astrology and your child. II. Title.

BF1729.C43 S68 2000
133.5'86491—dc21

00-060662

Llewellyn Worldwide does not participate in, endorse, or have any authority or responsibility concerning private business transactions between our authors and the public.
  All mail addressed to the author is forwarded but the publisher cannot, unless specifically instructed by the author, give out an address or phone number.

Llewellyn Publications
A Division of Llewellyn Worldwide, Ltd.
P.O. Box 64383, Dept. 1-56718-649-1
St. Paul, MN 55164-0383, U.S.A.
www.llewellyn.com

Printed in the United States of America

Contents

Acknowledgments

You're witnessing a rebirth! Since my original entry into the world of book-writing, my life has completely transformed (well, you'd expect that after fifteen years). This book is a rebirth of my first effort, but includes so much more information. My thanks goes first to my clients and students whose questions, comments, and interest helped shape the current state of this work. To my son, Chris, and husband, Richard—thank you for not complaining when you've lost me to long hours at the computer while I've written and you've fended for yourselves.

Then, there's a debt of gratitude from the bottom of my heart for all the people at Llewellyn who've been like family over the years. In this particular effort, thanks to Nancy Mostad, Llewellyn visionary, and to Joanna Willis, who has been a wonderful editor. My deepest thanks to the guiding lights of this family, Carl and Sandra Weschcke, whose encouragement and support mean so much. There's not enough room to thank my many teachers and mentors, but I'd like to extend a special thanks to Noel Tyl for urging me to continue to write. And to my colleagues, from whom I have continually learned, thanks for your insights and dedication to the great work of astrology.

Preface to
Astrology & Your Child

It does not seem so long ago when I sat down to write *Optimum Child*, but fifteen years has passed since the manuscript was written. Since that time, my life has undergone a series of changes and, oh, I've learned so much! In the process I have grown, and so have my own kids! I was simply delighted when my friends at Llewellyn suggested I revisit the material and determine whether or not I wanted to revitalize it. And revitalize, I have! But let me tell you a secret—it's been an internal, personal revision also, because rereading and working with the material has kindled memories of thousands of consultation sessions, just as many stories, and phenomenal shifts in the way I see these symbols. Astrology evolves because life is an evolutionary process. It was time to share my own evolution in thinking about developmental astrology.

Nothing has changed my feeling and belief that astrological insights are the most amazing gift we have to help us rear the earth's children. I feel that the time has come for the children to be embraced for the powerful beings that they are, and as parents, teachers, and astrologers, our hearts must be open to their questions and yearnings. Coupled with our slowly increasing wisdom, we—the parents, teachers, and counselors—can learn from the symbols of a child's astrological chart the magic and mystery of each child. In some ways, a child's chart is like a newly planted garden in early spring: the potential is there, the crops are chosen, but the garden needs care, light, water, and food to become what it can be.

For those of you who are familiar with the original text, you'll find it here. I have endeavored to leave as much as possible intact. However, there is so much more. Everything is more carefully and thoroughly defined, the aspects are clearly delineated, and I threw in a sprinkling of love for the work just to make sure it would take on a life of its own. I hope you enjoy this rendering of what I see as the astrology of childhood. Remember your own childhood. It's here in these pages. Find your own questions, too, and hopefully you can take it much further than these few pages.

I've never really seen myself as an authority on astrology. I like to think of myself as the person who steps inside the doorway and turns on the light. Astrology is a living science and art. I hope it beautifully illuminates every room in your life! Enjoy the journey!

Introduction

Why Astrology?

We all begin our lives in the same way: as small infants growing rapidly into children. At the moment we are born, we begin to express ourselves, experience our needs, and interact with our environment.

This moment is precious, and, for astrologers, important. For it is at the moment of that first breath, when we become dependent upon our physical environment to sustain our lives, that we set the astrological pattern known as the horoscope. The word *horoscope*, which has come to refer to the circular chart used in astrology, originally meant "to look at the hour." Over the years, I've been asked by countless parents why astrologers do not use the chart of conception. In many ways, there's a practical reason: determining the moment of conception is virtually impossible! However, as medical technology advances, I have a suspicion that there will be a time when we will be capable of pinpointing the moment of conception. Even then, conception is only the promise of life. Life for an individual begins when interaction with and dependency upon the environment occurs. This is the birth of the autonomous child—separate from the mother and committed to life in a physical form upon the physical plane.

Humankind has used the tool of astrology for thousands of years, yet our overall understanding of its symbols continues to expand as we gain a deeper understanding of what it means to be human. In this book, we will apply the astrological symbology specifically to children. A child's expression of the Self[1] is not yet mature, and the astro-logical symbols must be interpreted with this in mind. Just as psychologists have put forth theories dealing specifically with the behavior and developmental stages of chil-dren, astrologers must also redefine their usual adult focus when dealing with children.

The study of human psychology has revealed clearly defined developmental cycles and patterns of growth. Many of these are tied to physical development. In the young teen, for example, the explosion of hormones in the body creates tremendous emo-tional upheaval. This causes change in the child's level of awareness as the expression of the Self alters.

We also find different energies unfolding at different ages in astrology. These are the astrological cycles, which can be clocked by the movement of the planets. These cycles are specific for each individual, although there are some cycles which mark pas-sages for each of us at either generational or common developmental stages.

If you are new to the study of astrology, you may still have some questions about how a planet millions of miles away can have any significant effect upon your life. I struggled with this concept when I began my study of astrology, only to find that my approach to the question made it difficult to answer.

What we see in the astrological chart is a map of the heavens relative to the Earth at the time of birth. This becomes the map of our personal universe for the course of a lifetime. It symbolizes the lessons we need to learn for the growth of our souls, the special needs we have as individuals, and indicates our potential for development.

The planets continue their revolutions around the Sun, but for that special moment of birth we draw a map of the heavens and ask ourselves, "What does this mean? How do I fit into the scheme of the universe? Can this chart tell me something about who I am?" We are not asking, "What are the planets forcing me to do?" Rather, we are studying a symbolic pattern of the greater universe in order to gain some insights into our own personal universe. As astrologer Grant Lewi often said, "The planets do not compel, they impel."

Since we can study this map of the psyche, why not study it for the child soon after birth? Why not take advantage of its information to help the child of any age? Most people wait until adulthood to ask themselves these crucial questions of identity. Gen-

---

[1]When capitalized, *Self* refers to all aspects of a person, including those not evident on the physical plane (the Higher Self). When lower-cased, *self* refers to the personality currently being projected by the Higher Self.

erally we don't have sufficient consciousness to truly understand the importance of knowing who we are until adulthood. Many of us facing the challenges of parenthood have probably wondered why each child did not come with a handbook. The simple fact is that there is a guide!

We—the parents, therapists, teachers, and guides of the world's children—have a fabulous guidepost which symbolically indicates a child's physical, mental, emotional, and spiritual needs. This map, called the horoscope, can illuminate our ability to understand each child, and can help the child know herself better. It is important to allow a child to be who she really is, and I find astrology to be an excellent tool toward this end.

The birth chart, or *natal horoscope*, can give insights into the physical areas of the body which tend to be more easily stressed and which may require additional nourishment. This information has helped many of my clients with small infants help their children grow physically stronger. We can determine which areas indicate particular emotional dilemmas and vulnerabilities. We can see also how the child is likely to perceive the parents, and gain insight into the types of subconscious conditioning which would be most beneficial for the child.

In truth, having this wealth of information is only the beginning. Information is power, and must be used properly if it is to help instead of hurt. Parents must exercise great responsibility in using astrological information with their children so that each child's highest needs will truly be served.

Most parents I know are fine people who are genuinely interested in doing the best things they can for their children. Granted, parents have their own concerns and problems, but the ones who care find ways to direct positive energy to their children. They will avoid the ever-present temptation to bend the child completely over to their world view, rather than letting her experience her own unique way of being.

As a child you probably had secret wishes, but felt that expressing them might create difficulty with your parents. I talked with a woman recently who shared with me her childhood desire to be a dancer. She fondly recalled the times she would hear music in her head and dance in her backyard until she was physically exhausted.

Her parents stressed practicality above all else. The children were instructed to obey the rules, do their homework, learn what school had to teach them, and focus on "realistic expectations." While encouraged to study subjects which would provide financial security, she leaned toward a career in teaching. Her parents were supportive of this idea, because they felt it would help her be more "sensible."

She studied English literature in college and eventually became a professor. She had her first consultation with me when she was in her early forties. I mentioned that her chart indicated a love of dancing and music. With tear-glazed eyes she asked me, "Do you think it would be okay to begin studying dance at my age?"

She has now studied dance for three years. She does not expect to become a prima ballerina, but simply wants to fulfill a desire she felt was taboo in her family situation. I encourage her dancing, since I know it will aid in the opening of her creative awareness and give her a greater sense of wholeness. What if her parents had supported this particular inclination within their young daughter? Would she be a happier, more fulfilled person now?

One thing to keep in mind when using astrology with children is that we are dealing with a process of growth. I am not an event-oriented astrologer, but see myself as a "process aware" astrologer. We must take care to allow each child to grow into his unique expression of the Self. We will, of course, condition the child according to our lifestyles and philosophical systems. However, by using a child's chart in coordination with the changes you see in him, you can make a world of difference. Remember that as children develop willpower they can choose their responses to different situations and energies. We would do well to encourage this and learn to listen to the child.

There are so many different approaches to educating and rearing children. We now seem to have more choices than ever before in guiding a child's future. Each child has special talents—but how do we know which talents to support in the child? Where can we find insights into the shy, retiring child that will tell us which talents would be more beneficially developed? With astrology, we can more easily identify these talents.

An individual's astrological chart also indicates learning styles, and knowing whether a child will feel confident learning at her own pace or will need a more structured learning environment can make a difference in her feelings of success in school. With astrology, we can intelligently choose the best type of learning system for a child. The astrological chart indicates each child's natural approach to learning and communication, thereby aiding the parent in choosing the most suitable educational system for her.

I have found astrology to be a wonderful application of Divine Knowledge. We gain a broadened sense of ourselves with this ancient tool, and a more objective perspective of our own identities. In using astrology to understand children, we have a tremendous opportunity to help them learn about living in harmony with the Self and with others. This opens the child to his optimum potentials. And what better time is there to begin than at the beginning?

Rudimentary Principles of Astrology and the Houses

The fundamental principles of astrology are really quite simple, yet I have always been amazed at the number of students who overlook these basic concepts in their eagerness to grasp the more complex issues. The possibility that astrology can offer a glimpse into the future entices most students to try to speed through the basics to get to the juiciness of predicting. But unfortunately, without the basics, all is lost! When the student becomes sufficiently confused, he will either humbly decide to return to the basics or abandon the study of astrology altogether. Astrology is a complex language, and if explored with care and the intention of creating a solid foundation, it is a language which describes life at its fullest.

If you are well-versed in the basics of astrology, you may consider the following material a review. If you are just beginning to study this cosmic science, these fundamental principles will be the foundation of your understanding. These concepts represent the framework, and, as you study astrology over time, you'll add to that framework until you have a fully formed understanding.

An Accurate Birth Chart

In order to make the best use of the information in this book, you must have a child's natal horoscope. The astrological birth chart, or natal horoscope, is calculated using the precise time (hour and minute), date, and place of birth. Although we will not cover the mathematics involved in calculating the chart, I strongly suggest that you have an accurately calculated birth chart. If you are interested in learning the math, you will find references for further reading in the bibliography at the end of this book. Any professional astrologer can provide you with a chart, or, if you have a computer and computation software, you can chart the horoscope yourself. In most towns, libraries have programs on their computers that calculate charts, and access to this information is also available via the Internet. Metaphysical bookstores frequently offer chart calculation services, or you may choose to have your chart calculated through a mail-order computer service. For having purchased *Astrology & Your Child*, please see the back of this book to obtain a natal chart at no cost from Llewellyn Worldwide.

Correct birth times are necessary. Since they are not always paying attention to the clock during delivery, mothers may not be reliable sources for this information. (Being an astrologer, on the other hand, I was watching the clock very closely during the birthing of my children!) Generally, a birth certificate will indicate the time of birth. When requesting a birth certificate from vital records bureaus, be sure to ask for the *long form birth certificate*, since many states offer a shorter version of the birth certificate which does not include the time of birth. If a birth certificate cannot be found, hospital records are often available.

Orientation to the Chart Wheel

The chart itself is a circle with a variety of symbols placed within and around it. In Western astrology, we draw the map of the chart on a circular wheel. The wheel itself is symbolic, because the circle is a perfect structure with no beginning and no end. The circle is an ancient symbol, and is often associated with the concept of the human spirit. The chart itself represents the whole person.

Illustration 1 shows an empty astrological chart. This chart is divided into twelve segments called houses, which are numbered counterclockwise from one to twelve. The houses are indicators of the different facets of the individual—the environments, persons, activities, and experiences in our lives.

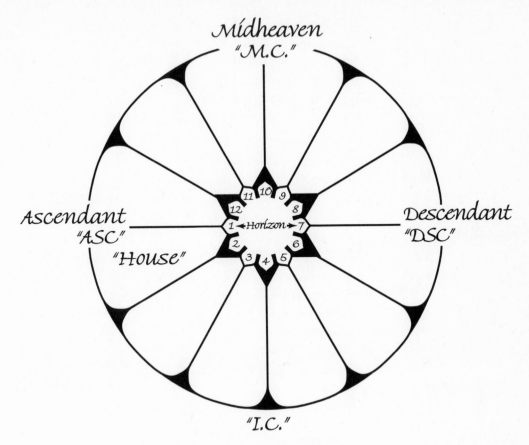

Illustration 1. The Wheel.

Mentally divide the chart in Illustration 1 into upper and lower halves. The axis dividing the two halves represents the *horizon*. On the left you will see the cusp, or dividing line, of the 1st House. This house cusp is called the Ascendant (ASC). Directly opposite the Ascendant is the cusp of the 7th House, which is called the Descendant (DSC). At the top of the chart you will find the cusp of the 10th House. This cusp is called the Midheaven, and is often abbreviated MC for the Latin phrase *Medium Coeli*. Opposing the Midheaven is the IC (*Imum Coeli*). These four house cusps are referred to as the *angles* in the astrological chart, and are sensitive points. They also denote the four points of the compass—the MC is South, the IC is North, the ASC is East, and the DSC is West. The directions are reversed from our usual view of a map because this is a map of our place in the heavens, not on the Earth.

The symbols for the planets, the Sun, and the Moon are placed within the houses. (The planets are discussed in chapter 3.) These represent the energies we experience and express in our lives. Energy is an extremely important concept in the study of astrology. We are each energy under the direction of consciousness. Each planetary energy symbolizes different aspects of the Self and offers us insights into our personal identity. The planets are placed within the houses according to their positions in the heavens at the time of our birth. Houses which contain planets indicate areas in our lives which will receive more of our attention and energy.

The twelve signs of the zodiac symbolize particular characteristics, qualities, and traits. Planets appear in different signs; therefore, a planet will energize the qualities of the sign in which it is placed. (The signs are fully described in chapter 2.) Much attention has been given to the signs, especially in "Sun Sign" newspaper and magazine columns. Although this widespread practice has brought the idea of astrology to many people, Sun Sign astrology is a very simplistic approach to a complex subject. There is accuracy in Sun Sign astrology, but it is limited. I have written Sun Sign material for many years, and there is definitely real astrology involved in this work. Because most people can relate to their Sun signs, this does provide a illumined doorway into the potentials of astrology. But when you study the complete horoscope of an individual, you're studying the Sun's sign along with other factors in the chart. The Sun only describes the ego self—why stop there?

You will also note the symbols for the signs at the cusps of each house. These signs amplify the meaning of the house by giving particular characteristics to that area signified by the house. For example, Aries on the cusp of the 2nd House would give Aries qualities to the energy present in the 2nd House.

Basically, the planets indicate *what* the energy is, the signs show *how* the energy manifests itself, and the houses identify *where* the energy is expressed in an individual's life. My favorite metaphor is to think of the Sun, Moon, and planets as the actors in your personal drama and consider the signs to represent the roles the actors are playing, the costumes they wear, and the props they're carrying about. The houses represent the setting and scene of the drama. Astrologers also study the interaction of the factors in the chart using geometric relationships called *aspects*. *Aspect patterns*, which identify themes in the birth chart, are also important and help to fine-tune certain issues and personality characteristics.

I suggest that students learn astrology using both intellect and intuition, since both are required to fully delineate a chart. The intellectual part requires a certain amount

GLYPH	SIGN	GLYPH	PLANET
♈	Aries	☽	Moon
♉	Taurus	☉	Sun
♊	Gemini	☿	Mercury
♋	Cancer	♀	Venus
♌	Leo	♂	Mars
♍	Virgo	♃	Jupiter
♎	Libra	♄	Saturn
♏	Scorpio	♅	Uranus
♐	Sagittarius	♆	Neptune
♑	Capricorn	♇	Pluto
♒	Aquarius		
♓	Pisces		

Table 1. Glyphs.

of memory work, such as learning the basic meanings of the houses, planets, and signs. To activate your intuitive understanding, try meditating on the astrological symbols (see Table 1). A good way to begin is by drawing one symbol on a piece of paper. Study the symbol; impress it in your mind. Then allow yourself to relax. Close your eyes and recall the symbol in your mind's eye. Focus only on this symbol, and surrender to your feeling for that symbol. Certain thoughts may come into your mind. You may also notice particular colors or special energies. After your meditation, make some notes about your experience with the symbol. A notebook may well become one of your most valuable keys toward experiencing astrology.

The Houses

The twelve houses in the astrological chart symbolize the multiple facets of the individual and her life. They represent the various environments, both internal and external, in which the personality develops and expresses itself. In the natural zodiac each of the twelve houses contains its complementary planetary and sign correspondences.

The Perspective of the Houses in Childhood

Since a child's perspective can differ dramatically from an adult's, the houses take on different meanings during childhood. Illustration 2 shows the viewpoint of the houses during childhood. Included are the elements, signs, and planets associated with each house in the natural progression of the zodiac. These correspondences are key factors to help you understand how houses, planets, and signs are related to one another.

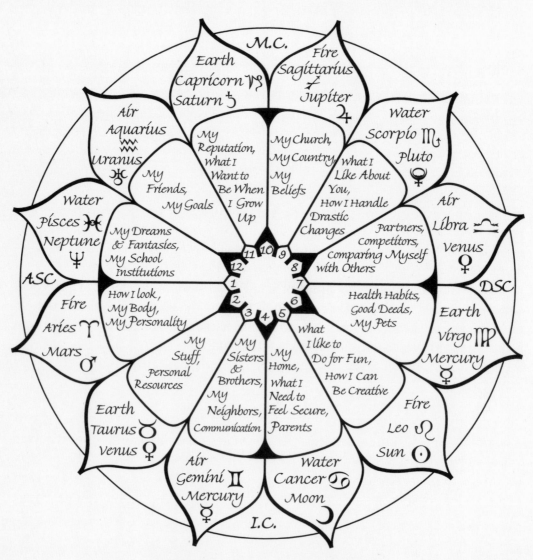

Illustration 2. The Houses in Childhood.

The houses that contain planets have greater impact since more energy is directed into those areas. If a house does not contain a planet, we interpret the meaning of the house using the sign on the house cusp. We can further extend this to the planet which is associated with the sign on the cusp in the natural zodiac. For example, if the 5th House contains no planets, this does not mean that the child is lacking in creative self-expression. We would look to the sign on the cusp to understand the child's approach to expressing her creative self. Looking further, the planet which corresponds to that sign and where it is placed will give us clues to the type of energy the child will direct into this area.

1st House and the Ascendant: How I Look, My Body, My Personality

In childhood, the Ascendant and the 1st House signify the physical appearance of the child and how other people view him. This is basically the same meaning we find when interpreting an adult's chart. This is not surprising, since for most of us our self-image is shaped by what other people tell us about ourselves. It is important to include the underlying reasons people see certain things about an individual: the ASC represents the attitudes which shape the way a person presents himself to the world. It is this attitude that shines through and is interpreted in this part of the chart. When we consider the significance of this area in childhood development, we can understand why environmental conditioning plays such an important part in the development of a child's personality self. The people strongly associated with the 1st House in a child's life are the grandparents, and the child's relationship to the grandparents is illustrated by any planets within the 1st House and the sign on the cusp of the 1st House. But basically the Ascendant's sign (rising sign) illustrates how others will perceive a child's physical appearance and basic personality traits.

> **Aries Rising**—The Aries rising child exhibits great independence and is quite strong minded. This child is right at home being a kid—sometimes for decades! Grandma and Grandpa may be favorite playmates.

> **Taurus Rising**—The Taurus rising child projects consistency and stubbornness. This child may enjoy natural surroundings and may have a special affinity for music. She may stay more to herself.

> **Gemini Rising**—The Gemini rising child's sense of mischief and curiosity are his key traits. There may be an impish quality about the personality, and distractions can be a problem in some situations.

Cancer Rising—The Cancer rising child's protectiveness and sensitivity are expressed through her personality. This child may enjoy hanging around home, with Mom, or doing family things.

Leo Rising—The Leo rising child's dramatic flair and personal pride are keys to his outward personality. This child needs a place to show off and shine, and may enjoy being the center of attention. It's difficult to ignore a Leo rising child.

Virgo Rising—The Virgo rising child's meticulous manner imparts a sense of perfection to the outer self. This child may have an extrasensitive body and may be overly concerned or worried when she does not feel well.

Libra Rising—The Libra rising child can show charm, grace, and consideration toward others and loves to feel beautiful. Boys and girls alike may have a strong idea of personal image, even at a young age, and will appreciate taking part in choosing wardrobe and colors. He can be too eager to please and may be insecure in competitive situations.

Scorpio Rising—The Scorpio rising child displays secretiveness and a sense of mystery. There may be a special curiosity about the way things work and a strong emotional sensitivity. This child can be more sensitive than you might realize, and encouraging her to express emotions honestly is very important. Grandparents may be the ones trusted with secrets.

Sagittarius Rising—The Sagittarius rising child's enthusiasm and free spiritedness will shape the view others have of him. This child may seem to always be in a hurry ("are we there yet?") and may love to travel. Grandparents instill a sense of adventure for this child.

Capricorn Rising—The Capricorn rising child may show a serious nature and wry humor. You may wonder how a child could laugh at adult things, but this child seems to understand the adult world. It's not an act! Take care in offering this child responsibilities to be sure that he is actually ready emotionally to handle the responsibility.

Aquarius Rising—The Aquarius rising child may delight in being different. Whether it's an unusual appearance or displays of eccentric behavior, she can be uncomfortable with conformity. Give this child a chance to include her special self-expression while encouraging a balance of responsibility as the child matures.

Pisces Rising—The Pisces rising child often exhibits shy behavior and may seem mystical. Music, drama, dance, and artistic expression are especially important. Provide an opportunity for this child to do things for others.

Rising sign qualities will be further altered by the planets found in the 1st House and aspects made by the planets to the Ascendant. I often find a strong correspondence between the rising sign of a child and the Sun, Moon, or ascending signs of the parents. This is especially noteworthy since it shows that the child is very likely to display many of the parents' traits.

2nd House: My Stuff, Personal Resources

This house deals with how the child's values are formed. Many of the child's attitudes concerning material possessions can be determined by the sign on the cusp of the 2nd House, the planet which corresponds to that sign, and any planets found within the 2nd House. (See Table 3 in chapter 2 for planet and sign correspondences.)

The 2nd House also corresponds to the child's developing sense of self-worth. It is a natural but dangerous tendency to tie one's self-worth to the material world, especially in our society. What the child needs to learn when developing this aspect of the Self is appreciation for who and what he is. As parents, we can attune ourselves to the child's special qualities and fortify them through recognition and praise. This will help the child develop a greater sense of self-appreciation. "My stuff" becomes "what I am inside" instead of "what toys I have on my shelf."

3rd House: Communication, My Sisters and Brothers, My Neighbors

This area of the chart indicates how we communicate the concepts we have developed about ourselves and our world. Babies and very young children cannot really talk, so they must begin by expressing themselves nonverbally. We must realize that we communicate in many nonverbal ways. A child whose chart shows planets in the 3rd House may be constantly trying to communicate, especially if this house contains active personal planets like the Sun, Mercury, or Mars.

We also see the child's sense of self being altered by relationships with siblings; the sign on the cusp indicates the types of relationships she will have with her brothers and sisters. For example, Mars in the 3rd House sometimes brings combativeness with siblings.

One way in which the 3rd House concepts of communication and sibling relationships operate can be seen by observing a family situation. Many communication skills are developed through interaction with brothers and sisters, since these relationships are significant on a daily basis. Older siblings may "translate" what younger children are communicating. Later, when the child becomes aware of the outside environment, neighbors come into play. These new playmates offer the child new concepts and varied opportunities for communication.

The 3rd House also deals with travel and transportation, and we can see the child's approach to travel by the sign on the cusp. The type of energy directed to traveling will be indicated by the planets in the house, or the one ruling it. (See Table 3 in chapter 2.)

4th House: My Home, What I Need to Feel Secure, Parents

The child's personal environment is his first impression of the world. The 4th House tells us about the people in that environment who create a feeling of security for the child, usually either Mother or Father. Planets in this house will indicate the specific energies the child will feel from the nurturing parent.

The sign on the cusp of the 4th House tells us what kinds of activities go on at home, and which qualities of the home environment the child identifies as "home" and what will be important in creating a comfort zone for him. For example, the meticulously clean housekeeping of Virgo might be important for the child who has this sign on the cusp of the 4th House.

5th House: What I Like to Do for Fun, How I Can Be Creative

This house relates to creative self-expression. One of the best ways to encourage this is through the types of play in which a child engages. Creativity flows more easily if it is free of unnecessary inhibitions and fears.

Look to the planets in this house to find the types of energy the child will have the best time with. For example, Uranus in the 5th House would really enjoy futuristic activities: planetariums, movies about space, and the unusual. If a child has Capricorn on the cusp of the 5th House, she might enjoy "working" or doing chores—something that feels constructive and purposeful.

Another concept associated with this house is giving love. Children need to learn how to give of themselves. As the child matures, she needs to learn that true creative efforts are indeed an expression of love.

6th House: Health Habits, Good Deeds, My Pets

Awareness of physical well-being is symbolized by this house. 6th House activities involve the development of good habits. The sign and planets affecting the 6th House will give clues to the child's basic well-being. They will also point to the areas which may be physically weakened and require further attention.

The 6th House is also traditionally the house of service, and it is through this facet of the self that the young child develops an awareness of other people and their needs. Children should be given opportunities to serve others by doing good deeds and favors for friends and family members.

One way to learn service is through caring for an animal friend. The child can be given the responsibilities of feeding, grooming, and sharing time with his pet. Children who have planets in this house should definitely have their own little animal friends. With Mercury and/or Neptune placed in this house, the child is likely to have a special ability to communicate with pets.

I have always felt that pets can play a special part in a child's emotional development. Part of this development comes through performing caring service for the pet. This helps the child begin to see needs in the world outside himself. It also gives the child a sense that he is vitally connected with life.

7th House: Partners, Competitors, Comparing Myself with Others

Children with planets in this house usually like to do things with someone else most of the time. It may be difficult for these children to feel comfortable just being by themselves. They are certainly not looking for a long-term relationship or a marriage partner—they are looking for themselves through others. The other people in her life provide vital feedback to the child with planets in this house.

This area of development also indicates the child's approach to comparing herself with others: "But Ginny has orange hair, Mom!" Seeking approval from others is something we all do to feel more secure. Ultimately, however, the approval must come from within the child. This self-acceptance does not just appear from day one; it initially requires an excellent support system in the child's personal environment.

The 7th House indicates the types of people the child will be competing against as she begins to be active in sports or other arenas where competitiveness may arise. Use the sign on the cusp of this house to determine if the child will have a strong, positive approach to competition. The fire signs (Aries, Leo, Sagittarius) are likely to be strongest in this regard. (The four elements are explained in chapter 2.)

As the child matures, this house also deals with her approach to the opposite sex. When the sense of personal identity becomes muddled by the rumblings of hormones, it is often difficult to even like the opposite sex. I think it is interesting that preteen boys and girls are "open enemies," (7th House) yet later become "potential partners."

8th House: What I Like About You, How I Handle Drastic Changes

The 8th house indicates the value we place upon other people in our lives. For a child, this would be the things he seeks out in others. It tells us what might be a real "turn-on" or "turn-off" for the child.

This facet of the self is also related to how a child may develop attachments, and the qualities radiating in and through this part of the chart indicate whether or not a child will do well adapting to changing circumstances or relationships. This is the part of the chart that deals with life-stage transformations. Parents would look to the 8th House to understand how to approach toilet training, among other things. A child with a cardinal sign on the cups of the 8th House might move quickly through this stage, the mutable sign would vacillate and need several tries, and the fixed sign might resist the idea entirely from the beginning! (The three modes are explained in chapter 2.) The sign on the cusp and the planets here are also good indicators of how to approach sex education for this child.

The 8th House is also the area of ourselves which undergoes deep transformational changes. Planets in the 8th House indicate that a child is likely to experience drastic changes, perhaps even the deaths of significant others, during childhood. The sign on the cusp of this house indicates the child's approach to drastic change and transformation and the way he will deal with it.

9th House: My Church, My Country, My Beliefs

The experience of the 9th House deals with what astrologers call the *Higher Mind*. This is an area of development which does concern the mind, but not at the basic conceptual level. These concepts are more expanded, focusing on the overview of the life a child might obtain through the teachings of her religion, the tenets of her nation, and the basic attitudes of her community.

During childhood, external belief systems usually take a back seat to the child's direct experiences. As the child matures, though, she will have more opportunities to experience other systems of thought just by spending time with other people. I can recall my own experiences as a little girl in church. I never questioned the teachings I was receiving, because I had no idea there was anything to question! When I grew into my teen years, however, I had the opportunity to visit other churches with friends and began to see other approaches to worship. This was a bit shattering at first, but then it became exciting. From that time on, I was inspired to study world religions and different philosophies—one of my passions to this day.

We also see the 9th House as the child's approach to travel, especially to other cultures. The person who has never left her own culture and spent time in another can never truly understand her own culture. Books, television documentaries, and the like cannot even begin to compare to the actual experience. The child with planets in the 9th House will truly benefit from travel, since the Self cries out to experience other views of life. Foreign language study may also be of interest.

I see this area of a child's life focusing on the manner in which she integrates the world into a sense of personal identity. This is also where she builds a bridge between the mind and the Source of All Knowledge and the experience of the Divine.

10th House: My Reputation, What I Want to Be When I Grow Up

This region of self-development is not usually focused upon until the child reaches school-age. At that time, interaction with others takes up most of his waking hours, and reputation and honor become issues the child must deal with.

As a child matures, he will also begin to consider what type of career might be rewarding. The primary role models are usually the parents. Secondary influences are significant others and famous people.

The child with planets in the 10th House—especially the Sun, Moon, Mercury, Venus, or Mars—will devote a great deal of energy to career considerations even in the early years. It's important that he is given a chance to find out how the world works, and to spend time observing how Mom and Dad do their jobs or the nature of their occupations. The 10th House cusp, or Midheaven, is the highest point in the chart. The sign placed at the Midheaven gradually develops more and more importance as the person matures and eventually becomes "my approach to establishing my place in society." It is never too early to learn how society works or to understand the types of demands society makes before it awards "success." The sign on this house cusp tells us much about how the child may handle success and what situations will affirm for him that he has reached a pinnacle.

11th House: My Friends, My Goals

Friendships are important at any age, but are especially so for the school-age child. Friends form one of the basic support systems at this time, and can dictate the standards and often the activities in which the child participates. The sign on the cusp of the 11th House tells what qualities the child seeks in a friend.

Goals are also the domain of this house. Helping a child set and master goals is important even in preschool years. I find that parents will often set goals which are inappropriate and/or unreachable for the child. The sign on the cusp of this house indicates the types of goals which will be truly interesting to the child, and better appreciated! For example, the child with Gemini on the 11th House cusp could have a variety of goals. Because Gemini enjoys stimulation of the mind, she might be especially motivated if the goals involved going somewhere or doing something different.

12th House: My Dreams and Fantasies, My School, Institutions

The 12th House is the realm of the imagination: the abode of dreams, fantasies, and secret desires. Here is where the "imaginary" playmates live, fairies dance, and dragons hide away.

Children should be allowed to have their secret spaces. These become their inner refuge in times of distress and difficulty, and their infinite playground for just plain fun. This is the private part of the Self, where one can let go of the pressures of the outside world and float in the peaceful space of the inner Self. Here the individual connects with the spirit of all humanity and feels the Oneness that lies beyond the illusion of separation.

The 12th House concept of "institutions" will probably apply most directly to the school the child attends. Children are generally aware of hospitals and other institutions, but usually have not spent much time inside them.

Sometimes a child born with several planets in the 12th House will have a clearer concept of what institutions are. I have a good friend, whose chart shows four planets in this house, who attended private catholic schools until graduation. She is now part of the Sisterhood of the Catholic Church. Another client with several planets in this house had two parents who were physicians. She spent most of her first six years staying with a nurse or secretary at the hospital while Mom and Dad worked.

Basically, this house ties into the deepest recesses of our consciousness, where we connect with the One. Children with personal planets in the 12th House may feel confused about their personal identities. Sometimes these children are hard to reach. If this is the case, music can often be a good tool to bridge the gap. The younger child with planets in the 12th House may be drawn out of his shell through musical games and action songs. Older children may prefer to study some musical instrument, which may later become the expression of thoughts and feelings that words cannot describe.

Although these basic house meanings can be extended much further, this introduction should be sufficient to get you started. Through the houses, we gain an understanding of the environments of our lives—both internal and external. The persons within those environments become an active part of our sense of Self. For the child, the person and the environment might be the same thing!

The basic concepts of astrology are the building blocks in our understanding of human nature. Since we are focusing upon children, our approach is a developmental one; we see the developing needs of the child expressed through the planets, signs, and houses of the chart. None of these factors stands alone, but must be integrated within a framework of wholeness. This will offer a portrait of a complete being in succeeding stages of growth and change.

2

The Signs in Youth

There are twelve signs in the zodiac. These signs embody the primary traits of the human personality. Through the signs, a human being expresses special qualities which set her apart from others. When reading this section, be aware that although you may associate the qualities of the signs with the Sun Sign of a child, these descriptive concepts refer to the quality of the zodiac sign itself. That is, all signs are not Sun Signs. The signs define specific *characteristics* and potential modifications; the planets, the Sun, and the Moon are *designated in* the signs in the horoscope; and house cusps are *defined by* the signs.

The basic organizational scheme for the signs of the zodiac comprises the qualities of the four elements and the three modes. The *elements*—fire, earth, air, and water— illustrate underlying factors which form the rudimentary substances in our lives. The *modes*—cardinal, fixed, and mutable—are styles of expression. Each sign projects the combined quality of an element and a mode.

The Four Elements

In the astrological scheme of things, everything in our world can be described using the concepts of fire, earth, air, and water. These four elements are present in our

17

environment and within our personalities. These are called the *elemental triplicities* (see Illustration 4 in chapter 4). Observing the interplay of the four elements on the physical plane can show us many fundamental truths about the life experience and also about the human psyche.

Fire—Fire is a powerful element in our lives, warming us when it is cold, providing us with light, and it can destroy things we consider useless. We have all experienced the positive qualities of fire, and we have also observed the destructive powers of fire burning out of control.

The signs of the zodiac associated with the fiery element are Aries, Leo, and Sagittarius. These three signs are active, energetic, and outwardly expressive. The fire element in children can also be felt physically (warm hugs are a pleasant trait of fiery progeny). Although each of the three fire signs will express a different level of fiery energy, there are common characteristics among them.

Psychologically, fire represents action, the outward expression of energy, and a desire to be noticed. Enthusiasm and inspiration permeate the fire signs and play an important part in motivating the child. There can also be selfishness with the fiery quality. One thing to keep in mind with fiery children is the fact that you must tend a fire: either to keep it burning or to keep it from blazing out of control.

Earth—The element of earth provides us with our sustenance on the physical plane. It is from the earth that we receive food, materials for shelter, and a foundation for our homes.

This principle in astrology is signified by the signs Taurus, Virgo, and Capricorn. Earth psychologically relates to the creation of substance in our lives. Earth signs need to apply knowledge in order to appreciate it. There is a conservative nature in the earth signs which can even be seen in childhood. The qualities of practicality and sensibility are strongly present, and there is strong sensitivity to the environment. Earth children frequently exhibit a stubborn streak.

Air—Air is also necessary for life on the physical plane. It surrounds us, filling our lungs with the oxygen we need to survive. The lungs help us purify the body by exhaling carbon dioxide. Air is difficult to contain, and escapes easily. It cools us, and can be harnessed to produce electrical power. Even though we cannot see air particles, we know they are there!

Children born in the air signs of Gemini, Libra, and Aquarius may exhibit abstract and often elusive qualities. Psychologically, air illustrates our need to relate to one another. It is a social, relationship-oriented element, and offers a sense of diversity in our lives. Air also represents the intellect, with all the air signs displaying a powerful mental energy. We must apply the intellect in a positive manner since the mind can be either our creator or our destroyer.

Water—We are also surrounded by water in our environment. It's important to remember that the human body is largely comprised of water. This liquid element knows no shape of its own, but conforms to the structures around it. It provides nurturance to the earth's life forms and can be soothing, cleansing, and revitalizing. Water can also bring destruction in the forms of floods and tidal waves.

Cancer, Scorpio, and Pisces are the water signs of the zodiac and represent the emotions and feelings in our lives. Psychologically, water signifies nurturance, emotion, receptivity, sensitivity, and depth. There is a need to experience and understand things below the surface with the water signs. There can also be a deceptiveness associated with the watery element, since it can easily conform to whatever (or whomever) is around.

The Three Modes

The modes determine *how* a particular sign manifests its energy. These qualities are known as *cardinal*, *fixed*, and *mutable*—the *modal quadruplicities* (see Illustration 5 in chapter 4). Each sign correlates with one of three modes of action.

Cardinal—Cardinal energy is motivational and gets things going. Much like the ignition of an automobile, the principle of cardinality is necessary to get things started. Initiative, assertiveness, ambition, and independence are all cardinal qualities. The cardinal signs Aries, Cancer, Libra, and Capricorn all have the ability to initiate or become immediately involved in whatever events may be occurring. When exaggerated or misused, cardinality can be impatient, restless, and opportunistic. There is also a strong desire to act without outside guidance. These signs correlate with the beginnings of the four seasons: In the Western and Northern hemisphere we associate Aries with spring, Cancer with summer, Libra with autumn, and Capricorn with winter. (In places like Australia and South Africa, these seasonal correlations are reversed.)

Fixed—Fixed signs stabilize and preserve. Taurus, Leo, Scorpio, and Aquarius, the fixed signs of the zodiac, are all concerned with maintaining the status quo.

There is consistency and patience in the fixed signs, but there can also be inflexibility, resistance, and obsessiveness that can be rather difficult to manage or accept. Positive natural tendencies of the fixed signs are those of bringing inner and outer reality into one and the determination to complete tasks. Fixed signs correlate with the duration of the seasons.

Mutable—The mutable signs Gemini, Virgo, Sagittarius, and Pisces are flexible and able to adapt easily. There is objectivity in the mutable signs which strengthens the ability to cooperate. The primary difficulty with mutable qualities lies in indecisive fence-sitting. The positive natural qualities of mutability such as versatility and teamwork should receive focused attention, while the negative exaggerations involving exploitation or dissipation should be guarded against. The mutable signs correlate with the changing of the seasons.

Determining the Balance of the Elements and Modes

You can use a simple formula to fully understand how much one element influences a child's chart. Locate the signs in which the Sun, Moon, all the planets, the Ascendant, and Midheaven are located. Give a value of one point for each planet, the Ascendant, and Midheaven and two points each to the Sun and Moon. As your study of astrology advances, you may decide that you want to give the Sun, Moon, and angles a higher point value, but for now, assigning one point to each of these energies and angles will suffice.

After finishing this step, add together all the fire, earth, air, and water signs to find the elemental balance in the chart. Use the same procedure to determine the balance of the modes by finding all the cardinal, fixed, and mutable signs which are energized in the chart. Use Illustration 3 to aid you in this procedure. You may even want to make a grid similar to this and note the number of planets or angles in each of the signs in the appropriate box.

Elemental Strengths

You may find one element to be extremely strong in the chart. If so, the qualities of that element will be more easily expressed by the child. For example, if air is very strong in the chart (greater than a value of four), the child's focus will be more intellectual, mental, and abstract. There may be one mode which is stronger than the

	CARDINAL	FIXED	MUTABLE
FIRE	♈	♌	♐
AIR	♎	♒	♊
WATER	♋	♏	♓
EARTH	♑	♉	♍

Illustration 3. Elements and Modes.

other two. If the child's chart shows a powerful focus in cardinal signs, he may be a great initiator, but will need to be encouraged to finish what he starts!

Fire Strongest

With fire the strongest element in the child's chart, expect high levels of activity. This child needs plenty of room and ample opportunities to assert herself. Sports may be a strong interest, but, at the very least, staying active is important. Encourage this child to funnel these active needs by providing plenty of options: from early gymnastics or dance classes to recreational activities that involve physical assertion. Babies with strong fire can be irritable if they are not given ample opportunities to get rid of physical stress (yes, babies experience stress, too!). Basically, this child loves play, and fiery temperament babies need active time with Mom and Dad.

Earth Strongest

The child with strong earth exhibits a more introspective quality and may be more cautious about new circumstances or situations. This child needs a hands-on connection to life. Hugs are especially important, and emphasizing security needs and reassuring the child that he can reach out and make contact will make a huge difference in this child's sense of identity. Touch is necessary for all children, but you're likely to see this child spending more time exploring textures, temperatures, and other physical evidence. Nature exploration can be especially stimulating, and learning in a natural environment helps forge strong memories. If your school offers it, give your child a chance to experience something like "nature's classroom," where environmental concerns are the focus of learning. Otherwise, occasional camping, hiking, or even spending time in the garden can be an amazing way to confer a sense of calm and focus to this child.

Air Strongest

When air is the strongest element in the chart, a child is drawn to make mental connections. Friends are exceptionally important, and social situations may always be a powerful feature of this child's life. Even during the early years, when sharing and cooperative play are a bit of a struggle, this child will enjoy being around others her own age. Later, you may discover that this child is the one who invites social interaction in the classroom or on the playground. While mental stimulation is important, encouraging this child to develop her own ideas may be somewhat difficult unless the child enjoys exposing her thoughts! The logical conclusion may be that this child is a natural at such experiences, but it's highly conceivable that presentations in the classroom or sharing her own ideas strikes fear. The reason may be a lack of confidence in whether or not the child is "correct." This child hates to be proven wrong or appearing "stupid."

Water Strongest

The child with water as the strongest element is definitely sensitive. At times, especially in very early years, you may see evidence that this child is uncomfortable around new people or in different environments, and the underlying cause is sensitivity to the "vibrations." Everything alive has a kind of vibratory rate, and the water child is highly attuned to the feeling of vibrations: sensing the underlying quality of emotionally charged situations is also evident. Encouraging artistic or creative expression is helpful, particularly if this can be experienced as pure fun and not a judged activity. Also, encouraging this child to trust his intuitive sense of things will serve him well.

What About Elemental or Modal Deficiency?

If an element is lacking or has a value of one in the chart, encourage the child to express herself in activities which involve that element. For example, if water is lacking in the chart, encourage the child to accept and express her feelings more openly. Astrologer Doris Hebel suggests directing a person into activities which involve the physical element itself, such as aquariums or swimming, to make up for the lacking water element. If fire is lacking, try burning candles, spending more time in the sun, and sitting in front of a fireplace. If earth is lacking, get in touch with earth's qualities through gardening, standing in green grass, hugging a tree, or building something out of wood. If air is lacking, the child could benefit from feeling the breeze (perhaps on the back of Mom's bike) or stimulating the mind each day by keeping a diary.

If one of the modal qualities is low or lacking, being around people who exhibit the positive aspects of those qualities might be helpful. Focusing on what the lack of any mode or element might mean for the child can prove beneficial, although this should not be interpreted as an actual deficiency. Rather, understand that this could indicate either a tendency to overcompensate or to seek what is lacking in some way. As your child matures, you might discover that she is drawn to others who express a quality which seems to be lacking in her own chart.

The basic concepts of the elements and modes are an excellent beginning for viewing the chart as a whole. We are trying to help the child become a whole person and a more complete expression of the Self. We must also begin to see the chart as an integrated structure rather than just isolated signs, elements, planets, and houses.

The Twelve Zodiac Signs in Youth

All twelve signs are present in each individual horoscope. Most charts will have more energy focused in some signs than in others. This is indicated by the placements of the Sun, Moon, planets, Ascendant, and Midheaven in the zodiac, since these are the "energy bodies" in the horoscope. The signs exemplify particular qualities and characteristics in our lives which will be modified as we mature. I think that planets in signs represent what the individual is striving to develop or perfect, not the promise of a particular quality. It's almost as though the sign placements indicate the lessons the soul has come to life to learn. The more planets and sensitive points found in one sign, the more energy will be given to developing an expression of those qualities.

GLYPH	SIGN	KEYWORDS
♈	Aries	Independent, commanding, teasing, direct, inventive
♉	Taurus	Stable, sensualistic, conservative, consistent, artistic
♊	Gemini	Intellectual, witty, quick, curious, changeable, flighty
♋	Cancer	Sensitive, intuitive, indirect, nurturant, protective
♌	Leo	Dramatic, loyal, proud, self-confident, courageous
♍	Virgo	Analytical, discriminating, orderly, precise, methodical
♎	Libra	Peace-loving, social, charming, artistic, balancing, relating
♏	Scorpio	Mysterious, intriguing, intense, transformational, secretive
♐	Sagittarius	Understanding, philosophical, expansive, optimistic, free-spirited
♑	Capricorn	Realistic, practical, organized, cautious, determined, persistent
♒	Aquarius	Friendly, innovative, eccentric, independent, humanitarian
♓	Pisces	Mystical, impressionable, imaginative, idealistic, dramatic

Table 2. Keywords: Signs of the Zodiac.

Each sign can be described by a few key concepts. Use the keywords in Table 2 when you need a basic idea of the way a sign might influence a planet or house cusp.

A child is unable to express these characteristics completely, but will gradually become a fuller expression of the Self as he grows. For this reason, our focus in discussing the signs is upon the early development of these qualities in childhood.

Each sign also corresponds in a natural way to a planet, the Sun, or the Moon. These correspondences are illustrated in Table 3. Use these affinities to help blend concepts together. These relationships are called *rulers*. For example, Aries is under the rulership of Mars.

To make the best use of this section, refer to the child's chart you are studying as you read. Note the placement by sign of the Sun, Moon, each of the planets, the Ascendant, and Midheaven. If you find a sign with two or more energies, these qualities will manifest more strongly. The personal planets—the Sun, Moon, Mercury, Venus, and Mars, along with the Ascendant—make up the aspects of the personality which will be the most dominant in a child's life.

	SIGN		PLANETARY RULER
♈	Aries	♂	Mars
♉	Taurus	♀	Venus
♊	Gemini	☿	Mercury
♋	Cancer	☽	Moon
♌	Leo	☉	Sun
♍	Virgo	☿	Mercury
♎	Libra	♀	Venus
♏	Scorpio	♇	Pluto
♐	Sagittarius	♃	Jupiter
♑	Capricorn	♄	Saturn
♒	Aquarius	♅	Uranus
♓	Pisces	♆	Neptune

Table 3. The Signs and Their Rulers.

Aries

♈ It is no accident that Aries is the first sign of the zodiac. In Western astrology, 0 degrees of Aries marks the vernal equinox, the new life of spring. The qualities of Aries are fresh and alive, with a sense of new beginnings. These include playfulness, leadership, assertiveness, enthusiasm and, often, impatience. Children whose charts have planets in Aries may be tremendously eager to try new things, perhaps before they have mastered the task before them! Here, fiery energy expresses itself by getting things started.

Aries shows a strong desire for freedom, a need to get there first. Watching the children at my son's preschool get into line before lunch, I noticed two children rush immediately to the front of the line. It was not surprising for me to learn that both of these children had Sun in Aries!

Aries often manifests in children as a high level of impatience. Planets in Aries will express more directly in an effort to waste less time and get to the point. Aries also enjoys teasing. You can even see this quality in little babies as young as nine months, already understanding how to play little teasing games with Mommy and Daddy.

Aries can be a physically active sign exhibiting a great deal of restlessness. When Aries is strong in an infant's chart, it is especially important for the parents to exercise the baby so she can sleep better. It's good to know that these babies will not enjoy being hemmed in by playpens!

Provide the Aries toddler with action toys. The Aries preschooler will enjoy playing ball with you or playing chase with the family pet. Elementary school-age Aries enjoy playing games such as Simon Says, or taking part in adventure scenarios such as Pirates or Cops and Robbers. Sports can also be a good outlet for an Aries child, and taking leadership roles in team sports may be a natural for the older child.

Aries needs to learn about the consequences of his actions, and parents should be alerted to this necessary lesson. Focusing on tasks which require some follow-through will also be helpful to the child with planets in Aries. You can find toys that will teach these actions for infants and children of all ages.

Brightly colored toys are favorites of Aries babies. Aries seem to be drawn to the color red. I've known many Aries children who love wearing fire helmets. I think this is because helmets are red and also because Aries rules the physical head. (Different signs rule different parts of the body. See chapter 5.) Hats in general might be fun for Aries children, especially since they help the child to identify with various roles.

Aries' natural leadership abilities can be encouraged in the school-age child. Give her ample opportunities to interact in such activities as team sports or running for school offices. Encouraged early, the development of these abilities will instill a high level of confidence in the child. This child loves to win!

Aries is strongly connected with willpower, and you may find these children extremely strong-willed. Sometimes this results in a combative attitude, with discussions quickly evolving into arguments. The child needs to learn that it is okay for another person to have a different opinion, and that he need not take sides all the time. Certainly, the development of willpower should be encouraged, but it needs to be balanced with an understanding of the consequences of one's actions.

Taurus

Taurus is drawn to the sensory and sensual experiences of life. Taurus is the fixed earth sign of the zodiac, and occurs at the time spring is showing her finest colors. All the greens are vibrant during this time of year, and the earth radiates life and sustenance. Taurus qualities include stability, conservatism, practicality, consistency, and creativity.

Children born with planets in Taurus like to involve the physical senses and to learn by experiencing. This allows the Taurean to integrate knowledge more completely. The Taurean child has a love for the earth and her life forms, as well as a sense of the stability found by attaching herself to the things of the earth. Babies with Taurean planets love walking in the warm sun, touching trees, smelling flowers, and crawling in the grass. As this child grows, so can her appreciation for the earth. Encourage activities like indoor or outdoor gardening and working with clay. Touching the matter of the earth helps to strengthen a child's sense of personal identity.

Taurus is not too happy with change, and should be encouraged to participate in changes in order to understand that change does not necessarily lead to loss. I think the fear of change for so many with Taurean energy stems from the fear of losing something, and consequently losing part of the Self. Taurus tends to be possessive for this same reason. Holding on means, "It's mine forever!"

This can carry over into emotional relationships and create difficulties later in life. Learning to share with friends is a necessary exercise for Taurus. A friend of mine related an experience that might help parents with children who like to hold on. She was standing in line at the supermarket behind a mother, her child, and the child's grandmother. Grandmother had to leave, and the child became hysterical upon her departure. The mother held the child closely, creating a sense of calmness. Then she said, "In our lives, things come and go. Sometimes, we have to let someone go in order to allow something different to happen." Simple games like Peek-a-Boo can help build trust that disappearing usually does not mean "gone forever."

Toys with varying textures and surfaces are wonderful for babies with Taurus energies. Taurus also loves to taste. Be aware that this sense can be carried too far, and could lead to a desire for too much food or too many "goodies!" (Chocolate is especially favored by Taureans, and these kids may also crave the natural sweetness of fruits.)

As the Taurean child grows, there will be an increased appreciation for building toys, as well as games that involve the accumulation of power. Whether board games or computer games, the fun of acquisition is a real game for this child! Since the lesson of gracefully letting go of things is so important for these children, games that teach cooperation and sharing is a good idea. Working with clay, growing a garden, digging in the sandbox, or making crafts can be enjoyable play. These children also adore music and may become fine singers or musicians.

The Taurean child will probably enjoy saving money once he understands its power. He might appreciate piggy banks at a young age, followed by a savings account later on. Offering goods in exchange for deeds works well in motivating Taurean children. Of course, the lesson that all deeds may not result in physical repayment will be a challenge to teach. The parents of the Taurean child are blessed if they can make him understand that "to give is more blessed than to receive."

Taurus has a knack for building things which last, and develops a tenacious attachment to concepts and ideas. Certain physical exercises can be a good way to attain mental or emotional resilience. The Taurus child would do well to learn yoga, tai chi, or any dance movements that will encourage flexibility. Learned early, this will teach the child how to create lasting impressions and stable values while functioning from a position of flexibility.

Gemini

Gemini is the mutable air sign of the zodiac, and possesses the qualities of diversity, mental curiosity, duality, wittiness, and changeability. Children whose charts show planets in Gemini are likely to be interested in many different things. There is a desire to explore something new as soon as it catches the child's attention. Gemini strengthens the child's need to experience variety and adds an ability to see several facets of an issue or idea.

In childhood, Gemini often has a sense of impish mischief. Although the young child with Gemini qualities may get into a few tight situations due to his endless curiosity, he can usually talk his way out of trouble or find a quick solution to extract himself from a jam. The rational mind seems to be activated from the very beginning.

A love of talking is often present—sometimes much to the parents' chagrin! Parents of Gemini progeny should be alerted that this child takes in every word, and is likely to repeat those words anywhere! The quality of Gemini can seem to be much like a monkey, and an ability to mimic can be very strong. Strong Gemini frequently leads to a tendency to use gestures and interesting facial expressions as punctuations to communication. These features are especially notable with the Gemini Moon.

Gemini characteristics in infancy seem to manifest as early desires to experience motion and stimulation. The baby with Gemini planets or Ascendant will need a variety in her environments during the day to avoid boredom. Often the infant will wail simply because she wants to go somewhere or needs to experience a change of scenery. A walk around the yard or a drive in the car may be just the thing to calm her.

Stories will be a favorite pastime from the beginning. There is almost always a love of books and a fascination with language. Toys that will take the child somewhere are a necessity: scooter cars for toddlers, tricycles and bicycles for older children, and eventually "a car of my own." In the future, Gemini children will most likely require their own personal space vehicles!

In learning situations, Gemini proves to be delightful and challenging. Materials need to be presented concisely and at a fairly quick pace. Since Gemini is easily distracted, a wide variety of subjects would be ideal. There is often a proclivity to abstract types of thought, such as mathematics. Computers and electronic games and devices may be an early fascination which extends into later life. Monitoring time on the Internet is necessary, too, since it may be much more fun to get into a chat room than to finish homework.

Gemini children should be encouraged to present their ideas in writing. Poems and short stories are generally the favorite forms. A diary is almost a necessity for the preteen and teenager. Working on the school paper might be fun, too.

Gemini often has restless hands and requires many activities to keep those hands busy. The tiny child might like the wide variety of blocks, brightly colored musical keyboards, or easy puzzles. As the child matures, offer him more complex puzzles, finger paints, pens, crayons (the variety of colors alone is often enough to draw the child), and any toy with finger keys. Toy telephones are a favorite. Later on, an Erector set or advanced Lego blocks would be enticing. Building models is a good idea for that active mind and those busy hands! There may be a desire to play a musical instrument such as guitar, harp, piano, or a wind instrument. Encourage these desires, but be aware that your child may lose interest if pushed too intensely, and needs room to experiment. Of course, budgetary considerations may have to be taken into account, and part of a Gemini child's learning is to understand that distractions can be costly if carried too far!

Gemini needs to learn concentration and the expansion of ideas. It is important to stress the joy of variety along with the necessity of integrating concepts. Learning to focus the mind and follow through will be very helpful to the child. The wit and cleverness of Gemini are special gifts, but there is very often a lack of tact when speaking. Teach Gemini the value of listening!

Cancer

 Cancer, also called the Moon Child, imparts nurturance, sensitivity, protectiveness, and resourcefulness. This cardinal water sign expresses a high level of emotionality. Cancer is generally drawn to Mother, home, and family.

Children of this sign are often kind and caring, and usually love to be around babies and small animals.

The child with planets in Cancer must learn how to deal with her emotional nature in a positive way. Her sensitivity can lead to easily hurt feelings and cause an overly protective nature to develop at a rather young age. The parents need to recognize this sensitivity and provide a stable, calm environment for the child. Excessive amounts of negative energy such as anger, loud noises, or other seemingly threatening experiences will be difficult for the Cancerian to tolerate, and may make the child irritable.

Cancer is symbolized by the crab, whose dominant feature is its protective shell. This shield was developed to lessen its vulnerability. Humans have their shells, too. Sometimes the child will use Mother as a shield (hiding behind her skirts is a common example). At other times, the shield is physical. Even a young child can begin developing an armor of fat. If your Cancerian is gaining too much weight, you should find out why the child is feeling vulnerable or hurt. This type of awareness early in life can help the child avoid such harshly self-protective and self-destructive patterns in adulthood.

Cancer, like the crab, moves most easily in an indirect manner. However, this behavior can manifest as manipulative and escapist if carried to extremes, resulting in confusion and mistrust on the part of everybody involved.

The Moon Child's penetrating awareness can be ripened early by encouraging the child to trust his feeling nature. It might be difficult to deceive such a perceptive child, so the best approach is simply to be honest at all times. Any attempt to hide the truth from a child, even when you think you are protecting him from hurt, may well backfire on you. Even delicate or painful situations should be explained in a thorough, reasonable manner.

I recall an adult client with both the Sun and Moon in Cancer tearfully sharing her pain about her parents' divorce when she was eleven years old. She spoke of knowing about the disharmony (of course, she could feel it!) long before her parents split up, but they tried to conceal their problems from her by acting as though everything was just fine. One day, her father bade her good-bye at breakfast with bags packed and trailer loaded. He never returned. Her mother would not even tell her that they were divorcing (she didn't until later), but just said, "Daddy is going away for a while." Imagine the hurt and confusion experienced by this sensitive young girl who, needless to say, has had trouble trusting in relationships throughout most of her life!

Children with Cancerian energies enjoy watching things grow. Nurturing small plants can be a joyful experience. Raising guppies or tropical fish might be delightful.

You can even purchase hermit crabs at pet stores or through toy catalogs, and this child might just love these little critters.

Helping to care for younger brothers or sisters could also be pleasant, but try not to take too much advantage of this service! Remember, this child also needs to receive personal nurturance and attention. Cancerian children often enjoy working with Mother, no matter what she is doing. The relationship with Dad can also be very strong, and an emotionally expressive father can be an exceptional asset in the life of a Cancerian child.

The infant with Cancerian planets will probably love to be cuddled and rocked. The tactile senses are strong, and should be stimulated by toys with varying textures and temperatures. These babies would really enjoy a crib aquarium hanging overhead. Music is also a particular favorite, especially singing.

As the child grows, toys which stack or fit inside one another will be fascinating. Cancerians love containers and boxes, especially pretty boxes for special things. Elementary school-age Cancerians might enjoy learning to cook, whereas the older child might like a chemistry set. Many children with planets in Cancer like sewing and crafts. Others also enjoy music, singing, and may have a knack for painting (especially watercolors).

What we need to encourage in these children is a desire to share love and caring with others without feeling threatened. In learning situations, there may be a reluctance to participate if the child feels emotionally vulnerable. The approach to learning begins at home. Accepting their sensitivity and using it to bring comfort and support to the lives of others is their special gift and challenge.

Leo

As the fixed fire sign of the zodiac, Leo radiates warmth, confidence, and power. Leo's virtues require maturity in order to express themselves in the most positive light, although children with strong Leo influence are the ones who make a very strong impression, even at a young age.

In the Western and Northern hemisphere, this sign occurs during the heat of summer, when everyone is enjoying the sun, playing summertime sports, and having a good time. Most Leos prefer warm climates to cool ones because this gives them greater access to Sol's rays. Children with the Sun, Moon, planets, or sensitive points in Leo are likely to be dramatic in self-expression, and are usually difficult to ignore! They, like the sun, enjoy being the center of attention.

Leo often demonstrates flair and style, and tends to be rather showy. The Leo progeny needs every opportunity to express that flair, and should be encouraged to build confidence and a sense of personal power. One warning: there is often a little prince or princess complex when Leo is the rising sign or is strongly energized by the personal planets.

Leo needs to learn that it is okay for others to own their own personal power, too. A family entertainment night, where everyone dances, sings, acts silly, or shows off would be a good way to teach the Leo child how to share the spotlight. This would also offer him a special chance to shine. After a while, he will certainly want to direct the show, although I am certain the family will handle this situation in grand style!

If the child with Leo energies is not allowed to shine, much inner suffering will arise. Self-esteem is confused and personal power repressed. To avoid these consequences, gentle affirmations of the child's worth need to be given on a consistent basis. Most people do not have problems giving special love and attention to a small baby. Mommy exclaims, "He's so cute! Look! He rolled over!" and claps her hands. "Watch her toddling over to the puppy. Isn't she a doll?" Yet as children mature, those little victories are not met with such open enthusiasm. The Leonine nature demands recognition and approbation for its victories, and deserves to receive it. If not given, Leo will gain the attention she needs through less-than-positive actions.

Small babies with planets in Leo will enjoy time out in the sun and strolls in the park in a carriage or backpack. There is often a fascination with animals, with a trip to the zoo being a choice option. Of course, a family cat would be a delight! Leo babies also love back rubs. My own son, with Leo rising, had a nightly ritual of a back rub, and often asked to rub my back when he was a young child.

Most of these children like large toys, especially large stuffed animals. Stacking blocks and nesting blocks would encourage Leo's organizational abilities. As the child grows, save the Halloween costumes for play time. Magic kits, microphones, and any stage paraphernalia will be relished. Dancing or acting lessons would probably be pleasurable for the child.

You might find the Leo five-year-old in his room, all the stuffed toys and dolls lined up at attention while he gives all of them directions or recites a favorite story. Leo children love stories, especially exciting tales told or read dramatically. Encourage the child to tell his own stories and, later, to write them. You may have a young Steve Martin on your hands!

Leo does need to learn about possessiveness, and should be encouraged to share friends as well as toys. These children sometimes have trouble coping with changes in their circle of friends. Leo likes to be the center of attention and have the controlling power with friends. Learning to use that power responsibly can be a real challenge for a young person. Leonine pride is often difficult to handle in youth, and can be the cause of disputes. To insult a Leo is grievous indeed. Since Leo is very likely to see everyone and everything as part of herself, to insult a friend, parent, or possession is tantamount to a personal affront. If other children are insensitive, Leo will probably set them straight.

Leo also needs to learn to appreciate the gifts and talents of others and share the limelight. This lesson can make the difference between a life of extravagant self-indulgence or an attitude of genuine philanthropy.

Virgo

In the Northern hemispheres, the summer is drawing to a close and harvest time is at its peak when the Sun is passing through the sign of Virgo. At this time the school year begins again, people start planning their schedules more precisely, and life takes on a more practical quality. The mutable earth sign of the zodiac, Virgo confers discrimination, analysis, criticism, precision, and organization. Virgo has a methodical quality which is observable even in the youngest children.

Virgo is highly attuned to the physical body, and appreciates physical wellness and comfort. Slight discomforts are readily discernible by this child, who will want the homeostasis (natural balance) of the body returned as soon as possible. These babies are quick to complain about soiled diapers or sticky fingers! As toddlers, these children may very well get dirty or enjoy play in the mud, but will not like staying messy. Also, the manner in which parents handle illness with this child is crucial. If illness marks the only time this child receives extra or special attention, the affirmation of being unwell can be extremely dangerous.

One concept I have always linked to Virgo is fastidiousness. This applies especially to the physical body, but can also extend into the personal environment. Being an earthy, mutable sign, Virgo is highly sensitive. This acute sensitivity knows when something is wrong, and generally will stay uncomfortable until the situation is remedied. You may then wonder why a Virgo child has a messy room or cluttered closet. There's a limit to how long these situations will remain. After a while, the clutter or mess will frustrate this child. Encouraging tidiness is helpful, but overemphasis can lead to excessive compulsiveness.

Virgo prefers to know what to expect in situations in order to make the most of them. You should let toddlers and preschoolers know each day what their schedule is likely to be. Virgo can adapt to changes (it is a mutable sign), but adapts much better with advance notice!

The young child with Virgo emphasis can be a great help in keeping the house clean and organized. These are the children for whom little brooms and mops were invented! Let this child know you appreciate his efforts, since it is very easy to take advantage of Virgo energy without saying thanks. However, if the child does not show an interest in spending lots of time cleaning, do not assume that this is wrong. Some children with strong Virgo tendencies seem to crave disorder, and the most you can expect is to help them learn to use this quality to become more organized.

Even the preschooler would benefit from some type of reward system for jobs well done. A chart in the room listing chores or behavior appropriate for the child's age would be helpful. This can be made from construction paper or poster board, listing things such as "picking up my toys," "feeding the puppy," and "dressing myself." Colorful stars and stickers could be awarded to indicate achievement. The recognition can be its own reward, or the child could have a goal which could be achieved by accumulating a certain number of stickers. Earning fifty stickers, for example, could be rewarded by a trip to the zoo. This will give a sense of increased self-esteem to the child. Since Virgo often has problems appreciating the self, such an exercise would be extremely beneficial.

The self-esteem of children with Virgo energies is often lowered due to self-imposed expectations of perfection. These children do not enjoy doing anything less than perfectly. There may be a reluctance to share their creative projects, drawings, or other work with parents, teachers, or peers if it does not meet their own high standards.

I, with my Virgo Sun and Ascendant, can recall my feelings in first grade when my teacher asked us all to draw a picture of something we enjoyed doing. I set to work with my crayons and construction paper and began drawing one of my favorite activities. There was the green grass, the blue sky, the bright sun, and, in the foreground, a clothesline. I just loved taking clothes down from the line, smelling their sun-sweetened freshness, and tumbling into the kitchen covered with sheets, towels, and Daddy's big shirts.

As I drew the picture, I took great care to draw one of everything on the line. After I had completed my work of art, however, I noticed that the clothespins were bigger than Daddy's shirt. I was crushed! The teacher asked to see my picture, and I ran out of the room into the hall outside crying. Fortunately, I had a patient and understanding teacher. She gently coaxed me to share my drawing and was delighted. My picture was even displayed in the city children's art show. Yet there I was, humiliated in my own eyes because everything was not perfect. As an adult shuffling through the papers my mom saved in my keepsake box, I came across this picture and clearly recalled the incident. However, as an adult, my thoughts ran more along the lines that I had the makings of a good surrealistic artist when I viewed the lack of proportion.

Talk with your young Virgo about his attitudes toward learning and doing. Let him know that you have no conditions except that he does the best he can. With Virgo, unconditional acceptance and love is more than important—it is absolutely necessary.

An infant with Virgo energies will enjoy toys that can be disassembled and/or serve more than one function. Toys requiring a high degree of manual dexterity are excellent choices. Toddlers will prefer things such as puzzles, sewing cards, and books. The preschooler will probably be eager to read, and may also enjoy art supplies and building toys. Young children whose analytical minds are ready to blossom may be challenged by math and science, and will be fascinated by the human body. Musical instruments may also provide an excellent and positive challenge, and this child may enjoy learning to play more than one instrument, or may become an excellent singer. Working with design tools can be great fun, and model-making may be a favorite pastime. Computer programs which facilitate drawing or drafting—and playing computer games in general—may be entertaining. These children really do like technical toys and tools!

Give Virgo opportunities to help other children. These kids are often fabulous teachers of younger brothers, sisters, and neighbors. I have always thought it would be excellent to implement helping situations in the classroom. The Virgo child can be an excellent tutor to fellow students. If there is a sick friend or family member, the Virgo may act as a concerned nurse. These types of activities stimulate the need to be of service. Older children and teens should be encouraged to write and speak publicly.

Virgo's main challenge lies in the need to appreciate herself and others. This appreciation should have its inception in early youth, and be based on the examples set by the parents. Often, whatever Mom, Dad, or school indicates is "the right way" will be unquestioningly incorporated into her life. Helping the child to understand the reasons behind these criteria is important, since it will enable her to create her own standards as she matures rather than blindly following someone else's.

Libra

Libra, the cardinal air sign of the zodiac, is directed toward maintaining harmony and balance. This sense permeates the majority of Libra's qualities. The child with an emphasis in this sign needs to experience situations in which beauty and harmony abound. This child will love pretty things, and may collect things just because the color is appealing. There can be an aggressiveness with this sign, but it is often disguised by an air of sweetness—hence, the concept of charm arises!

Relationships are important to Libra. The omnipresent sense of balance almost always requires another person to give reflection and diversity in life. Young children with planets in Libra are likely to be very sociable, enjoying parties and other gregarious activities. The childhood tea party is a good example of a Libran activity. Even if there is not another person, the child will socialize with dolls, the family pet, or stuffed animals. Yet even with this desire to relate, these children often exhibit a pronounced fickleness. This is due to the changeable nature of this airy sign.

Babies with a strong Libran emphasis are soothed by beautiful surroundings and will be delighted when someone talks to them. They will probably prefer being in a room with someone else rather than being left alone. Musical toys are favorites, as are toys which are pretty and visually interesting. Toddlers and preschoolers will like stories about princesses and princes, especially when they end happily ever after. Providing a positive archetype of relationships, in which each individual brings his best qualities into the relationship, is an exceptionally important lesson for this child. Even small Librans should be encouraged to draw, paint, and develop an awareness of color. Often, talents for design show at an early age.

Balancing toys are almost a necessity. One excellent toy I've seen was designed to teach math through balance. It consisted of a hanging scale from which numbers were suspended on each side. The child would hang a number on one side of the scale, then would have to balance it with the same number, or two or more numbers which equaled it, on the other side. The Libran concepts of balance and equality were taught very effectively. Building blocks are also good tools for learning a sense of balance. Physical feats encouraging balance may also be positive challenges (dance, gymnastics, bicycle-riding, and yoga are good examples).

Musical toys, art supplies, and other toys which provide the Libra child with a chance to make something are a necessity. Be sure to allow this child to have a say in decorating her room. You may decide that you'll ultimately employ her sense of style elsewhere. These children usually have an excellent eye for color, quality, and beauty.

Most Librans enjoy music, especially songs with lyrics so they can sing along! Music with beautiful harmonies is a heavenly experience for the Libran ear. Ballroom dancing might be enjoyable, too. Visiting art galleries and museums, attending art festivals, and going to concerts would delight this child.

The Libran desire for harmony carries over into interpersonal relationships as well. Libra hates to rock the boat. He will use placating behavior in early childhood just to avoid unpleasantness. He will also have difficulty dealing with harsh words, loud mannerisms, and obnoxious behavior. The refinement of this sign creates a desire for quality in all aspects of life. Distastefulness in any form can be repugnant.

One attitude children with Libran energies should develop early is learning to avoid the trap of comparing themselves with others. It is easier for the Libran to see what she considers "perfection" in another person, than to feel less than perfect if they are not doing exactly the same thing. If everybody else is wearing short sleeves and the Libran arrives with covered arms, she will feel uncomfortable and out of place. Sometimes these children have a natural sense of inferiority because they believe that someone else is better than they are.

Teach the child to appreciate the changes and growth within himself, using himself as the guideline. Make it clear that using another person for one's own individual standards is often dangerous and counterproductive. This is especially true in the case of external appearances. In our society today, the model of "perfection" as projected by advertisements and the mass media is far from the reality most individuals perceive about themselves. An impressionable young child may believe that all little children have to dress or look a certain way in order to be acceptable.

Libra is continually seeking balance, and other people usually provide one side of it. This can be helpful in relationships, as it confers a considerate attitude. Learning to be considerate of others can be a positive and special focus for the child with Libra planets. A lack of consideration from others may be hurtful to these children. An open dialogue with parents can aid the child in understanding a situation more easily.

Children with Libra energies need to learn to shoulder responsibility for their own decisions and actions early in life. There can be tremendous difficulty in accepting responsibility and scapegoating may be exhibited ("The dog ate those cookies, not me!"). Children with Libran Moons and Mercuries are notorious for their difficulty in making decisions. The decision has to be perfectly balanced to be right, and it may seem easier to not take responsibility for the decision and let someone else take care of it! To aid these children in decision-making, try some simple exercises such as choosing clothing for the day. Once a decision is made, help the child stay with it as she goes about getting dressed. Sometimes parents become so frustrated with this slow decision-making process that they make all the decisions themselves in the name of efficiency. This, however, can eventually cripple the child psychologically. When the preschooler is getting dressed in the morning, offer a limited choice of clothes, then walk away. Allow the child to decide. Once she is dressed, remember to extend a hug and compliment the child on her choice.

Scorpio

Scorpio, the fixed water sign of the zodiac, presents us with the qualities of intensity, mystery, passion, and resourcefulness. Scorpio brings powerful emotions into play, although children with the Sun, Moon, or planets in Scorpio may not show all that is brewing beneath the surface. This can create a sense of mystery or secrecy about the child. Even very young children with strong Scorpio influences may seem enigmatic.

For the child with Scorpio energy, life is experienced at a very deep, intense level. This intensity can be frightening for a child since it penetrates the Self so completely. Another person's barely noticeable sensation could be experienced as overwhelming pain by this child. Because of this increased sensitivity, the parents and significant others need to be especially tuned in to him. These children probably will not tell you their feelings all the time, especially if they are hurtful ones. It is more comfortable for the child to repress the memory of the sensation and go on to something else.

Psychology has shown us some of the negative results of emotional repression: withdrawal and depression which sometimes lead to periodic explosions of extreme violence. Parents of children with the Sun, Moon, Venus, or Mars in Scorpio should begin a dialogue with the child about emotions very early. This will help give the child a workable escape valve. An understanding, patient, and loving parent is a true jewel for the child with Scorpio planets. There is sometimes an overwhelming fear of abandonment which may stem from the powerful emotional attachment the child feels to those close to her.

I have worked with many adults with the personal planets (Sun, Moon, Mercury, Venus, or Mars) in Scorpio who have real problems with emotional relationships. This is often due to the overwhelming experience of pain when a relationship ends. Rather than easing in time, the pain just seems to penetrate more deeply into the self, creating an excruciating wound. This repressive behavior can be self-destructive.

The pattern or repressed emotion generally has its roots in childhood. The child needs to learn effective ways to release pain. If there are hurt feelings, hold the child lovingly. Perhaps a massage would help. Sometimes a bath is just the thing to ease away negative feelings. If the pattern becomes repressive, it will be extremely difficult to change later on.

This intensity also has its positive channels and opportunities. It is the passion of Scorpio which gives him the ability to be highly creative. The progeny of this sign don't just put mental energy into a project—they tend to throw themselves completely into the creative act. Children with personal planets in Scorpio should be encouraged to express themselves artistically or creatively. Painting and drawing can be ideal outlets. This is also a good way to release pent-up emotions—just get some finger paints, about thirty feet of paper, and let it all out!

Music is also an excellent choice to complement Scorpio's sensitivity. The baby with planets in Scorpio would appreciate powerful but soothing music. Classical forms are often favored. Whether or not the child shows musical talents is not so important as exposure to this form of expression!

Toddlers would probably enjoy playing with toys in which things are hidden (the Barrel of Monkeys is a good example). Puzzles are also a good choice. Toys that transform one thing to another can be fascinating.

Scorpio children like to watch things grow. Planting a small garden indoors with your child can be a magical experience as the seed transforms itself into a flower. Since Scorpio needs to understand the process of metamorphosis, real cocoons enclosed in transparent protective containers from which live butterflies emerge would be an excellent choice. Or, this child might enjoy watching a tadpole transform into a frog!

As the child grows, microscopes, chemistry sets, or anything which will aid her exploration of life would be perfect. A spelunking adventure would be fabulous for the teenager; until then, family trips to caves and caverns might be great fun. Computer games which represent power struggles and quests may be especially fascinating for this child.

Scorpio's abilities often extend to the positive transformational process of healing. There is usually a fascination with the human body and the processes which can heal it. You may find that these children are interested in medicine or anatomy at a very young age. Encourage this interest since it may result in a very fine physician, counselor, or healer. Early on, this may be the child playing "doctor" with everyone.

Another reason why a Scorpio child would be playing "doctor" is because Scorpio's sexual expression is very powerful. It is extremely important that children with Scorpio planets be approached honestly about sex. An open, positive attitude is necessary for all children, but especially for those who live daily with such intensive sensitivity. Since Scorpio projects the qualities of transformation so intensely, the child will be especially interested in this most fundamental level of human transformation. Small children will want to know where they came from, and this information must be presented accurately and honestly. As the child matures, the potential to create of life through sexual sharing can be discussed in a frank manner with him. If the parent represses his sexuality, the child will most certainly absorb this attitude. Given knowledge, the young person can choose to act in a responsible and mature manner when relating sexually.

Sagittarius

The mutable fire sign is the most freedom-loving sign of the zodiac. Sagittarian traits include aspiration, foresight, optimism, versatility, and open-mindedness. I've often thought the song "Don't Fence Me In" was a good example of the Sagittarian theme. Sagittarian children will exemplify some of these qualities, but are likely to be a bit capricious in their behavior until they learn the importance of positive limitations.

Children with the personal planets (Sun, Moon, Mercury, Venus, or Mars) in Sagittarius will exhibit a fascination with learning early in life. This is stimulated by the natural need to understand as much as possible. Learning does not have to be associated with school or traditional educational systems: Sagittarians tend to be philosophical, and believe that there is much to be learned in every experience. Travel is also high on the list of favorite things to do, especially to places or events that are fun. Places like theme parks—Disneyland, Disney World (especially Epcot Center), or adventure parks—are fantastic examples of Sagittarian fun.

Most children of Sagittarius will be attracted to horses, which are often associated with this sign due to their free spirit and fleet-footedness. There is a general love of nature, wild animals, and the great outdoors. Activities attractive to Sagittarians must provide new experiences and opportunities. These expand the personal universe and enhance the sense of personal freedom.

One aspect of this sign which can create difficulties is the ease with which distractions can occur. Focusing is sometimes a huge problem for these children, especially for those with the Moon or Mercury in Sagittarius. But the tendency to get distracted can be positively employed. For the very small child, realize that her attention span will be limited and plan a series of things to do with the child. Once the child is in school doing homework, schedule breaks into her study times. Scheduled "distractions" sometimes make it easier for the child to focus on schoolwork. If absolute freedom is allowed with studying, though, it may never get done!

Children with Sagittarian planets often resist limitations. Playpens are frustrating for the crawler with his needs to explore and move about. Although it will require the parents to be more attentive, the baby would prefer the less restrictive environment of a blanket on the floor. Although the infant may enjoy the feeling of movement in a backpack or babypack strapped close to Mom or Dad, fussiness can result from too much time spent strapped in. The same is true of strollers. Riding for a while can be fun, but these are the toddlers you frequently see pushing their strollers!

Once the baby begins to expand her horizons, she can be taught limits gradually. If you want the child to respect and understand these restrictions, you will have to tell her why they are necessary. My daughter, with four planets in Sagittarius, nearly drove me nuts with her incessant "Whys" beginning at about age two. When I finally realized that she honestly needed to understand, I became more pliable about answering her questions. In fact, it got to the point that I would often give her the answer before she asked the question!

By appealing to reason, parents offer the child a sense of personal power and this will build a more understanding relationship with the child. Open communication will be especially helpful when dealing with the toddler who would run headlong into the street unless tethered. Use cooperation and understanding to build the fences inside the child and there will be less need for a leash!

Sagittarian babies and toddlers enjoy action toys, as well as toys they can take with them. Sometimes a wailing infant can be calmed by a walk around the block or a stroll in the park. I have had many parents of Sagittarian children ask me why their baby cries for long periods. This may be partly an early exercise in oration! A bigger reason may be that these children have a strong spiritual light energy, and simply resist having such a large, expanded consciousness crammed into such a tiny body!

Small children with Sagittarius' influence will enjoy walkers, since they are eager to be on the go from the very beginning. As the child gets older, he should be given opportunities to experience many different environments. A trip to Grandma's, a jaunt to the park, or just a change of scenery would be enjoyed.

Toys should include books and records (especially storybook tapes and records), rocking horses, pull toys, and little cars. A racetrack will be a delight for the older Sagittarian (boy or girl). While computer race games or flight simulators might be fun, ultimately this child will want the real thing.

The characteristic Sagittarian resistance to limitations can also extend to speech patterns ("talking a blue streak"), overeating, or overextending the physical energy. Sagittarian children do not want to miss anything, and will probably resist scheduled bedtimes and nap times.

The lessons the child must learn—and they are not easy ones—involve learning to know the Self and developing a sense of positive limits. Personal freedom must be balanced with a true sense of personal responsibility. Teaching the Sagittarian child horsemanship in the preteen and early teen years would not be a bad idea. The child would learn that a horse cannot just be "ridden hard and put away wet," but must be fed, watered, groomed, and loved. The physical maneuvers involved in horseback riding (especially English style) are also rigorous and require personal discipline along with a keen attunement to the animal. Gymnastics, martial arts, and track and field sports also seem especially well suited to these children.

Most children with Sagittarian energies enjoy stories and reading, especially tales of adventure. The *Black Beauty* books are especially attractive to these children. Writing flows easily, as do the other language skills. Learning at least one foreign language is advised. Although adhering to the rules of spelling and grammar may be a problem at first, these too can be mastered.

There can be a love of game-playing, even in infancy. Other activities which are enjoyable involve interaction with nature. Camping, hiking, and spending time outdoors in natural surroundings is important for the child influenced by Sagittarius.

Even the young Sagittarian may find the study of religion fascinating. The child should be taught the spiritual truths of life, since Sagittarius constantly searches for the truth.

There can be a wonderful generosity and optimism in Sagittarian children, as well as a contagious sense of positivity. These children can teach us much about the Law of Abundance (the concept that the universe always provides), since they seem to have a natural understanding of it. Their directness of speech can be a two-edged sword, although very refreshing at times. We often do not want to hear the truth. However, if there is a Sagittarian child around who thinks she knows the "truth" about something, be prepared to hear about it!

Capricorn

♑ The sign of Capricorn initiates the winter solstice in the Northern Hemisphere. This cardinal earth sign has the qualities of determination, practicality, ambition, reliability, and persistence. Capricorn children have a need to be respected, and truly admire adults who have earned respect. It is often said of children with Capricorn planets that they are old when they are young and young when they are old.

These children want to be in control of everything in their lives. This can be frustrating for parents with Capricorn toddlers who already want control but are not ready for it! There is an outgoing yet cautious independence in these children. My son, who has both the Sun and Venus in Capricorn, would quietly assess a situation before getting involved in it, even when he was very young. At a new playground, he would slowly walk around the perimeter, observing how the other children climb up the ladders and chains, then will cautiously try one thing at a time until he feels confident. Then, however, he would dive in full force, running and squealing with delight as he enjoyed the now familiar situation.

One way to encourage the young child with Capricorn energies is by offering him appropriate responsibilities for his age. For example, the three-year-old can be given the responsibility of dressing himself. As the child grows, his responsibilities can be increased, such as helping with chores around the house or feeding the family pet.

Capricorns become radiant when they receive something for their efforts. They will respond well to a "reward chart," or, once they understand the value of money, actual cash. This must be handled with care, however, since a sharp Capricornian can drain Mom's cash reserves in a hurry! Self-esteem is strongly associated with physical and material results for these children. They need to feel that they are creating, building, or improving something.

Capricorn enjoys making use of available assets. These kids will definitely keep the leftovers cleared out of the refrigerator! If something is "useless," however, Capricorn wants nothing to do with it. Toys for Capricorn might include various types of building blocks, especially ones which interlock. Erector sets, interlocking blocks (like Lego) and other building toys are suitable. Building projects like birdhouses or sewing may also be fun. Sandboxes, digging in the dirt, working with modeling clay and other "earthy" activities would also be enjoyable. Computer games like *SimCity* might be enjoyable.

Toys that are like Mom's or Dad's business tools such as calculators, cash registers, typewriters, tools, or computers, are natural choices. At age five, my daughter, with Venus in Capricorn, would set up her toy cash register in her room on laundry day. She would "sell" her dirty clothes to me for a penny per piece. I thought that was pretty resourceful, and catered to it until she found she could make more money making pot holders and selling them to the neighbors!

One challenge for the child with Capricorn energies is maintaining a positive attitude. This is absolutely necessary if the child is to express the more advantageous qualities of the sign. Because of the strong tie to the physical and material aspects of life, the child can quickly become depressed if she does not have some particular toy or does not get something which she strongly desires. The child must learn to be grateful for what she has, and would be blessed to understand that appreciation is the first key to abundant living.

All children of earth signs will enjoy contact with their natural elements, and Capricorn is no exception. Gardening or spending time in nature is an absolute. There will probably be a love of trees, especially those that are very large and ancient. The older Capricorn child might enjoy a tree house, especially if he can proudly say, "I built it myself!" Climbing is also a favorite pastime of Capricorn. Even the infant can be observed climbing, sometimes before he can walk! These children also love rocks and crystals.

The sense of smell is often highly developed, and small children with Capricorn planets love anything they can "scratch and sniff." Watch these children as they grow older: the first thing they may do with a new pair of shoes is smell them!

Children with Capricornian influences often have a great sense of humor. (This must be the "corn" part of Capricorn.) Given encouragement, these kids will offer parents and friends ample opportunities to find humor in almost any situation. Sometimes the humor centers around puns, so be ready to groan. One never knows when a Capricorn may be lurking about, ready to transform serious dialogue into her next play on words!

Children with Capricorn energies are often loners, or may prefer the company of older children or adults. Parents and significant adults will be observed as the models for behavior. Learning self-respect is important for children with strong Capricornian qualities, and having a positive relationship with parents, teachers, or mentors is crucial to the development of self-respect. However, this child will continually test and probe to see whether or not the parent is worthy of respect. If a child is disappointed in a parent or teacher and loses respect, he will put the parent through rigorous testing before deciding that he deserves that respect. Once that respect is earned, however, it will endure.

Aquarius

Aquarius introduces us to the fixed quality of air. Children with inventiveness and original thinking are this sign's trademark with the intellectual thrust strongly focused. Children with Aquarian energies are independent, idealistic, unique, and often unconventional.

Life can be an exciting challenge for the child with Aquarian influences, offering endless opportunities to find alternative ways of approaching everything. The often rebellious quality of Aquarius will not be as readily apparent in the infant, although even then the parents may be aware of an unusual detachment emanating from the baby. One mother of an Aquarian baby commented to me, "My baby seems to be out in another dimension much of the time." Perhaps he was! These babies need plenty of human contact, but they also need to feel true freedom to be themselves.

Present the young Aquarian with unusual toys of varying shapes, sizes, and textures. Toys with moving parts will encourage the child to study them to see how they work. Give the baby plenty of room to crawl about and explore. Most of these babies are friendly, and will enjoy the company of many people. Playtime with other children can be a highlight of the toddler's day, and school may ultimately be enjoyed as much for the social interaction as the learning.

As the child of Aquarius grows, her sense of independence also expands. The mind is very active and inventive. Toys which can be used in inventive ways will be necessary: interlocking blocks or erector sets which may be transformed into robots, creatures from another galaxy, or intergalactic radios. There is also a fascination with technological developments. If it has buttons, knobs, or dials on it, the Aquarian child will want to know what it does, how it works, and in what other ways it might possibly be used. Safeguard the stereo, the video equipment, and the computer until you are ready for the child to start manipulating them! Calculators, radios, computers, VCRs, synthesizers, and video games are also likely intrigues for the Aquarian mind. Interactive, multimedia experiences will be pure delight for this child.

Air and space travel may also hold a special fascination. Encourage these explorations, as they may be a necessary part of the Aquarian child's identity. Astronomy and astrology are also natural areas of interest and study.

Geometry is often a favorite study of those with Aquarian leanings and should be encouraged in a participatory manner when the child is very young. Have the toddler walk around the perimeter of a large triangle. Find geometric shapes in daily life—the octagonal stop sign, the circular Moon, and so on. Other mathematical subjects may also interest the child, especially if Mercury is in Aquarius. These should be supported and encouraged as the child is ready for them.

Aquarius is not an emotional sign, and often seems rather distant and aloof. This detachment offers the child an opportunity to understand the concept of unconditional love. He may be directed more to groups of people than to just one person, thereby indicating a need for several playmates. Later, larger groups of friends might be enjoyed. Becoming involved in organizations such as scouting might be worthwhile for the child. Not only would this offer him an opportunity to be involved with other young people, but would provide humanitarian activities in which to participate.

Aquarius needs to focus on humanity and the masses. Given a cause, the revolutionary nature of Aquarius can be directed to facilitate needed changes within a system. Teaching the young child advantageous methods of bringing about change is a challenge, but a necessary one. If the child cannot distinguish between the creative and destructive sides of revolution, she may later direct energy destructively.

One aspect many grown-up Aquarians have shared with me is that they often felt like the oddball or misfit among their peers. Feeling different can be hard for a child because he does not feel included. Help the child feel comfortable with his uniqueness and special qualities. Encourage his natural inventiveness. Now that we are on the threshold of the Aquarian Age, these children are likely to lead the way into humanity's new expression on this planet. The child should be supported in his unique approaches to problems and in his concern for humanity and the planet.

Because of Aquarius' fixed nature, ideas and concepts may become rigid once they are formed. Learning to listen to others' ideas and consider them as potentially valid until proven otherwise may present a challenge. Sometimes there is a know-it-all attitude when Aquarian energies are present in the chart. This can be damaging in many ways, mostly because it creates unnecessary limitations for the child!

If this type of attitude persists, it would be wise to challenge it at every opportunity to help the child broaden her perspectives. Also, those with Aquarian energies must learn to trust the intuitive aspect of the Self early in life. Logic can too easily become the king for Aquarius. We certainly need logical, pragmatic thinking, but not to the exclusion of the all-important attunement to the Higher Self.

Pisces

 The twelfth sign of the zodiac is the mutable water sign Pisces. Pisces represents the idealistic, intangible qualities of life: spirituality, imagination, mysticism, and romanticism.

For the child with energies in this sign, life presents the challenge of staying in touch with physical reality while remaining attuned to the powerful inner guide. There is often a dreaminess or otherworldliness with Pisces children, as well as a sense of magic. With a heightened sensitivity to the physical, mental, emotional, and spiritual levels, Pisces can experience an enhanced awareness of life.

The infant with energies in Pisces may be very peaceful, especially if his personal environment is calm and pleasant. If an environment is boisterous, this child will feel it more intensely than most children and may react with surprisingly strong signs of discontent. Transcendent music is almost a necessity for these babies to help them maintain a strong sense of inner peace. The soothing sound of an evening lullaby can be just what this child needs at the end of the day.

Walks near a pond, lake, or the ocean will feel wonderful to this baby. Bath time can be a special treat. Encourage an early rapport with the element of water. Pisces babies enjoy swaying movements, and might be delighted to be held or carried while Mom, Dad, or a sibling dances with them. Sensations of all types are heightened. There may be a special delight when she finds her reflection in a mirror.

The toddler with energies in this sign will adore fairy tales. Stories of angels and other light beings will be mesmerizing. Aquariums may fascinate the child for long periods of time. Encourage the imagination with dressing up and games of make-believe. Since Pisces often has problems relating to physical reality, the aspects of the physical plane should be gently, but definitely, introduced. For example, the difference between a pretend bear and a real bear could be easily identified during a trip to the zoo.

Be especially sensitive to these children when allowing them to watch movies or television. Those with Pisces energies have a highly impressionable consciousness. It is too easy to allow the television to become the baby-sitter. Try to spend time viewing programs with your child in order to help him distinguish between reality and fantasy. I am not suggesting that fantasy and imagination be repressed—in fact, they should be encouraged. But you must be a conscientious censor, since the graphic images in motion pictures and television can alter an impressionable consciousness for life.

Toys for Piscean children should encourage the imagination and creativity. Costumes, make-up, and other role-playing aids will be enjoyed. Drama, dance, or singing lessons will probably be well received by the child over age four or five. Although an older child might enjoy playing video games, setting limits on the amount of time spent may be necessary, and definitely governing the qualities of games is important. This is true for all children, but a child with strong Pisces sensibilities is especially prone to integrating the experience of the games into her life as reality.

It is easy for the child with Pisces energies to escape into an inner world to avoid interaction with others. Provide ample opportunities for the child to play with other children to balance this tendency. New situations can be a bit frightening, and should be presented to the child gradually. As the child grows, and a new activity or different situation is planned, talk with him about what changes are about to take place. This child has an amazing ability to adapt to new situations, but the imagination is so strong that the child may withdraw inside the self if he feels too afraid.

For example, if the four year old is about to begin preschool, a preview trip to the school is strongly advised. Then you can talk with the child and have her imagine what it would be like to be there. Generate positive, exciting feelings in this exercise. Then, when the child is dropped at preschool, it will be familiar and pleasant since she has already been there in reality and in the world of imagination.

Encourage young children with Piscean influences to share stories and fantasies with you. This cultivates the sense of imagination while maintaining a connection between you and the child. By giving these children opportunities to flow into their special worlds, we encourage the positive use of their talents.

Dance is often an excellent release for the Piscean. Swimming, scuba diving, or other aquatic activities would also be good outlets. There may be an interest in painting or photography—a camera would be a welcome gift. Music education might include not only dance, but voice, string instruments, or synthesizers. Growing exotic flowers or caring for tropical fish is often a favorite hobby for the young Piscean. These types of hobbies can last a lifetime.

The quality of Pisces is a channel for divine compassion. Offer these children opportunities to care for and help others. Let them know that they can make a difference. The power of their love, accompanied by the vision within them, can truly make the world a better place!

3

Energy: The Sun, Moon, and Planets

The Concept of Energy

In astrology, we focus on the concept and qualities of energy. Life itself is an expression of many forms of energy. Each human being is spiritual energy incarnate. We are each a complete universe, and the power of that individual universe is directed by the Higher Self in coordination with the power of mind energy. Mind energy, which is expressed as thought forms, is focused through the willpower of the human being. Learning to focus and use our individual power requires the development of personal awareness. We gain knowledge and understanding of ourselves as we mature and become more comfortable with who we are and how we function.

For the child learning to express the energies of the Self, a sense of identity has not yet formed. We must view the individual energies within the child as *potentials* for development. These energies are symbolized in each individual horoscope by the Sun, Moon, and planets in our solar system. By understanding these symbolic concepts, we gain access to a deeper insight into human nature and human needs.

Developmental psychology has taught us much about a child's various stages of growth. In the very early stages, the child is dependent upon others for physical survival. This dependency is usually focused within the child's immediate family, especially through the father and mother.

As a child matures and gradually becomes more adept in controlling bodily functions and movements, this dependency lessens somewhat. The child gains mastery over the self through a gradual process of self-unfolding until, finally, he can demonstrate full responsibility for his basic survival needs. Continuing maturation gives the ability to meet other needs until a state of independence is reached and the child has "grown up."

This developmental process continues throughout life, and can be studied astrologically by observing cycles of energy called *progressions* and *transits*. Once again, we use the symbols of the Sun, Moon, and planets to understand this continual unfolding of the Self.

Clarifying the basic meanings of the Sun, Moon, and planets when applying astrology to children offers a fresh perspective in astrology. Certainly, the archetypal qualities of the planetary energies presented through astrology remain, even in childhood. The basic keyword concepts for the planets apply in all stages of life (see Table 4). However, a child will not express each of these energies completely in youth, since her needs and energies are evolving during the stages of childhood development. Astrology offers a framework from which to examine the needs of a developing child, to be used with loving guidance in helping the child to fully express a sense of personal wholeness.

The Sun and Moon

The Sun and Moon are referred to as the "luminaries" or "light bodies" in the astrological chart. The Sun emanates light, while the Moon reflects it. Within the human being, the Sun is the light of the spirit. It projects the individual ego, willpower, and sense of individuality. It is a primary indicator of conscious self-awareness. The Moon symbolizes the reflective nature of humanity. It is the absorbing, subconscious mind, and reflects the needs of the soul.

We also experience an understanding of ourselves through interactions with other people in our lives. For the child, the Sun and Moon are first experienced as the father and mother. Father illustrates the assertive sense of willpower (the Sun) and Mother illustrates the receptive nurturance of the Moon.

GLYPH	SIGN	KEYWORDS
☉	Sun	Individuality, ego, willpower, drive, vitality, Father
☽	Moon	Receptivity, nurturance, emotional security, highest needs, feelings, subconscious, Mother
☿	Mercury	Communication, senses, ideas, humor, inventiveness, intellect, transportation
♀	Venus	Love, values, emotions, aesthetics, harmony, beauty, artistry
♂	Mars	Physical energy, drive, assertiveness, temperament, strength
♃	Jupiter	Confidence, generosity, enthusiasm, optimism, prosperity, consciousness, understanding
♄	Saturn	Discipline, control, structure, responsibility, karma, testing
♅	Uranus	Independence, originality, intuition, uniqueness, revolution
♆	Neptune	Idealism, imagination, illusion, escape, sensitivity, beliefs, spirituality
♇	Pluto	Transformation, regeneration, power, extremism, compulsion, healing

Table 4. Keywords: The Planets.

As the child grows and externalizes the personality self, it is easy to identify parental influences. How many times have you heard someone say, "Why, she laughs just like her mother!" or, "When he said that, he looked just like his dad!" How often have we, as parents, had to remind ourselves of our negative habits when we observe them in our own children? The small child will not be spending time analyzing why he behaves in a particular manner; he largely just mimics what he sees and hears. Sometimes, that mimicking behavior is like practicing expressing the self. If it seems to fit, it may be integrated into the way the child ultimately expresses his unique identity.

The Sun and Moon in the child's chart do not tell us exactly what the parents are like—they only indicate how the child perceives the parents. The child's perceptions of the parents will almost always be somewhat different from the parents' perceptions of themselves. Yet it is this framework of perception which determines the child's understanding of not only who the parents are, but who she is. We will examine these perceptions in depth in chapter 10.

When we study the Sun in a child's chart, we are looking at how the sense of individuality and drive for significance might ultimately be expressed. We can understand what might motivate a child by looking at the sign in which the Sun is placed. A child with the Sun in Leo, for example, could be motivated by recognition for his achievements. The father will provide the pattern the child is likely to follow for his idea of recognition and how to achieve it.

The sign in which the Sun is placed will also indicate which qualities the child is seeking to identify within the father. A Scorpio Sun child may easily identify with Father's repressed emotionality. But if Dad can show an acknowledgment of his emotional needs, the child may find it easier to accept the intensity of his own emotional nature. The qualities of Scorpio indicate a powerful ego, but one that feels vulnerable if exposed.

By studying Jungian psychology, we gain a sense of the archetypal patterns in our lives. *Archetypes* are models for unconscious needs which we usually project onto others in our lives. These significant others are the models we use to develop an understanding of ourselves. This projection can be identified through astrological symbology and is tremendously important in understanding the needs of a child. Parental attitudes and behavior toward a child are critical in shaping a child's emotional matrix. The archetype of the Sun may be difficult for the child to "own" early in her life. Imagine the child's impressions of individual will as exercised by someone five times her size! A small child may not be ready to expose her personal ego into the world when faced with such potentially stifling possibilities! It's much easier to project the psychological ownership of the Sun onto a parent, especially Father: give it to the "big guy!" However, qualities of a child's ego emerge early in life, albeit in a still-developing form.

The subconscious mind is symbolized by the Moon in the astrological chart. This is the matrix from which our habit patterns emerge. The archetypal projection of the Moon is Mother, who provides nurturing, comfort, and security. Good keywords for the Moon are "nurturance" and "mothering." Mother is the model for the child's developing sense of how he will nurture and care for others, and, most importantly, how the child will nurture himself.

By analyzing the Sun and Moon signs in the child's chart, we observe the qualities the child needs to express through these particular energies. The energy of the Sun—willpower, drive, ego, and personal power—and the energy of the Moon—receptivity, nurturance, emotional security, and highest needs—form the basic building blocks in understanding the child's real needs. Too often, parents will project their own needs onto their children, thus overwhelming the child's true nature. Living vicariously can be dangerous!

Although these two energies definitely show how the child perceives the parents, they indicate even more strongly who the child really is and what she needs and will ultimately strive to develop as her identity and personality emerge. In counseling divorcing parents, I appeal to them to allow the child to see each of them as individuals. I encourage them not to "have it out" in front of the child, or badmouth the absent parent to the child. Doing this inevitably traumatizes the child. The parents should keep any hostility they may feel toward a spouse or ex-spouse to themselves.

The Sun

The Sun in the chart shows us how the child would like to be perceived, what the child needs to feel motivated toward achievement and what makes the child feel significant in the world. While the full expression of the Sun's ego self takes quite some time to develop, certain qualities will definitely be apparent, even in young children and babies. However, it's important to remain mindful that this aspect of the personality will be more apparent after the toddler years. Characteristics identified by the signs and their elements will indicate how the child is likely to go about meeting the needs of expressing will, recognition, and ego. The Sun placed in fire signs will encourage a child to be active in expressing needs for recognition. These children may seem to shine more easily. The child with the earthy Sun is more grounded, and may take a practical approach to expressing the ego needs. With the Sun in water signs, a child may be more emotional about himself. This sensitivity creates a quieter approach to expressing willpower and drive. Air sign Suns express verbally and intellectually, and tie their identities to their thoughts ("I think, therefore, I am.").

The Sun in the Signs

Sun in Aries—The fiery nature of a small child with Aries Sun is presented through a quality of impatience. Waiting can be simply intolerable. During the "terrible twos" when toddlers are testing limits on a moment-to-moment basis, the Aries Sun can be extremely temperamental. But in the next moment, once anger is burned off, the Aries Sun may be quite charming. Even as a baby, Aries loves to tease. You may even think this baby winks at you! The elementary school years provide the perfect chance for this child to develop a drive to compete, meet challenges, and test limits. Sports may be fun, and staying active is important. In preteen years, this love of physical activity may continue, but if other factors draw the Aries Sun child to participate in more intellectual activities, that same desire to win and need to prove himself still shines through. Encourage the young Aries to exercise the drive to move forward and get things started.

Sun in Taurus—Taurus babies may, at first, seem rather placid. Certainly this child will prefer that things go smoothly, but when it comes time to make changes, a surge of stubborn resistance can appear. Too much jostling about right after waking may be unsettling for this baby. During the toddler years, that resistant attitude is likely to be experienced as a firmly spoken "no." While the tiny Taurus may actually mean it, it's possible that "no" is just the first response! Give this child time to get used to any changes to encourage cooperation. Preschool and primary school years can be the best time to offer early artistic education, since creating things can be a favorite pastime. Musical education can be an excellent opportunity to encourage any talents in this arena. Preteen Taurus may be especially interested in social relationships, although she can be somewhat shy in new situations or uncertain when it comes to matters of appearance.

Sun in Gemini—Busy Gemini Sun babies need plenty of distractions. Crib toys, interesting mobiles, and rattles (which, when finally quiet, are the clue that this child is asleep) ultimately give way to tricycles and bicycles, since moving about is a top priority. Then, early on, a preference for social play with other children is likely in preschool years. This child may talk early, and whether or not he speaks understandable language, seems to always have something to say or questions to ask. Primary school years can be pure joy, since the chance to learn new things is usually met with great enthusiasm. However, focus can be a problem, but this will be further defined by other planetary qualities. Preteens may seem to change friends as interests change, although a good friend who's fun to be around and understands this child's humor will be cherished.

Sun in Cancer—Cancerians generally enjoy childhood and may be especially fond of family and family experiences. As babies, Cancer Suns prefer close physical contact and may be fussy in the presence of strangers, since the familiar comforts of Mom, Dad, or siblings are much more soothing. The toddler may not like separation from family or home, and may be especially clingy when Mom needs to leave for work or errands. But if there's a safe, comfortable substitute, the child can just as readily seek shelter in that familiarity. (Mother does not always know this as she walks away to the sound of sad whimpers.) During the elementary school years, attachments to teachers are the norm, although working with parents on school projects can be the stuff that makes lifetime memories. This child will also want to invite playmates to share family gatherings when friendships grow strong. Preteen Cancerians can be especially moody as hormonal changes flood her with unfamiliar emotions. Maintaining open lines of understanding and communication is absolutely necessary.

Sun in Leo—Make way—this child needs to be noticed now! Leo Sun babies may even like the spotlight, but one thing's certain: when this child wants or needs attention, you will know. During the toddler years, a demanding quality can emerge, and setting reasonable limits can be frustrating if this child gets dramatic. Nonetheless, lovingly defining who has the power is important from a very early age. Yes, you're reading this correctly: these children sometimes seem to demand to be spoiled. Granted, they shower you with warm smiles and big hugs, so it's easy. By the early school years, if given opportunities to take center stage, you may have a budding performer or young leader growing up before your eyes. Preteen Leo's can sometimes become insecure if they're noticed for the wrong reasons, and, if they're not given proper attention, can become especially disruptive in order to gain notice. If there's any inclination shown, encourage this child to run for class president!

Sun in Virgo—Most children with Virgo Sun are studious, even as babies. While a young Virgo can be talkative, you may also see that this child is watching everything very carefully. This child can be a keen observer, and learns by watching every detail. You may assume that with all this attention to detail that your Virgo child will be neat, but it's best to avoid jumping to conclusions. While there are definite preferences for cleanliness and for things to be in their proper places, neatness is something that may have to be learned. And be warned: Virgo babies are not likely to tolerate physical discomfort. Some of that fussiness can even be due to irritation from a tag in the back of Baby's shirt. (You may think I exaggerate, but trust me on this one!) This child will appreciate parents and teachers who enjoy developing the intellect, and your young Virgo may like school for learning itself. Yet it is crucial that this child be given plenty of outside interests and encouraged to develop hobbies and skills. Hands-on exposure to learning is best, and dealing with nature up close and personal is right up young Virgo's alley. Virgo children may enjoy small toys, miniatures, or toys that can be carried in their hands. Preteen Virgo may also have an interest in health and nutrition, which is uncommon for children of this age group. Opportunities to lend a helping hand will shape what is sometimes best about Virgo: a desire to make things better!

Sun in Libra—A child with the Sun in Libra will crave the company of others. While a Libra baby may not be social in the strict sense of the term, feeling the presence of others, listening to conversation, and being taken along to share excursions and experiences will instill a sense of connection which is deeply important to this child. Even at a young age this child can become rather charming, and may have a winning smile. Artistic leanings may be apparent early on, and, at the very least, this child will appreciate beautiful things and may have a keen sense of color. Once in school, the Libran may enjoy the social aspect of education the most, although these are the children who also seem to appreciate literature and the arts. Exposure to cultural experiences can stimulate lifelong interests. Preteen Libra can be inclined to place too much value on social status and may fall into the trap of exclusive cliques or may feel deeply hurt if excluded from the "in crowd." Early on the Libra child needs encouragement in the realms of self-esteem and personal values.

Sun in Scorpio—Babies with the Sun in Scorpio may seem intense! That intensity is not necessarily a detriment, since with it comes a keen awareness and sensitivity. Even though you may not be fully aware of it, this child, even in infancy, can be extrasensitive to the emotional atmosphere of any situation. In the midst of high-tension, the baby can seem fussy for no apparent reason (and only adding to the tension!). In early childhood, Scorpio Sun is drawn to the power archetypes—superheroes to super villains! You may even notice a fascination with things some people find scary—like insects, snakes, or not-so-fuzzy critters. This child likes to probe and look under the rocks instead of just stepping on them. Science can be fascinating. There can be a reticence when it comes to developing friends, although during elementary school years some very solid friendships may begin to emerge. Jealousy can be a problem when young Scorpio feels threatened within the context of a relationship, and if he learns to deal with these feelings during a younger age he will find the complexity of relationships much less intense as time moves on. Even during preteen years, Scorpio Sun can become unusually attached to others or to situations. Learning to cope with change may be one of his great challenges.

Sun in Sagittarius—"Let's go!" may be the consistent request from a Sagittarian child. This is the baby whose fussiness can likely be calmed by a walk around the block or a ride in the car. Motion feels natural, and a change of scenery can prove fascinating. Trips to the zoo or wild animal park may be among favorite pastimes, but amusement parks are also likely to rank high on the priority list as the child grows. The Sun in Sagittarius stimulates a desire to experience life in the broadest sense. Ideas can be just as adventurous as actually going somewhere for a Sagittarian youngster. While this child might enjoy school if the teacher makes things interesting, she can just as easily become bored if the subject material is too repetitive or lacking in interest. Distractability can be a problem. Preteen Sagittarius loves to be around friends, and may have a keen desire to get a driver's license as soon as possible.

Sun in Capricorn—Childhood years can be frustrating to the child born with Sun in Capricorn, since it takes a while to figure out the true nature of control and this child innately desires it. This is a determined child who is not likely to take "no" for an answer if he really wants something. Positively directed, this can be an excellent trait, but if left unchecked, can develop into an intractability which can be frustrating to others. Structure is of primary importance, but that does not mean that Capricorn likes restraint! Even in early educational settings, illustrating the principles of continuity will be helpful to a Capricorn. Since one of the lessons of Capricorn is learning self-discipline, early disciplinary measures which provide sensible boundaries and reasonable restraints will be helpful when they are necessary. However, excessive restraint will only encourage him to develop greater willfulness. Nurturant consistency is the key to creating a safe and healthy haven for young Capricorns to grow. In preteen years, this child may be a bit shy and can even be awkward in social situations. While he may want to be respected and accepted, it's not likely that he will take the lead unless there is real encouragement and a safe situation for pursuing such ends.

Sun in Aquarius—For a child with Sun in Aquarius, childhood can provide the perfect backdrop for experimentation in a protective setting. Aquarian babies can exude a kind of brightness that is rather engaging, especially when communication skills are developing. These are the kids who seem to have a language all their own, but somehow, others understand it. Sometimes this child may seem a little detached, especially if she is occupied with a fascinating toy, and later on, a project. Early childhood interaction with other toddlers can be enjoyable, although you may not see much attachment to any particular friends in the beginning. However, by the elementary school years, she may become extremely drawn to friendships, especially with those who appreciate her special talents and unique abilities. Some Aquarian children express the sentiment that they feel out of place, and helping this child appreciate the value of uniqueness can go a long way toward stabilizing her sense of self. Preteen Aquarius may be the perfect class officer taking on school projects or working in community endeavors. Involvement with others can be a mainstay for this child, but time to allow individuality to shine is just as important.

Sun in Pisces—From the beginning a child with Pisces Sun seems to radiate a quality of enchantment. There is a sensitivity which invites imagination, and if given ample encouragement and the right environment, even a very young Piscean may seem musically or artistically inclined. Free-flowing self-expression is the mainstay of self-affirmation for Pisces, and allowing this child to use his imagination can prove to be purely delightful. Of course, illustrating the differences between what is "real" and what is imagined can be a challenge for the parent or teacher, since this child innately operates in the realm of what psychologists would define as "magical thinking." It is also quite conceivable that young Pisces will be extrasensitive emotionally, and he may seem to cry too easily. Although it's not a good idea to stifle this type of emotional expression, reaching out to comfort or console can help affirm feelings of safety and security. Exploring the problems that were hurtful can help this child gain objectivity about what has transpired, especially by the elementary school years. Music, dance, and the arts can be crucial to this child's intellectual and emotional development, and during the preadolescent years when a young identity is emerging, these types of expression can provide a secure backdrop for Pisces to fit into the world.

The Moon

The Moon represents the subconscious mind. This aspect of ourselves operates on automatic pilot and represents the internal matrix we call our habits. Examples of subconscious processes include the simple tasks woven into daily life—we learn how to tie our shoes when we are young, then never really have to think about it again. The subconscious mind directs the body's actions, and we can tie our shoes without thinking. Emotional responses develop in much the same way. We are conditioned to feel confident or fearful by our experiences.

The developing child has a very open subconscious mind, but is not just a blank slate. Rather, this aspect of the self is most impressionable in the early years due to the dependency upon others for survival. Even small infants soon make their particular warbles and cries meaningful to the receptive parent. Observing a mother and child tells you much about their intuitive links with one another. Baby cries the cry which tells Mother, "I'm hungry!" and Mother responds by feeding her.

Yet Mother still has more power than Baby. Imagine the small infant, alone in the crib at night. Awakening hungry in a dark room, the baby cries. Mother awakens, arises, and silently touches a switch. Voila! Light magically appears! What is the baby to think of this all-powerful being who brings light into the darkness and provides warm milk for his nurturance? The impressions from Mommy are very important, since she provides the primary matrix for the child's habit patterns and emotional security. Mother is the Moon.

Moon energy is most significant in the first few years of life. If we can attune to the child's true needs by understanding the sign and house in which the Moon is placed, we can offer the child an optimum set of stimuli. Astrologer Noel Tyl has described the Moon as the "reigning need" in the chart. This highest need must be fulfilled if the child is to achieve a sense of inner security.

The Moon in the Signs

Using the Moon's sign to understand the things a child needs to feel secure can be an excellent guideline for parents:

Moon in Aries—Aries Moon will be more secure when given independence and room to move. Establishing boundaries may be difficult with this child, and caretakers will need to be especially watchful, since Aries Moon children seem to run away rather quickly when given too much room to move!

Moon in Taurus—Taurus Moon needs the Rock of Gibraltar, and feels best when the environment is predictable and recognizable. Accepting new things can be difficult for this child. You'll notice this early on when introducing new foods to the diet.

Moon in Gemini—Gemini Moon needs variety and intellectual interactions with others. Reading, storytelling, and conversation can be self-affirming.

Moon in Cancer—Cancer Moon feels secure when protected and cuddled. Different environments can feel threatening, hence something that's carried along will be emotionally stabilizing. These are the "blankie"-carrying toddlers!

Moon in Leo—Leo Moon is most secure when she is the center of attention. However, this child will not enjoy being onstage at the times she does not want to be in the limelight!

Moon in Virgo—Virgo Moon's security depends upon smoothly running circumstances. This child will feel best in a sparkling clean environment and is likely to be very particular about diet.

Moon in Libra—Libra Moon is more secure when someone else is around. Emotional security is balanced by another person, and decisions are more easily made when confirmed by others (even if it's only a knowing nod).

Moon in Scorpio—Scorpio Moon's security comes from a deep-level bonding with the mother, who is the archetype of the Great Mother. However, this child also has trouble distinguishing whose emotions are most important and may respond quite strongly when there are high levels of emotional tension.

Moon in Sagittarius—Sagittarius Moon's security is best achieved with lots of room and ample opportunity for expansion. Confirming this child's intellectual growth and rewarding learning in positive ways builds stability.

Moon in Capricorn—Capricorn Moon's security depends upon consistency and reliability. This child functions best when he knows the rules.

Moon in Aquarius—Aquarius Moon needs mental stimulation and a strong mental and intuitive tie with Mother. This child also needs independence, since she usually can intuit how to get help if needed!

Moon in Pisces—Pisces Moon needs to be one with Mother, who symbolizes Divine Love and Compassion. Saying good-bye to Mommy can be frightening and may be accompanied by great wailing. Yet this is also the child who can become attached to the baby-sitter! Watch for drama.

The types of schedules most suited to each child can be understood through the Moon sign as well. For example, a child with the Moon in Capricorn might prefer a fairly predictable and disciplined schedule, whereas the child with the Sagittarius Moon may enjoy more time for spontaneity and games. Study the keywords in Table 2 (chapter 2) to gain an understanding of whether a child might prefer a rigid or flexible schedule.

One way in which a child expresses Moon energy is through eating habits. The child with a fixed Moon sign is most likely to be stubborn about trying new foods, and knows exactly what she does and does not like. My daughter, with her Scorpio Moon, would eat only yogurt with fruit and whole grain breads from age two to three! If a child has a Gemini Moon, however, tastes may change from meal to meal.

House Placement of the Sun and Moon

The luminaries—Sun and Moon—are vitally important in understanding a child's sense of self. By examining them as a unit, we can see how both the inner and outer needs will be expressed. While the sign placement provides information about the qualities which are likely to be expressed through the conscious (Sun) and subconscious (Moon), the house placement shows which facets of life experience will support these expressions and needs.

Examine the Sun's placement by house and the sign through which its energy is directed to expand your understanding of the child's ego self. The Sun's house position also illustrates the child's perception of the assertive parent (usually the father) and the manner in which the child will ultimately exercise assertiveness.

The Moon's sign and house placement indicate the types of habits the child is most likely to develop. This placement provides insights into the child's perceptions of the receptive parent (usually the mother) and how the child expresses security needs. Where the child feels at home and the relationships and environments which stimulate a child's emotional is signified by the house placement of the Moon.

The Planets

Mercury

 The planet Mercury signifies communication, inventiveness, transportation, and sensory impression. It is through the vehicle of Mercury that we share our thoughts, ideas, and impressions of the world.

The qualities of Mercurial energy involve the translation of internal experience to external expression, hence the concept of communication. We communicate in many ways—through spoken or written words, gestures, body language, and other expressions. We can also communicate an idea through a photograph or pictures. The function of Mercury is to provide that communication, in whatever form. Mercury also represents the energy of transportation, which has a variety of options on the physical plane. We can transport ourselves by using the physical motion of the body (walking) or by employing a vehicle.

For the developing child, Mercurial energy brings about a series of transformations. Unable to speak in sentences or execute elaborate drawings, the tiny infant has two primary methods of expression—the voice and generalized body movements. As the baby grows, several forms of Mercurial expression develop. Cries, gurgles, and coos are transformed into sounds which are recognizable to the parents, and Baby's first words are formed. Eventually, the child learns the language of his world and engages in more advanced forms of communication.

The eagerness and security with which a child chooses to communicate verbally is indicated by the quality of the sign in which Mercury is placed. In air signs, Mercury is more readily expressive and verbal. In the earth signs, there may be a quietness of speech. A fire sign Mercury is strongly and often dramatically expressive. Mercury in water signs is often expressed with more reticence.

Mercury offers clues to the child's sensory input. The five senses are our physical mechanisms for observing and assimilating to the external environment. Small crawling babies are known for their tendency to put almost anything into their mouths in order to explore it. This inventiveness in exploring the world is the operation of the baby's Mercury energy.

Mercury in the Signs

The sign in which Mercury is placed indicates how the child approaches sensory exploration. Mercury in Aries children are likely to jump right into situations, just following the impulse to know what that thing is! Mercury in Taurus is driven by the physical senses ("How does it taste or feel?"). The Gemini Mercury is highly curious, and may try two sensory impressions at once. Leo Mercury identifies with self and explores through ideas like "this is small like my toes." The child with Mercury in Virgo might sit back and study an object before letting the senses of taste, touch, and smell have their turns. Mercury in Libra compares everything ("This is warm," and "This is cold."). Mercury in Scorpio is wary before allowing the senses to become involved, and rarely forgets any impression. Mercury in Sagittarius can jump in before any assessment is made. By contrast, Mercury in Capricorn takes the cautious approach. Mercury in Aquarius may seek out visual impressions first, whereas Mercury in Pisces is almost purely vibrational.

Mercury is associated with the hands and handwriting. Sign language is an effective means of communication when verbal expression is impossible. The use of the hands as the primary communication tool is another Mercurial expression.

The sign in which Mercury is placed indicates the types of things a child will enjoy doing with the hands. Mercury in Aries might like working with paper and scissors. Mercury in Taurus loves the feel of clay and may have very expressive hands or may like making music with the hands. Mercury in Gemini is well-known for hand gestures, and may also be a good placement for writing. Mercury in Cancer might enjoy the feel of yarn, and might like creating things out of fibers and fabrics. Leo Mercury may use more grand gestures. Mercury in Virgo is a great placement for crafts or writing. Libran Mercury enjoys creating beauty with the hands, perhaps by painting or writing poetry. Scorpio Mercury's hands can be kept productively busy studying nature. Sagittarius Mercury needs to keep all those fingers busy. Mercury in Capricorn may like to build things, while Mercury in Aquarius may enjoy playing music or computer games. A child with Mercury in Pisces may love making music, drawing, or painting. Use the basic concepts of the signs and extend them to the meaning of Mercury to understand the many ways Mercury operates for the child.

As a child grows, a refinement of Mercurial energy develops. Mercury's sign indicates the types of subjects a child enjoys learning and talking about. It is the nature of Mercurial energy to bring about improvements. When observing the child's approaches to problem-solving and improving her environment, we are observing Mercury at work. Understanding the sign placement of Mercury will aid the parent, guide, or teacher arrange particular types of situations in which a child will feel more inventive. We also have clues to the concepts which the child will find most interesting. Chapter 7 expands on these concepts of intellectual needs.

Mercury in the Elements

Mercury in Air—Children with Mercury in air signs may be the most talkative, although they might not necessarily be the best listeners! These children are interested in learning about a variety of concepts. Primarily, they want to have someone with whom they can have an interchange. These children love identifying and classifying.

Mercury in Fire—Children with Mercury in fire signs may speak without thinking (with the possible exception of Leo, who always enjoys sounding like an authority). These children are interested in ideas which can inspire them to create.

Mercury in Water—Children with Mercury in water signs often have their feelings mixed up with their thoughts, and may have difficulty separating them. There is a highly impressionable quality to their minds. These children like learning subjects with deep meanings.

Mercury in Earth—The earthy Mercury is interested in thinking and talking about subjects which have a practical application. Hands-on experience is worth a thousand words to this child.

In Homer's *Odyssey*, Mercury was the messenger of the gods. He carried messages, but did not originate them. In the astrological scheme, Mercury is also a messenger. This energy is the translator, communicator, and illustrator of our thoughts. In dealing with children, we study Mercury to find a child's easiest mode of communication. Insights into the child's areas of interest are provided through this symbology. By stimulating the child's thinking in ways she can identify with, we bolster the child's intellectual self-esteem. This can make learning more enticing. Through the clues Mercury offers, we can find ways to motivate the child's desire to learn and help her develop an understanding of this incredible world in which we live.

Venus

The planet Venus symbolizes the value systems in our lives and the manner in which we express feelings of affection and love. Venus inspires creative efforts as well, and is the energy of artistic expression. Venus is one of the primary feminine principles in the astrological chart. Children express Venus through their experiences of love and what brings pleasure and value to their lives.

While Venusian energy does not seem to be easily expressed by the very young child, it is certainly experienced. Although children can be tender, and do display love and affection, it is not always the enduring love we think of in the mature, intimate sense. However, the pattern for a child's future intimate expression is set during the childhood years. This is one area of the child's life which is sensitively open to development, and will definitely be colored by the child's influences and experiences. Venus is often associated with the concept of beauty, and we can certainly expose a child to things he will appreciate as beautiful or ask this child his preferences, likes, and dislikes.

Venus in the Elements

The elemental quality radiating through Venus in the signs describe the preferences, artistic leanings, and circumstances which bring pleasure into a child's life.

Venus in Air—The child with Venus in air signs loves ideas, stories, airy colors, spending time with friends, and visual arts.

Venus in Earth—The earthy Venus is stimulated by the things of nature and will find trees, mountains, and natural surroundings beautiful.

Venus in Water—Watery Venus is sensual, and appreciates the feeling of water, the bright colors of spring flowers, the sounds of the ocean, and a mother's embrace.

Venus in Fire—Venus in the fire signs is more showy, and enjoys things which sparkle and glitter. It loves to be active and may be enticed by candlelight or the flames of the fireplace.

Creating surroundings which appeal to the child's Venusian nature will make creative and artistic expression easier. Ideal surroundings include not only physical structures, but compatible types of people, appealing colors, and an overall energy which is comfortable to the child.

Additionally, the sign in which Venus is placed is also a good indicator of creative talents. The references in chapter 8 will be helpful in this determination. As we develop an understanding of the interactions between planets through the planetary aspects, we can help to perpetuate and fine-tune a child's expression of creativity.

Emotionally, Venus indicates the child's ability to show his feelings. Emotion is the outward expression of inner feelings. The sign in which Venus is placed indicates the qualities that emotional expression will take. The child with Venus in Gemini, for example, may talk about feeling a certain way while seeming quite detached from the emotion itself. The airy nature of Gemini is not comfortable with deep levels of emotions. For this reason, I suggest to parents that this child be given ample opportunity to express himself when confronted with emotional situations. (Of course, this encouragement is necessary for all children.) However, Venus in Capricorn may be a difficult placement for a child, as this sign tends to be overly structured and cautious in its qualities. A good outlet is to encourage the child's sense of humor at times when the emotions seem restricted, since Capricorn enjoys puns and corny jokes!

Venus energy is often directed to the things we value, and is expressed in the adult years by the types of material goods we desire. In the formative years, we can use the astrological indicators from Venus (its sign and house placement) to understand the kinds of things a child holds in high esteem. Sometimes we can use this revelation to offer the child a more positive reward. A child with Venus in Leo, for example, might be overly possessive of friends. She could be encouraged to enjoy the friend when she is there, then focus on a new activity when the friend chooses to leave. It should ultimately aid her when developing mature relationships in adult years to know that people cannot be possessed.

Venus in the Signs

Venus in Aries—This child seems to exhibit a pure *joie d'vivre*. He is attracted to situations and people which stimulate play, spontaneity, and which may also be a bit competitive. This child will love playing games (a good outlet for that competitive drive), and may also be a very charming flirt. In the very early years, the child may burn out or grow weary of any situation or person which seems too repetitive. Warm hugs are appreciated and are likely to be forthcoming even in early childhood. But displays of dislike are also easy to demonstrate!

Venus in Taurus—This child stimulates a strong desire to experience the beautiful side of life. This child may love singing, music, working with modeling clay, and can develop close attachments to people and situations. Getting into nature is rejuvenating for Venus in Taurus. Encourage her to grow something! Hugs and closeness mean a lot when it comes to expressing affection.

Venus in Gemini—This child will enjoy time spent sharing ideas, and may be very talkative and expressive. As a baby, Venus in Gemini may seem to be telling amazing stories with all those hand and arm motions—just fill in the blanks! This child will enjoy exploring different places, and is likely to find meeting new people exciting and stimulating. Gushing expressions of affection are not the style for this child.

Venus in Cancer—This child enjoys all the delicious things of life. Warm hugs, good food, family dinners—all these comfort experiences are the realm of Cancerian Venus. During childhood, he may thoroughly enjoy cooking and gardening as part of play. Keepsakes are meaningful even in the early years, and shows of tenderness are always appreciated. This child may adore stuffed animals.

Venus in Leo—This child enjoys being the entertainer and being entertained. This child is looking for a great time, and can radiate the warmth and enthusiasm that will attract some spectacular experiences. Expressing affection through hugs, laughter, and grand gestures seems to develop in the early childhood years for Leonine Venus.

Venus in Virgo—This child has a good time taking things apart. (Putting them back together can become tedious, though!) It's probably a good idea to allow this child to have a pet if she shows an interest, since taking care of something living can impart a good feeling. Later on, training a pet to do special tricks might be fun. This child may also enjoy collecting miniatures or making models. While some children are emotionally demonstrative, this child can convey a world of affection by holding hands.

Venus in Libra—This child loves pretty things and is drawn to beautiful people and expressions of beauty. Even in young childhood this child may be fascinated by art and music. Interactive play will be enjoyed by the toddler with Venus in Libra. Kisses and hugs in appropriate settings are comfortable for this child.

Venus in Scorpio—This child imparts a desire to experience deep connections to people, places, and things. You can usually tell precisely what this child does and does not like, since doing something just to please someone is not really on his agenda. The arts can be especially important in helping the child express emotions that could be difficult to articulate. Expressing affection is usually done cautiously until trust is developed, when the child can be highly expressive.

Venus in Sagittarius—This child may be drawn to adventure and travel. Zoos, theme parks, and places with plenty of things to do will be much more rewarding than sitting quietly while other people do things. Wilderness or nature experiences can hold a special fascination, and summer camp can make the rest of the year worthwhile. This child can be very exuberant about expressing affection.

Venus in Capricorn—This child needs his outdoor time, but does prefer being physically comfortable. This child may also be fascinated with what's happening in the real world and may seem interested in finances and things related. Games like Monopoly, *SimCity*, or role-playing games which allow the child to be in control are quite appealing. Emotionally, this child can be reserved and may have difficulty showing affection. However, sharing back rubs or mutually cuddling a favorite teddy bear are good excuses to allow this child to feel good about getting close.

Venus in Aquarius—This child inclines toward enjoying groups of friends more than just one special playmate. While enjoyable activities can range from playing games to making crafts, the child may also be drawn to storytelling and theatrics. Displays of affection may seem a bit stifled, although it is easy for the child to express what's on her mind. Preteens may be embarrassed by the gushing of emotion displayed by some friends.

Venus in Pisces—This child is tenderhearted and will love sinking into a warm cuddle during storytime. Play-acting is great fun, and dance, music, and art may be more to this child's liking than math or history. Even in early childhood, Venus in Pisces can learn to enjoy doing nice things for others, and may show a special sensitivity in situations calling for extra care and concern.

Mars

The energy of Mars is direct, active, and assertive. Children express Mars energy through bursts of physical activity and through their basic temperaments. Mars is the energy we use to get things done. Anger is a Martian expression, and the sign in which Mars is found will indicate how anger is likely to be expressed.

Physically, Mars represents the basic energy level in the individual. While the Sun shows general vitality, Mars is the more accessible energy. The fire signs seem to be the most physically assertive signs, conferring a powerful sense of energy and a direct expression of physical power. Earth signs seem to have a more moderate energy level and can develop strong endurance, while the air signs tend to dissipate physical force and can scatter energy. In water signs, Mars holds in physical power, and indicates a good reservoir of physical strength. With water signs, however, there can be too much holding back when release would be more desirable.

In determining the types of sports or recreation a child might enjoy, use the sign in which Mars is placed for a basic guideline. (See Table 8 in chapter 5.) Basic guidelines using Mars to indicate preferred physical activity or sports can be determined by sign and house placement alike. Using sign placement alone, for example, you might consider Mars in Capricorn as being drawn to sports which require endurance such as marathon running. Capricorn is attracted to mountains and heights (like the goat which symbolizes it), so climbing and snow skiing are likely prospects. Finding a sport the child will enjoy is the key to aiding him find ways to generate more physical energy for himself. Mars' house placement will indicate the types of associations which might be more desirable when asserting the self. For example, group sports might be preferential when Mars is in the 11th House, whereas those with Mars in the 1st House might favor individual sports such as tennis or track and field. Combining sign and house, Mars in Pisces in the 1st House might enjoy swimming or dance as an individual athletic activity. But that same Mars in Pisces in the 7th House would prefer to dance with a partner!

Dealing with a child's temper is one task which most parents handle with discomfort. Anger is an emotion we all have, and which we all need to express. The key to dealing with anger is to release it in a constructive way whenever possible. During the second and third years of life, children are learning to assert themselves and are beginning to exercise willpower. Psychologically, they're testing limits at this time. These years—the "terrible twos"—can be key times to help a child learn healthy ways to express will without creating destructive results. Later, in preschool years, parents, nannies, and teachers can begin to teach cause-and-effect in relationship to expressions of anger. The elementary school years continue these lessons, with social situations creating the perfect backdrop for gaining an understanding of the way anger can be expressed.

Mars in the Elements

>   **Mars in Water**—Children with Mars placed in water signs often have the most difficult time releasing anger; instead, they tend to repress it. Work with these children to find ways to let off steam. Exposing the child to the element of water itself by splashing or swimming away the tension can be helpful. Fussy babies with Mars in water signs may be soothed by a bath.

>   **Mars in Air**—Whenever a child with Mars in an air sign is angry, he may scream, shout, and speak wounding words. Generally, Mars in air will be very open about feeling angry. Appeal to the child's need to understand this feeling by talking about what created the anger after things have cooled down a little. Discuss what the child would like to do to change the situation which led to the outburst.

>   **Mars in Earth**—Children with an earthy Mars may hold onto anger, and can be tremendously volatile when the anger is finally released. These children are the best candidates for working off angry feelings by doing something constructive or simply kicking a ball around the yard.

>   **Mars in Fire**—Fiery Mars is open, direct, and concise with anger. Once the anger is expressed, it will probably be completely released. It is rare for a child with Mars in a fire sign to hold onto anger, and she can be exceptionally volatile. Aspects from the other planets can, of course, alter these basic tendencies.

All children learn about the destructive side of anger after a while, but may not know how to avoid it. We can aid them by understanding the basic form the anger takes and finding creative ways to direct it. For example, the child with Mars in Leo could be encouraged to dramatize these angry feelings, becoming a lion for a while and getting in touch with the primal level of this feeling. The Mars in Virgo might be able to direct the same energy in a more precise manner, perhaps by playing drums. As the child matures, the possible ways of directing anger become more varied.

The use of physical energy begins at the moment of birth, although control of that energy is a challenge until the early teens. At this age, the developing adolescent may find the more negative qualities of Mars surfacing. When the physical body grows stronger, assertiveness may get out of hand. Learning to control one's temperament is more difficult during these years. Fights often result. Sometimes exercises such as martial arts are helpful to the teen who has problems positively directing physical force.

Mars also represents sexual expression, which is not fully realized until the hormones begin their inevitable awakening. However, children of all ages have some fascination with human sexuality and are, at the very least, curious. The emotional and physical sexual drives do not emerge in a strong manner until hormonal changes occur during the years of puberty and adolescence. This new force can be confusing for the young teenager, who may often feel uncontrolled, or controlled by what seems to be an alien force! It is at this time that we also alter our approach to ourselves and begin to assert the self in a more powerful manner. Sexual energy may be openly expressed with the Aries Mars, or more covertly expressed through Mars in Cancer. How the adolescent youth deals with Mars energy will affect his sexual expression in the adult years. Although much of this behavior will be learned through the adult role model, it is the basic needs of the youth which must be considered. Just because a young man has an openly assertive father doesn't mean that he tends to be openly assertive himself.

Take the example of the adolescent with Mars in Cancer. She will need to express her sexual and assertive interests and feelings in a somewhat indirect manner. When confronted with a group of friends who are more outward and direct in their Mars expression, she may feel that something is wrong with her. There's nothing wrong, only a different approach and a less straightforward expression of energy. Cancer is sensitive, and does not blend easily with the direct, assertive quality of Mars—thus, the emotional discomfort of all those urges pushing to be outwardly expressed!

By understanding Mars in a child's chart, we find clues for dealing with his needs for expressing physical force, temper, and sexuality. The manner in which the child makes demands is seen through his expression of Martian energy. By focusing on the positive qualities of the sign in which Mars is placed, we can help the child deal with feelings of anger in a constructive way.

Mars energy is challenging to humans—it exudes a raw, primitive power. Fortunately, we have other aspects of the self to support and temper the development of this physical force. We must learn to confront and deal with the beast of the Self in order to be fully expressive. This process begins in childhood. When the child learns to accept all aspects of the Self, and learns creative ways to deal with her own power, there is no limit to her potential development.

Mars in the Signs

Mars in Aries—Mars in Aries is likely to be expressed in childhood through impatient attitudes and bold actions. This child can seem fearless and he may end up in accidents, compromising situations, or circumstances sure to leave Mom feeling unnerved. It's crucial to teach this child the importance of safety and reasonable caution (although you have to hold his attention long enough first!). Anger is usually burned off quickly, but can also be quickly ignited! This child can be competitive, even during the preschool years. Competition is not necessarily personal but just an expression of desires to have what he wants when he wants it!

Mars in Taurus—Mars in Taurus stimulates a mellowing influence, which can be helpful during the more tumultuous years of childhood. However, the stubborn nature of Taurus can become a strong feature of this child's personality. Learning to cooperate with others is important, and team sports could be a good outlet for this type of learning experience. Sharing is not easy to learn during the early years (ages two to five) when "things" are considered part of the self. Releasing anger can be difficult for this child, and jealousy can arise if the child feels displaced.

Mars in Gemini—Mars in Gemini adds a restless, nervous quality to a child's temperament. She can also be a real chatterbox, or may have habits like fidgeting which prove to be distracting to others. Anger expressed verbally can get this child in trouble, since words may be spoken which were intended as a release but provoke hostile responses from others. Exploring places, ideas, and people actually gives this child energy. Staying quiet can be a challenge, and maintaining interest and focus can be a lifelong lesson.

Mars in Cancer—This child is most comfortable in circumstances which are non-confrontational. Sports may not be enjoyable if injury is a possibility, since this child really does not like getting hurt. If he gets into an argument or brawl with anyone, he can become exceptionally upset emotionally and will need time to cool down and get settled.

Mars in Leo—Mars in Leo can be seen as a strong assertion of will and desire to be in control. However, not only does this child need to be given full attention, but the lesson of sharing the spotlight with others can be especially valuable to the development of a positive self-image. Even at a young age, Mars in Leo will prefer to be noticed for positive reasons and will not enjoy being placed in embarrassing situations. Therefore it's important to gauge whether or not the child is in the right circumstances to show off. Family settings may provide the perfect audience. Self-confidence can be strongly developed with proper support.

Mars in Virgo—This child needs to keep the hands busy. A baby with Virgo Mars may be fussy if she is physically uncomfortable. The toddler years may find this child fascinated with dexterity building toys, puzzles, and gadgets. As the child grows, developing skills which require dexterity and attention to detail can be extended into sports like gymnastics, dance, or art and music (or all of the above). Do not expect that this child will be neat, since keeping all those tools and toys organized may not be as much fun as pulling them off the shelf and putting them to use. This child can become excessively critical of herself and others and needs to develop patience with the process of becoming skillful.

Mars in Libra—This child likes sharing activities with others, but can also be directed toward exceptional skills. Developing grace is important, and social skills can be of interest as the child matures. While it may be assumed that this child prefers peace, the undercurrent of this energy is highly competitive. If he feels that a situation is unfair, strong protests are likely to be the result. Working as an equal partner on projects or as a team member in sports can be helpful, although he will appreciate some time in the spotlight when he has shown excellence.

Mars in Scorpio—This child inclines to be especially willful, even in infancy. If this baby does not want you to do something, you'll have a battle of wills. However, the most consistent feature of her personality can be persistence. When she wants something, there's little that can dissuade her. Accordingly, when an interest develops, she will tend to put everything into it and may not be easily distracted. In relationships with family and friends, jealousy can be a problem, but only if the child feels threatened or insecure. Personal preferences are likely to be very strong—no gray zones!

Mars in Sagittarius—This child enjoys adventure and may love being outdoors. Even in the early years there's a sense of daring, although it is usually accompanied by a friendly attitude. What is most noticeable is a marked desire for freedom. This child will not easily tolerate the confines of a playpen, although later on a fenced yard may be fine if there are interesting things to do outside. Individual and team sports which help him develop a sense of fair play, cooperation, and moral idealism are attractive and can provide positive developmental outlets.

Mars in Capricorn—Mars in Capricorn can confer a kind of self-contained quality of energy, and in childhood can be seen as caution or even fearfulness in unfamiliar circumstances. She may resist first and cooperate later. This child craves consistency and may develop exceptional physical skills through practice and focus. Ultimately, self-discipline becomes a personal goal, since it represents a kind of self-control and power which is appealing to her. The importance of learning to set and develop realistic goals cannot be underestimated. Rules can seem to innately make sense, and ultimately she will enjoy situations where she can be the one to define the rules or boundaries.

Mars in Aquarius—This child appreciates freedom. He may be interested in activities which are extraordinary, and can have goals like piloting a space shuttle or creating the ultimate virtual reality game. As an infant, he will enjoy being around other people, although in toddler years may seem to play alone, even when among a group of children. Team or group activities can be enjoyable, especially if he feels that his skills or ideas are appreciated. At any age he may exhibit defiance and rebel against authority, especially if the situation inhibits personal expression.

Mars in Pisces—Mars in Pisces adds physical and emotional sensitivity to the personality. As a baby, this child can seem especially quiet and will appreciate a serene environment. She is highly impressionable and may respond dramatically to frightening or confrontational situations. It's important to take special care with the choices of movies, stories, and music. Sometimes Mars in Pisces inclines a child to enjoy sports, but primarily those that are somewhat self-contained. Swimming, dance, and gymnastics can all be excellent choices, since the fluid body movements are more natural for her. Expressions of anger are uncomfortable for this child, and learning assertiveness can require extra effort.

Jupiter

♃ The energy of Jupiter offers the individual an opportunity to expand his personal universe. Jupiter's energy provokes the desire to understand the meaning of life and gain an awareness of Universal Laws. This energy helps us pass beyond the limits of individuality and reach an understanding of Universal Truth.

Through Jupiter we achieve a sense of honor and establish a basic philosophy of life. Jupiter demonstrates the sense of confidence, enthusiasm, and optimism which gives us the hope of a brighter day, even in difficult times. Generosity of spirit is an outpouring of Jupiterian energy.

For the child, Jupiter expresses the desire to expand and grow. This energy definitely requires a period of maturity to realize, although it does operate at basic levels within the child. Even the small child of four will wonder about God or universal principles as he contemplates the "whys" of life. Jupiter energy aids us in finding divine principles in our lives, and is often signified by a special teacher or guide. For the child, the parents are usually the first guides. As interactions with others increase, other teachers appear. Jupiter also illustrates the type of person a child may appreciate most as a mentor.

I have always associated Jupiter with a sense of divine protection, and encourage parents to teach their children about the protective energy of Truth and Understanding. The light of truth can be illustrated through stories. The *Star Wars* theme of the dark and light sides of the Force is a good way of introducing young children to universal principles. Fairy tales and other allegorical stories have illustrated moral lessons for centuries.

I am often amazed at the level of awareness I observe in young children. Too often, parents and teachers forget the natural ability the child has to expand consciousness beyond the physical level. Given opportunities to share their understanding, children are wonderful and surprisingly insightful teachers.

Jupiter is often illustrated in the behavior of the child by the sense of "I want." The child must be taught to balance his long list of "I wants" with personal responsibility. Too strong a desire to expand our possessions causes us to become motivated by the materialistic aspect of Jupiter rather than by the principles of harmonious abundance. Expectations are a primary feature of Jupiterian energy, and helping a child define expectations which are realistically possible will enhance his confidence when setting goals.

Appeal to the energy of Jupiter when motivating a child. Look to the house and sign position of Jupiter to find the types of rewards that the child will like. For example, the child with Jupiter in Aquarius in the 3rd House might be easily motivated by the promise of a trip to the local planetarium with friends. This reward would appeal to the Jupiterian sense of expansion since it deals with the vastness of the solar system. Spending time with friends is important to Aquarius, and the travel this activity would provide is a perfect 3rd House activity.

Jupiter also indicates the child's desire to learn and enlarge her concept of the world. We can use Jupiter's placement by sign and house to gain insights into increasing these desires within the child. When used effectively, Jupiter energy provides continuing understanding and a sense of wisdom. If not properly channeled, Jupiter can confer a sense of wanderlust and a lack of direction.

The house placement of Jupiter may also indicate what the child takes for granted. Help the child develop a sense of gratitude, especially in the area signified by Jupiter's house placement. A child with Jupiter in the 2nd House may take the material things in life for granted. By helping the child learn the values of things, including the management of money, the potentially difficult side of this placement can be avoided.

Generosity is a significant feature of Jupiterian energy. It is important for any child to experience the true meaning of giving and sharing. There can be a fine line between generosity and wastefulness. We can be wasteful of energy in many ways through physical, material, spiritual, and emotional outlets. The house and sign in which Jupiter are placed will offer indicators of the areas in which the child needs to expend (not waste) energy. Sometimes a child does not know the difference!

Jupiter, representative of the energy of expansion, abundance, optimism, and generosity, is known as the "greater benefic" in old astrology texts. For the truly beneficial aspects of the energy to be used, the person must develop a sense of reasonable limitations. This can be enhanced or altered by other planets which support or detract from the energy of Jupiter (planetary aspects will be discussed in chapter 4).

It is generally not until the child has developed some measure of cognitive skill that the awareness of Jupiter can be taught. During elementary school and preteen years, this energy begins to blossom. Jupiter is a function of the higher mind, the part of our consciousness which can connect with the Divine. The early awareness of Jupiter deals primarily with the concepts of sharing, positive thinking, enthusiasm, and hope for reward.

Jupiter in the Elements

The element of the sign influence on Jupiter gives clues to the most positive avenues to help a child learn about higher principles and moral issues.

Jupiter in Air—In air signs, Jupiter's energy can be addressed and developed through reading, discussion, and social activities. Doing things with others whose values and ideals are similar will feel positively confirming for the child with Jupiter in air signs. Objectivity and fair-mindedness can be features of Jupiter in air signs.

Jupiter in Water—Jupiter's energy can become overly fervent when flowing through the water signs, since emotionality can influence ideals and beliefs. While this placement can add a sense of compassion to the personality, it's also easy for this child to develop prejudice, judging situations and people according to feelings (including fears) rather than employing more objective means.

Jupiter in Fire—When Jupiter is in fire signs, a passion for ideals and beliefs can be present. When this child holds certain principles strongly, she may be quite zealous about morals and ethics. Enthusiasm and confidence can be strong.

Jupiter in Earth—Placed in earth signs, Jupiter's energy can seem too contained or restrained. This child needs belief systems and moral values which are anchored in practicality. However, it can be easy for the child to become stuck in a belief system or to have difficulties accepting that another belief system is as valid as her own.

For Jupiter in the Signs, see chapter 7. House placements are described in chapter 10.

Saturn

The energy of Saturn is disciplined, structured, and responsible. For the young child, Saturn is initially signified by the structures, limits, and expectations imposed by the parents. Later, social systems such as schools and institutions take on a Saturnian role. The teachers become important disciplinarians, preparing a child for further integration into society.

Children do not usually like restrictions and limitations, yet the necessity of learning the positive use of limits is critical. At every stage of growth, pushing limits is an integral part of the process, and learning those limits can be a crucial part of the structure of life. It is truly a challenge for the parents to provide the limitations necessary for the child without inhibiting the child's creative self-expression. In the child's chart, we can see Saturn operating as the force of discipline, responsibility, and structure. It provides the child with a sense of inner security.

Saturn acquaints us with the realities of existence on the physical plane. Tiny babies are concerned primarily with the basic functions of survival, but they, too, have Saturn in their lives. In fact, it is at this time that a child may feel the most restricted. The baby's consciousness, which is adjusting to the reality of life in the physical form, may feel tremendously inhibited by the restrictions of physical plane existence. We need to become aware of the frustrations of the tiny infant, with his limited ability to express his wants and needs. Too often, parents are acutely aware of the limitations a child places on their lives, but forget the frustrations of the baby.

Babies learn rapidly when adjusting to their needs. One aspect of Saturn deals with daily routines and schedules, and there have been some interesting debates concerning whether or not a baby needs a definite feeding schedule or on-demand feedings. Even in the beginning of life on Earth, Saturn begins to set its limits!

The awareness of time is another function of the developing human being which requires some maturity to understand. Saturn is symbolic of time in our lives, and deals also with our awareness of it. Children have difficulty understanding time. When you consider that a child can base her perceptions of time only upon personal experience, it is no wonder that Christmas seems eons away to a child of five. A year represents one-fifth of her life! Patience is a Saturnian concept, and is generally not seen in great amounts among small children. When dealing with the sense of time, children are aware of the present moment, their desires within the present moment, and very little else. As the child matures, she learns that some things require waiting. This aids in understanding the operation of Saturn.

Discipline is a primary feature of Saturnian energy. We can look to the child's house and sign placement of Saturn to understand the areas which will be most disciplined and what form the discipline will take. For example, Saturn in Leo in the 5th House may approach creativity (5th House) in a structured (Saturn) way, and could be responsive to discipline which is dramatic and consistent (Leo). Also, we can see how the child will discipline himself and how much responsibility he will take for his own actions. This is further fine-tuned when we examine the aspect Saturn makes with other planets in the chart. For Saturn in the signs and houses, see chapter 10.

Since Saturn represents restraint, we can view the areas where a child may feel most limited and restricted. Saturn in the 1st House may restrain the projection of the personality. Children with Saturn in the 1st House very often take on responsibilities at an early age, because of younger brothers or sisters or due to other reasons. It is important that the child be able to cope with the restraints she feels; otherwise a self-defeating attitude may develop.

A child truly begins to integrate a sense of Saturn around age six or seven. There are cyclical patterns represented by Saturn's *transit*. The transits are the positions of the planets at any given time in life compared to the pattern of the natal chart. When Saturn is making contact to the natal Saturn or to other planets by transit, the individual tends to develop a stronger sense of limitation and responsibility. This sense will be focused in the areas and energies symbolized by the planets and houses involved. These cycles are measured in increments of six to seven years.

There are two basic Saturn cycles which occur at age six to seven and at age thirteen to fourteen. At the first Saturn cycle (about age seven), the child is beginning to feel very aware of the Self and of personal responsibility. Many parents do not realize the tremendous responsibility a child feels at this age. The awareness of the world is centered strongly on the self, and the child usually feels responsible for almost anything that goes wrong. A family trauma, such as a divorce, might be interpreted by this child as being entirely his fault. It is crucial that the parents be aware that this age is critical in order to give much needed support to the developing child. If a grandparent or other adult becomes ill during this cycle, the child may feel that he is somehow responsible. While the adult viewpoint may be that this is illogical, a sensitivity to this emotional vulnerability can help a child draw important distinctions, especially when feelings of guilt arise.

At about age fourteen, the second Saturn cycle occurs. By this age, the child has developed physical abilities which allow her to feel rather powerful, but does not yet have a complete understanding of the nature of personal responsibility. There are generally many restrictions (Saturn) placed upon the teen which she does not appreciate.

Some of the problems inherent in this developmental cycle can be avoided if the parent and teen can sit down together and form open lines of communication. They need to work out a system in which the teenager feels he is allowed adequate personal responsibility, along with some measure of freedom. The teenager will probably respond well to a balanced system of freedom and responsibility at this age, but is likely to rebel against a highly restrictive situation.

It is the function of Saturn to confer an awareness of the physical plane. Not only does it provide restriction and discipline, but it also builds the foundations and support systems which offer a sense of personal security. Many people place security exclusively in the realm of material form, such as financial and material security. This is only one level of security, and one which is never totally reliable!

The most reliable level of security is the inner sense of security. This comes from learning to attune to the universal principles which teach us harmony within life. Granted, attaining a measure of material security aids in a sense of personal security, but it is not sufficient unto itself.

Saturn also symbolizes guilt and fear. Because of the restrictive nature of this energy, our response to it often comes through these negative reactions. Certainly, caution is a worthwhile form of Saturnine energy, but too often children are taught overwhelming fear. If allowed to be paralyzed by fear, the child cannot react in creative ways when dealing with obstacles in life.

Guilt's paralyzing effect makes it a close cousin to fear. Guilt usually results when a child is reprimanded for disobeying the rules. Understanding that certain behavior is irresponsible or inappropriate need not produce feelings of extreme guilt in the child.

For the developing child, the archetype of Saturn is played through the parents. Traditionally, astrologers have considered this energy as a projection of the father, although I think that mothers in our society have provided the emotional structure while fathers have symbolized the structure and power in the outside world. This is changing as men and women take their places in careers. The roles both parents play in teaching a child respect, consistency, and reliability are crucial to a child's sense of safety and security. The way in which Mother and Father provide messages of consistency, reliability, personal responsibility, and caution will determine a pattern which the child will probably follow for the remainder of her life. The sign, house placement, and aspects of Saturn in the chart tell us much about the child's developing need for security and structure in life. Structure and inhibition are two separate concepts, but often become confused in the formative years.

Consider the analogy of building a house. A strong, level foundation is laid, then the framework is built. Saturn provides the foundation and framework in the life of the child. In order to have a level foundation and a solid frame of reference in life, the child needs to receive consistent messages from the parents. Later, institutions like schools can reinforce these messages. Ultimately, peer relationships may challenge them! Saturn represents a need for consistency, reliability, and dependability. Without a clear sense of Saturn, the child has no real reference points for the developing self. In later chapters, we will explore aspects of Saturn and the ways in which this structure can be built or undermined.

Uranus

Uranus symbolizes supercharged energy. It provides us with a sense of the rare, eccentric, and unique aspects of life. Through Uranus, we gain an awareness of Universal Brotherhood—the common bonds of humanity.

Uranus' energy operates very strongly at a level of intuitive awareness, and confers a "knowingness." It is this aspect of life that psychologists are describing when they speak of the "other" side of the brain. This right-brain functioning is not logical, but is the aspect of the Self which attunes to a higher level of awareness. A child is not likely to possess a conscious connection to Uranian energy, but this will develop during the early adult years (around age twenty-one).

Until the discovery of Uranus, Saturn was accepted as the boundary of our solar system. The planets beyond the bounds of Saturn—Uranus, Neptune, and Pluto—are called the *outer* or *transpersonal planets* in astrology. We enter the realm beyond the personal self once we pass the boundary of Saturn. These transpersonal energies operate at the level of expanded awareness in the individual, and require a directed approach in order to be fully utilized. In childhood, Uranus is expressed as the strange, exceptional, and ingenious.

Children with Uranus placed in an angular house (1st, 4th, 7th, or 10th) may feel out of step with their peers. They may complain that they just don't fit in. If this is the case, assure the child that his uniqueness is simply different. I will never forget the new sense of confidence I felt in my early teens when I read Thoreau and realized that it was okay to be different! We are so geared to become like everyone else and be a good clone (the workings of Saturn)! It feels secure to have a group, a belief, or an ideal which is acceptable.

Uranus in the Signs and Generations

Since Uranus spends about seven years in a sign, members of a child's peer group usually have Uranus in the same sign. This sign placement offers the unique signatures which distinguish differences in kids. I have a number of friends and clients who are teachers and who have commented to me about the changes they see every six or seven years in the overriding qualities of their kids. In many ways, the sign placement of Uranus indicates the challenges these groups will face in bringing about evolutionary, and sometimes revolutionary, changes.

Uranus in Scorpio (1974–1981)—These children are, at this writing, entering into society as young adults. They've been challenged, even at an early age, to deal with issues around sexuality, violence, death, and psychology at levels which may, to some adults, have seemed premature. One thing we grow to realize with astrology is that everything has its time! To develop truly awakened attitudes about human sexuality, the stereotypes and barriers which have existed for several generations will be challenged by those of this generation. These are likely to be the adults who create revolutionary actions, laws, and social situations around issues like family planning, abortion, genetic engineering, and sexual preferences.

Uranus in Sagittarius (1981–1988)—With Uranus in Sagittarius, education, religion, spirituality and the law become the realms of revolutionary challenge. The children of this generation may seem to cry out for changes in education which will provide not only the information and skills they require to make it in a rapidly changing world, but also for a kind of moral direction which stems from true principles of acceptance, tolerance, and humanity. Balancing new uses of technology with higher principles is important. These kids are growing up in a world where information is expanding and the sense of one world is emerging. However, the ideal and reality are unlikely to occur at the same time! We humans evolve more slowly than the rate at which our ideas about change emerge.

Uranus in Capricorn (1989–1996)—These children are the ones who will ultimately change the established order. They will become adults when there are more elderly people alive than have ever lived before! Integrating the exuberance of youth with the experience of age may become the hallmark of this generation. As a global economy emerges, this generation will create the structures of business and commerce which may become the new battle zones, but also the new arenas for growth and opportunity. Environmental concerns may also be especially important for this generation.

Uranus in Aquarius (1996/7–2004)—These children are truly the children of the New Age. This generation is most likely to see developments in experiences like space travel and exploration, but here on earth, they're met with the clear challenge of creating a more humanitarian society. Old structures are certainly likely to give way to innovation, and by teaching these children how to create change within existing circumstances, it's more likely that they will be capable of addressing the issues of making alterations which are more constructive. However, in some instances they are also more likely to try things that are completely different, and need ample encouragement to push their limits in the best possible manner.

Uranus in Pisces (2004–2011)—Uranus in Pisces opens the way for heightened creativity and will mark a time period when some of the boundaries between the people of earth will be erased. These children will appreciate a special emphasis in the arts, but will also respond to situations which allow them to feel more connected to one another. Music is a prime example of this kind of energy since the vibration, sounds, and flow of music can completely alter the moods and expressions of the people experiencing it. It may be more difficult for these children to break out of collective experiences. In fact, their desire to be alike may be important in some instances. These shared experiences can confirm an unexpected quality of power, and learning to direct consciousness and mind may play a significant role as these children reach their maturation.

On an individual level, Uranus represents the unique—the part of us that is exceptional and not like everybody else. Uranus gifts us with special intuitive talents which enable us to attune to the Universal Mind. When strongly placed in the chart, the individual may feel called to become a spiritual teacher. Dealing with this can be difficult and confusing for a child who is struggling to maintain a sense of personal identity in the face of continual change. Uranus is another energy which may require some time to develop and appreciate fully.

The house in which Uranus is placed will indicate the facets of the self which will be most unique. A child with Uranus in Libra in the 5th House may have outstanding talents in expressing artistry (5th House) through painting or other art forms (Libra). (Of course, we would analyze other aspects and planets to completely decipher the creative potential, although Uranus is a good indicator of special genius.) The ease of flow of the talents suggested by Uranus can be determined by the aspects Uranus makes to the personal planets (Sun, Moon, Mercury, Venus, and Mars) in the chart. In chapter 6, Uranus' expression is described in each of the houses.

Uranus energy is sometimes unmanageable until the individual knows how to flow with it. Flowing with this uniquely charged aspect of the Self requires a strong sense of self. Therefore, parents and significant others will do well to offer unconditional support of the child's creative genius and special qualities until the child can provide that support for herself. The independent nature of Uranus is also one aspect of the Self which requires some maturity to handle. However, babies with powerful Uranian vibrations seem independent even in the crawling stages!

Directed in an irresponsible manner, Uranus is disruptive and destructively revolutionary. This energy can bring about radical change within the individual, as well as offering him the ability to bring about changes within society as a whole. "Freedom" and "individuality" are the watchwords of Uranus.

To positively express these aspects of life, one must have a greater understanding of the reasons for change and accept the responsibility that accompanies personal freedom. These lessons are not easy ones for the young child or adolescent. In fact, it is the balance between freedom and responsibility which is the most difficult lesson during developing years. Parents, guides, and teachers can give the child opportunities to express personal individuality and uniqueness while also demonstrating the necessity to understand the demands of society. This can be a rather tricky proposal, since most adults do not understand how to do this either!

Neptune

The illusory, mystical, and otherworldly aspects of life are symbolized by the planet Neptune. Neptune's vibrations have a sensitizing effect. This sensitivity has its effects on all aspects of life—physical, mental, emotional, and spiritual.

Neptune is Divine Compassion. Through this energy, we can attune ourselves to the principles of Universal Love. Neptune can also operate as the deceiver, resulting in disappointments when the deceptions and delusions are revealed. It is hard to determine from the chart alone how the child will use any of these energies. Neptune, like an elusive, mystical butterfly, requires special development to be used in its highest form.

Neptune in the Signs and Generations

Neptune moves very slowly through the zodiac, and its sign placement has a generational effect. During the passage of Neptune in Libra, from 1942 to 1956, the "Flower Children" were born. Now, at the turn of the twenty-first century, Neptune is in Aquarius where it will remain through 2012. Understanding the sign placement of Neptune will provide clues to the beliefs of the generation in which a child is born.

Neptune also tells us about the things we worship and the concepts we hold sacred. The Flower Children held the ideals of love and peace as sacred—a very Libran attitude. Those born with Neptune in Capricorn are more likely to hold the Capricornian concepts of determination, consistency, and material success as sacred. The generational influences of Neptune through the signs are noted below:

Neptune in Sagittarius (1970–1984)—These children are now young adults and all soon will be entering their adult years. They have grown up in an era when knowledge of different religious ideals has been more widespread, but they have also seen vestiges of excessive religious zeal. For example, the knowledge of heightened terrorism stemming from perceived insults from radical religious groups is part of the collective psyche of these kids. Since Neptune's energy can help to dissolve barriers and locate the higher thread of any principle, this generation can have a profound influence on the way media exposes truth and information.

Neptune in Capricorn (1984–1998)—These children's ideals are focused on things that can be proven, felt, or tangibly manifested. There is likely to be a very conservative quality in these children. They will innately understand the need to appreciate and care for the things of the earth if they want to keep them. These children carry the torch for the new structure of modern society, but can also fall victim to the tendency to use religious principles to create divisions among people. Political ideals have also been strongly intertwined with religious beliefs during this cycle, and it may be up to this generation to find the most effective ways for religion and government to exist harmoniously in the world.

Neptune in Aquarius (1998/9–2012)—These children are the visionaries and will be exposed to the realm of dreams and possibility. While distinctions between science and religion may carry an interesting development during this time, these children bear the burden of finding the common thread which binds us all together.

The house placement of Neptune indicates the areas that are especially sensitized, and in which a more refined aspect of the self operates. For example, Neptune in the 3rd House brings an intuitive and mystical quality to communication. There may be a special intuitive link with the siblings. Neptune in the 6th House often brings a heightened intuitive sensitivity to animals. Complete descriptions are noted in chapter 8.

The imagination is the special realm of Neptune. We all know that children have wonderful imaginations. This is because they are more easily attuned to their inner realms of consciousness—the rational mind has not yet dominated the imagination. In order to maintain imaginative creativity, the child can be taught ways to distinguish between physical reality and the alternate reality of the inner planes. In the past, parents and society have given strong messages that the special inner world is inferior to the "real" world. They were mistaken, however: reality has many levels of expression!

Neptune's energy is intangible. The illusions created on a movie screen, for example, are Neptunian, but create a powerful impression on the conscious and subconscious mind. Does this mean that this impact is not real? As we understand the multiple facets of human consciousness, we begin to tap into the realm of Neptune. The ongoing argument about the depth of influence music, television, and the movies have on the developing consciousness of a child stems from an understanding of this principle of impression and consciousness.

The world of dreams is also Neptunian. If you tell a child that a dream is not real, you shatter a level of the child's awareness. But explaining intangibles is difficult, so for centuries parents have been throwing up their hands and telling children, "It's not real! It's only a dream." Yes, it is a dream, but on its own level it is quite real. Until the age of six or seven, distinguishing real from imaginary is difficult for any child. (Is this not the age when many children discover the difference between the myth and reality of Santa Claus?) What we have to explain to the child is that the horrifying beast in a nightmare is only a fear inside himself. We can show the child ways to banish these beasts.

My children shared their dreams with me from their earliest years. We did all kinds of things with dreams. In many instances, we would use images from a dream to create a story or paint pictures about a dream the next day. When a child wakes up frightened from a nightmare, physical caresses and a soothing voice will help bring her into a different level of reality. Tell the child that she is okay and give her some special comfort. Talk about making friends with the growling dog or scaring away the yucky monsters. Some children will be comfortable with the idea of turning the tables on the monsters and making friends with them. I was so delighted when my three-year-old awoke one morning to tell me, "The monsters were after me, but I just threw pink flowers on them and then they were my friends." Another child actually liked monsters, and images like those created by Maurice Sendak in the book *Where the Wild Things Are* were his favorites. "I'm not ascared by the mon-ter," he told me, "since I like the place where the wild things live!"

The child must also learn when imagination is and isn't appropriate. Imagination can be encouraged through art, storytelling, music, or dramatic performance. I think children are naturally attuned to Neptunian vibrations even more than to the coarser physical plane vibrations. We should encourage every child to maintain this attunement with the Higher Self through creative expression. At the same time we should also encourage the child's understanding of physical principles. By doing so, we avoid the tyranny of rational thought over intuition and imagination. This cultivates the evolution of a more complete, balanced person.

Pluto

Pluto is the extremist of the zodiac and operates at a very deep, intense level. The energy of this planet is normally inaccessible in a direct manner by the human consciousness. With attention to development of the inner realms and the awakening of the intuitive Self, the energy of Pluto's realm is more readily expressive and more easily directed. The energies of Pluto take some time to manifest, but act as a powerful catalyst for transformation and regeneration when they do emerge.

Pluto represents the evolutionary energy of the zodiac.[1] Evolution occurs at all levels of life—physical, emotional, mental, and spiritual. For the child, directed

---

[1] See Jeffrey Green's book *Pluto: The Evolutionary Journey of the Soul.*

awareness of this energy is virtually impossible, since the personal self must be well developed before awareness of this deep plane of consciousness awakens. In fact, most adults have difficulty with this! Although the energy of Pluto may be felt during the childhood years, it is not usually directed consciously at this time. Yet, even in childhood, an individual is responding to the stimulus of these powerful, primal forces.

Pluto symbolizes the primordial essence of man. This energy flows from the Great Mother (the feminine principle of Divine Power) and is responsible for the radical changes brought about by birth and death. As human consciousness has matured, we have come to realize that these transformations take place more frequently in our lives than we thought. We experience many deaths and rebirths as we grow spiritually and psychologically. Often, the energy of Pluto is the stimulus for drastic changes in individuals when they move away from one level of functioning and into a radically new one.

Pluto in the Signs and Generations

In childhood, Pluto is felt as a compulsive, sometimes overwhelming force. Pluto is a generational planet, moving very slowly through the zodiac. Therefore, the placement by sign tells more about the transformational influence Pluto will have on a particular generation than it will about the changes in the individual.

> **Pluto in Libra (1972–1984)**—These children feel the challenge to break down societal barriers concerning human relationships. This generation was born at a time when the concept of dysfunctional families and relationships, co-dependency, and other previously denied relationship patterns were brought into the open light of understanding. Of course, the changes in these patterns require some time to manifest, and these are the kids who bear the burden of what has happened as these levels of awareness have been brought to the surface. On a personal level, this generation may feel responsible for the creation of a renewal of marriage built upon balance (Libra) and equality. Alterations in the legal system may be one of the historical markers created by this generation as they come into power.

> **Pluto in Scorpio (1984–1995)**—These children were born during the time when life's ultimate issues have reached a boiling point. The occurrence of AIDS, open discussions about the right to die, the right to life, cloning—all these processes have created a need to bring what was once in the closet to the sur-

face. While sex education may have been part of the previous school curriculum, this time period saw the need to be more explicit, since there are now truly life-threatening sexually transmitted diseases! This era also saw the end of the Cold War—the time when the superpowers held the survival of the world in a touch of a button. However, outbreaks of terrorism have also become a fact of life for these kids, and they're dealing with it not only on a global level, but in their neighborhoods. These children are the healers, and may ultimately be the ones whose job it is to transform our environment as well, healing the damage done by previous generations.

Pluto in Sagittarius (1996–2008)—These children are confronted with quite a task. During this era, a true global economy is emerging and new definitions of power are coming into play. This is the generation challenged to transform the educational systems, the courts, and the legislative bodies once they come into their power within society. The important distinctions between religion and spirituality will be emerging during this era, and these children are hungry to know the truth. If we cannot teach it ourselves, they will help us uncover the myths that mask it.

When interpreting the child's astrological chart, the house placement of Pluto indicates the personal expression of Pluto's energy. The house in which Pluto is placed will be the area of life in which the most drastic changes and transformations will take place. It will be this facet of the self which will most likely be permanently altered in some way. To further understand the workings of Pluto, we examine the aspects between Pluto and the other planetary energies. (The sections that follow give aspect examples.)

Pluto was discovered at the same time human beings learned to split the atom. This discovery coincided with the beginning of the Atomic Age, a period in human evolution in which we developed the power to annihilate all life on the planet. Such is the power of Pluto to bring about change at the deepest levels of existence.

In the life of a child, Plutonian energy is experienced through changes in both the external and internal environments. Even children must often cope with death in their lives. If we can teach the child the truths of life, death, and transformation, he can accept this aspect of deep, inner change more readily.

One good way to acquaint the child with Plutonian concepts without creating fear is through the story of a tadpole's metamorphosis into a frog. The child can be shown this miraculous transformation, and see the gradual development of one body structure into another. Also available are butterfly kits, which provide a Lucite container, caterpillar, and food. The child can observe the caterpillar, the creation of the cocoon, and the ultimate emergence of the butterfly—a perfect example of transformational change. Watching another dramatically changing life cycle—egg to hatchling to chick to bird, for example—is also a good lesson.

We have other transformational processes to share with children. We can plant seeds together. We can have rituals at the time of death which are celebrations of change, yet which still allow the release of personal grief. Often, an opportunity to deal with death presents itself when a family pet dies. To hide these things from a child is damaging. Children have a remarkable way of understanding truth if it is just presented to them directly! Parents so often shield their children from truth because they fear their own pain. Love and understanding heal pain much more quickly than repression and fear.

Because of the deep level of Plutonian energy, many people fear it. Here truly lies the beast in the underworld, the dragon within the Self. Sometimes that dragon is placed in the child's inner consciousness through the fears of the parents. This can manifest as repressive and obsessive behavior and can also manifest as the instillation of shame and guilt. I know many adults who are dealing with the removal of these old dragons, often in painful ways. Perhaps we can implant more positive images in the minds of our children and teach them ways to banish these overwhelming fears.

Pluto is the darkness from which light emerges. To avoid the dark places within the Self is to avoid the ability to truly open to the Light! All children can be taught a sense of personal power in very positive terms, without experiencing the fear of annihilation.

Working on continual self-improvement promotes positive self-transformation. This can be encouraged even in early childhood. Where there are shadowy fears, illuminate them with the light of understanding. Where there is dark despair, carry the bright torch of hope. Now, more than at any other time in history, we must equip our children with these powerful tools. They are the ones who must use the evolutionary energy of Pluto to determine the fate of all humanity. Avert the possible destruction of the Earth by creating a planetary awareness of the deeper meaning of life.

Retrograde Planets

Because we calculate the astrological chart based upon the positions of the planets relative to the Earth, we often encounter a phenomenon called *retrogradation*. Retrogradation means to move backward, and planets in retrograde do in fact appear to be moving backward. (Of course, a planet does not really back up, but it does give that illusion from our viewpoint here on Earth.) When a planet is in apparent retrograde motion, we note it in the chart by the symbol "℞." We encounter this phenomenon frequently in our everyday lives. Have you ever been passing another automobile and experienced the sensation that the other car was going backward? This illusion is especially notable when two cars are passing on a curve.

When planets are in retrograde motion, the faster planet (the one closest to the Sun) is passing a slower planet in its orbit. A typical chart contains two retrograde planets. However, one exception is that the Moon does not retrograde in its orbit around Earth. And while the Sun is never in retrograde because we are in orbit around it, there is a kind of retrogradation of the Sun astronomically. But we do not note this astrologically.

Interpreting Retrogradation

When a planet is in retrograde, its energy seems to turn inward before it externalizes. This can be a useful quality in personal development, since it allows a deeper level of introspection regarding the essence of the energy. Sometimes, however, there is a sense of frustration during retrogrades.

Mercury Retrograde—Mercury retrogrades about three times each year. When it is retrograde in the natal chart, the reasoning and thinking processes are more sensitive. There may be more deliberation in decision-making. Parents and teachers may feel that a child takes too long to answer questions. Extra patience on their part will encourage the child to communicate more openly. Sometimes those with Mercury retrograde at birth find that it is easier to write than talk. Rather than impeding the ability to communicate, this placement often enhances the ability to express ideas through the written word. Many notable writers have been born with Mercury retrograde, including Norman Mailer, Anne Frank, Isak Dinesen, and Henry Miller.

The child with Mercury retrograde at birth needs to learn to trust her ability to express thoughts and ideas, and should be given plenty of opportunities to communicate. This chart placement often leads to some ingenious ideas and concepts. Letter-writing may be a favorite pastime, and diaries can be helpful in objectifying thoughts.

Venus Retrograde—Since Venus is the expression of emotion, an involution of this energy adds intensity to the feeling nature. There is sometimes a reticence in expressing affection. Retrograde Venus can be challenging for the female teen since she may mistrust her own sense of femininity and may question her self-esteem too much. However, boys with Venus retrograde can have their own issues, like a tendency to hold back their demonstrative loving feelings.

Values can be on the unusual side, with an attraction to unique art forms. Artistic expression (through music, painting, acting, poetry, etc.) is often a positive approach in dealing with Venus retrograde. Songwriter Carole King and actress Sally Field both have Venus retrograde in their charts. Encourage the child with Venus retrograde to reaffirm his self-worth. As a parent, give strong messages to establish positive self-esteem within the child.

Mars Retrograde—The outgoing, assertive, competitive energy of Mars is often frustrated when retrograde. When this planet retrogrades, the physical energy is often slowed. Self-confidence may seem blocked, and needs to be boosted by establishing a firm sense of personal strength. Expressing anger can be difficult and uncomfortable.

Physical assertiveness is not always easy when Mars retrogrades, but there can be great success when the individual learns to thoroughly visualize an action before physically performing it. Affirmations which increase personal confidence will prove helpful in achieving a sense of positive direction. Actor Jack Nicholson and tennis champ Billie Jean King were born with Mars retrograde.

Jupiter Retrograde—There can be a strengthening of personal faith with Jupiter retrograde, because ideals and philosophical beliefs are developed within the self. These ideals and morals may run counter to those of society at large. Writers William Butler Yeats (who wrote extensively about mystical philosophical concepts) and Upton Sinclair were both born with Jupiter retrograde. The expansive energy of Jupiter is positively enhanced when retrograde, because the inner search for truth is strongly empowered.

Saturn Retrograde—Trusting inner security is a primary lesson for the child born with Saturn retrograde. These children may also innately mistrust authority. Saturn provides structure, direction, and discipline, and teaches us about our priorities. Having this planet in retrograde sometimes makes it difficult to learn these lessons at first.

Saturn retrograde may indicate problems relating to the parent who provides this structure in the early years. With our changing society, we are seeing Saturn's structuring influence being expressed through both the male and female parents. Very often this parent is inaccessible to the child, either because she is absent, constantly working, or emotionally distant. The child must learn to go within and achieve her own sense of structure, direction, and personal discipline.

Questions about safety can be paramount. Affirmations which confer a sense of confidence, achievement, and personal strength can be powerful tools. These children can be remarkably self-disciplined and focused once this sense of self-doubt is overcome. Pianist Van Cliburn, actor Sean Connery, dancer/actress Leslie Caron, and singer Dionne Warwick were all born with Saturn retrograde.

Uranus Retrograde—The sense of uniqueness and individuality exemplified by the energy of Uranus can be strongly accentuated in retrograde. There is a powerful urge to break free of all forms of restriction and achieve true personal freedom. The knowledge that external freedom can only come when inner freedom exists is inborn with these individuals.

Many individuals born with Uranus retrograde have achieved positive recognition for their special talents. Some examples are Sir Winston Churchill, Johnny Carson, Katherine Hepburn, and Anne Morrow Lindberg. Children born with Uranus retrograde will need acknowledgment of their uniqueness, especially if Uranus retrograde is placed in the angular houses (1st, 4th, 7th, or 10th).

Neptune Retrograde—Neptune's energy draws us into the inner self where we dream, visualize, imagine, and escape. When Neptune retrogrades, this introspective energy is even more deeply sensitized. There can be an intensified desire to escape the ordinary world and its pressures.

The positive use of creative imagination is absolutely essential in this situation. These children also need to learn very early in their lives the difference between physical plane reality (what we usually think of as "real") and imagination or illusion. Imagination should certainly be encouraged, but in ways that are constructive to the child's growth.

Neptune's house placement will indicate the area in which the child needs a creative escape and how he can effectively use the imagination. Farrah Fawcett, Yoko Ono, and Ralph Waldo Emerson were all born with Neptune retrograde at birth.

Pluto Retrograde—Pluto spends about half of each year in retrograde motion. In dealing with Pluto retrograde, parents can help the child understand her sense of personal power in relationship to other people and situations. The child may feel somewhat mistrustful of this life process and needs to develop a trust of herself. Developing honesty is quite helpful in this regard.

Planetary retrogrades stimulate the child to develop an inner awareness of the energy involved. Often, there is also a counterpoint between how the child will use the energy and how society expects the energy to be utilized. This can be positively useful or disruptive, depending on how the energy is channeled. The planetary expressions which seem to be positively intensified by retrogradation are Jupiter and Uranus, with Mars and Saturn being the most frustrated by retrogradation.

4

Planetary Aspects and
Aspect Patterns in the Chart

Defining the Aspects

Planetary aspects in astrology are the geometric relationships between the planets and sensitive points to one another. Aspects modify the basic meaning of the planets.

A simple example of a planetary aspect is the cycle of the Moon. We can see the Moon's aspect to the Sun from the amount of light it is reflecting. The "dark of the Moon" is the time the Moon begins its cycle, the New Moon. At this time the Sun and Moon are in an aspect called a conjunction. We then observe the Moon becoming apparently larger in the sky, with the crescent changing to the Quarter Moon. This illustrates the square aspect between the Moon and Sun. At the time of the Full Moon, the Moon is in opposition to the Sun, making a 180-degree aspect to it. When the Moon begins to wane, or decrease in light, other aspects between the Moon and Sun are seen. Astrologers measure these aspects in terms of degrees of the zodiac, giving several of the degree correlations names and meanings.

Understanding the basic meanings of the planets, signs, and houses allows us to integrate various factors in the chart. Aspects are the next step in this process of integration. Blending the concepts of planets, signs, and houses together gives us a general overview. Adding the aspects, however, gives us a much more detailed and meaningful view of the person. These relationships between planets are tremendously important in comprehending the whole person. Different aspects have particular meanings, and can significantly alter the basic surge of a planetary energy. Some aspects create harmony, while others create tension.

Identifying aspects is sometimes a challenge for the beginning student of astrology. To some extent, you have to train yourself to look at the circle and its geometry. Now, for those of you with math fears, it's actually easier than you may think! Begin with the simplest aspect to find: the conjunction. The conjunction is the 0-degree aspect, with the two planets appearing adjacent to one another in the chart. It is rare that two or more planets are exactly the same degree and minute. In our example, we find two planets in conjunction which are 3 degrees from each other. This allowance of 3 degrees is called the *orb*. A list of aspects, their degrees, and suggested orbs is found in Table 5. See below for more discussion about orbs.

Interpretation of the aspects follows a very logical assumption which is related to the geometric angle itself. To continue our example of the conjunction, consider the concept of what happens when two points are joined together. Apply these to the con-

Glyph	Name	Aspect Degree	Degree of Orb
☌	Conjunction	0	7
⚺	Semisextile	30	2
∠	Semisquare	45	2
✳	Sextile	60	4
Q	Quintile	72	1
□	Square	90	7
△	Trine	120	6
⚼	Sesquiquadrate	135	2
⚻	Quincunx	150	2
☍	Opposition	180	7

Table 5. Table of Aspects.

cept of energy, and there you are—more power! The conjunction is a powerful aspect, uniting two planetary energies so that they empower each other. A conjunction of the Sun and Mars will unite the active, assertive energy of Mars with the vitality and willpower of the Sun. This adds a positive assertiveness, a sense of impatience, and an increased drive to the personality. When delineating the conjunction aspect, using the keywords "unites" or "is united with" will help you in determining the basic meaning of the aspect.

Aspects can be qualified as harmonious and flowing, or as dynamic and tension-producing. Two planetary energies which are supporting one another through a flowing aspect would be easier to handle than two planetary energies which form a dynamic, tension-producing relationship.

The conjunction is the only aspect which, in itself, is neither harmonious or dynamic—its quality is determined by the nature of the two interacting planets. A conjunction of two personal planets will often be harmonious. Conjunctions of personal and outer planets may create a bit more distress, however, since these involve integrating the outer and inner self. Saturn conjunctions often bring frustrations and delays. I have found that most aspects between the personal planets and Saturn will reflect the restrictive nature of Saturn, regardless of the aspect. More information on specific aspects will be found in the following chapters.

The Question of Orbs

It is rare for any aspect to be exact—for example, two planets in conjunction at exactly the same degree and minute of the zodiac. Astrologers allow for variations in this exactness and call this variation *orb*. The orb of influence of any aspect is determined by the relative strength of the aspect. The aspects defined as Ptolemaic are also called the *major aspects* and are the angular relationships which seem to have the greatest strength. As a rule, astrologers allow more orb for these major aspects than for the so-called minor aspects. The tighter the orb of the aspect, the more strength the aspect will have. Therefore, two planets in aspect which are less than one degree of orb will be more intense in their influence than two planets whose aspect has a wider orb of 4 or 5 degrees.

GLYPH	NAME	BASIC MEANINGS
☌	Conjunction	Focus, unity
Harmonious Aspects		
⊻	Semisextile	Continuity, rapport
✳	Sextile	Cooperation, productivity
Q	Quintile	Potential, talent
△	Trine	Ease, opportunity
Dynamic Aspects		
∠	Semisquare	Irritation, contrast
□	Square	Tension, frustration
⬐	Sesquiquadrate	Disruption, aggravation
⊼	Quincunx	Adjustment, reorientation
☍	Opposition	Challenge, separation

Table 6. Keywords: Aspects.

The Major Aspects

Conjunction

The conjunction has been introduced above. To find the conjunctions in a chart, look for planets which are adjacent to each other. Remember that conjunctions represent a unity of two energies—they operate as a unit.

Two planets can be conjunct even if they are not in the same sign. There are 30 degrees in each sign of the zodiac. Once we reach 29 degrees 59 minutes of Aries, we move to 0 degrees 0 minutes of Taurus. If we have the Sun at 28 degrees Aries and Venus at 2 degrees Taurus, the Sun and Venus are conjunct within an orb of 4 degrees. These two energies are united in their expression, with the vitality of the Sun giving power to the artistic nature of Venus. This aspect would be one indicator of an artistically expressive individual. Conjunctions represent focus and unity.

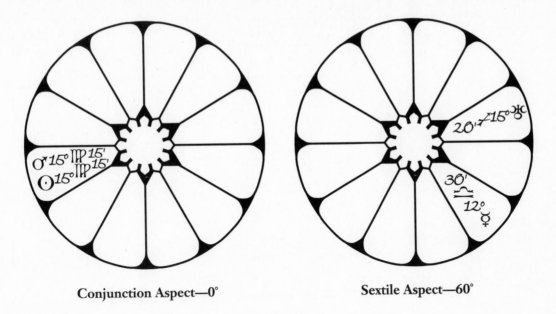

Conjunction Aspect—0°   Sextile Aspect—60°

Sextile

The sextile is an aspect of 60 degrees. This aspect provides a support system for the individual, with the two energies working in harmony and producing a cooperative effort.

When we find planets sextile in the child's chart, we need to encourage the child to activate and express those energies. These are the energies within the self which flow easily and can create increased confidence. For example, if Mercury and Uranus are sextile to one another, the mental energy of Mercury is supported by the inventive, intuitive energy of Uranus. The child should be encouraged to try out spontaneous ideas and trust the intuitive flow in her thinking processes. Sextiles represent cooperation and productivity.

Square

The square is an aspect of 90 degrees between two planets or points in the chart. This dynamic aspect produces a powerful tension between the two energies involved, and creates a need to resolve it. It is difficult to ignore energies which are squaring one another—the tension can sometimes be explosive!

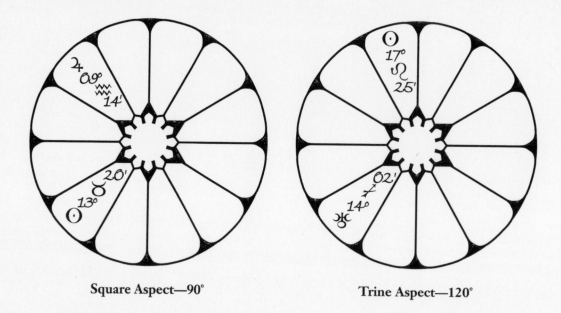

Square Aspect—90°   Trine Aspect—120°

Squares drive the individual to improve the parts of himself signified by the planets involved, thus stimulating growth in the individual. Planets which are squaring one another offer very powerful opportunities for growth within the child. For example, a child with the Sun squaring Jupiter (see "Square Aspect" example) will need to overcome tendencies to overindulge himself and overextend himself emotionally. Once this is learned, he will have a better sense of his boundaries in personal relationships. Tension and frustration are the keynotes of the square.

Trine

Planets which trine one another are 120 degrees apart and the energy flows together harmoniously. The ease with which these energies support one another gives increased confidence to the child, although the gifts of the planets involved may be taken for granted too easily. In order to create opportunities through the trine, the child must learn how to apply herself and make the most of situations. Trines are special gifts which must be used to be appreciated. This is the aspect of ease and opportunity.

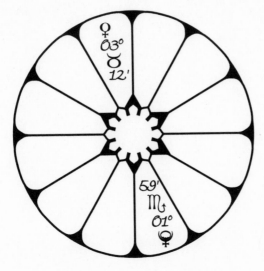

Opposition Aspect—180°

Aries	Libra
Taurus	Scorpio
Gemini	Sagittarius
Cancer.	Capricorn
Leo	Aquarius
Virgo	Pisces

Table 7. Opposing Signs.

Opposition

It is also easy to spot oppositions in the astrological chart. An opposition aspect is 180 degrees. Oppositions represent the principles of polarity and duality. This opposition/polarity principle is also illustrated in the natural progression of the zodiac where each sign has its polar opposite (see Table 7). This aspect is dynamic, with the tension produced between the two planets providing a heightened sense of awareness in the individual. Achieving balance is the challenge of the opposition. The child may vacillate from one side to the other, much like a seesaw, until he learns to find a balancing point. The opposition is an aspect of awareness and balance, and gives thrust to achieving goals.

The Minor Aspects

The so-called "minor" aspects are a bit more difficult to locate in the chart. I use a smaller orb of influence in these aspects, since the angles are not as strong as the angles of the major aspects. Although these angles are less prominent, the aspects still have a notable effect.

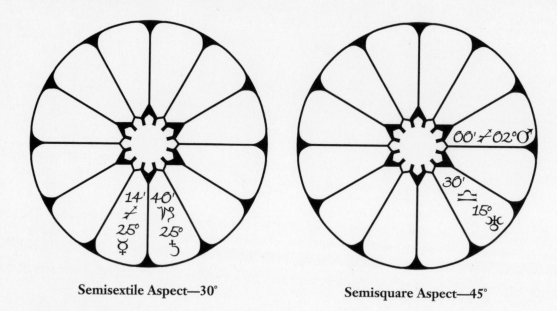

Semisextile Aspect—30°   Semisquare Aspect—45°

Semisextile

The semisextile is an aspect of 30 degrees. Here the planets represent qualities which are dissimilar, but which naturally flow into one another in the natural progression of the zodiac. This is an aspect of continuity and flow which works like steps moving us from one level to the next. Two planets in semisextile represent the potential for developing rapport and continuity.

Semisquare

The 45-degree aspect is called the semisquare and is an aspect of friction and irritation. A good analogy for the semisquare is the discomfort one might feel when wearing heavy wool against bare skin in the summertime.

To work with the semisquare energies, one must learn how to appropriately apply the energies involved. If a child has Mars and Uranus semisquare to one another (see "Semisquare Aspect" example), she might be stimulated to act rashly or take dangerous risks. The quick-acting nature of Uranus could be helpful in some applications, but the child must learn the proper times and places to do her daring deeds. (She should skateboard on a quiet sidewalk during the day rather than on a busy street at night, for

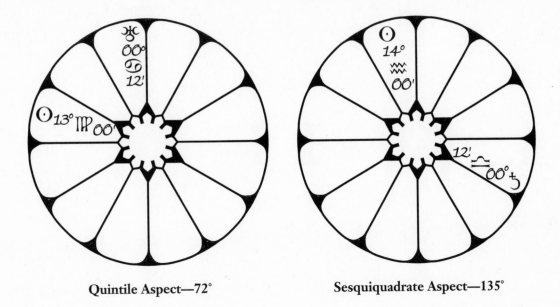

Quintile Aspect—72°   **Sesquiquadrate Aspect—135°**

example.) Keywords for the semisquare are "irritation" and "contrast." For the most part, semisquares are not operating on a clearly discernible level during childhood with the exception of those aspects involving the personal planets and luminaries.

Quintile

Quintiles are aspects of 72 degrees and represent a child's special talents and potentials. These talents generally require maturity and inner balance to be developed with any consistency. Planets which are quintile to one another are automatically fine-tuned. These qualities may operate on an unconscious level, but they can be activated. Usually the qualities are refined during adult years.

Sesquiquadrate

Sesquiquadrate aspects are 135 degrees apart and are disruptive and aggravating. Planets which are sesquiquadrate are like a pinch, and are sometimes difficult to resolve. These planetary energies disrupt the status quo and can undermine personal security if the disruptive energy is not consciously replaced by more positive and harmonious action.

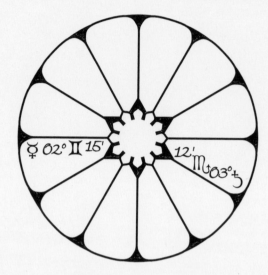

Quincunx Aspect—150°

Quincunx or Inconjunct

Quincunx (sometimes called inconjunct) aspects are found between planets which are 150 degrees apart. The quincunx is like itching, requiring that the individual make adjustments to deal with the energies. Be warned, though—sometimes scratching only irritates! This is an aspect of adjustment and reorientation.

How to Interpret Aspects

The interpretation of aspects is initially difficult for most students. By approaching aspect interpretation very methodically, though, you will find it much less confusing. What we are doing is blending many levels of concepts together to create a more complete picture. Delineating an astrological chart without using the aspects will certainly offer some good information, but it will be incomplete. It's like comparing an ordinary scrambled egg to a veggie supreme omelet. The eggs by themselves will make do for a quick meal, but the addition of fresh mushrooms, green peppers, shallots, and monterey jack cheese certainly makes for a delicious difference!

Mercury	Aquarius	1st House
Communication	Inventive	Personality
	Unusual	How others see me
	Eccentric	
	Inventive	

In aspect to:

Saturn	Scorpio	10th House
Structure	Intense	My reputation
Discipline	Powerful	Parents
		What I want to do

Table 8. Blending Concepts Using Keywords.

To begin the task of aspect interpretation, first consider each planet, its sign, and house separately. Then blend the ideas of these elements together, using the basic meanings of the aspects (see Table 6).

For example, if we are studying an aspect between Mercury in Aquarius in the 1st House squaring Saturn in Scorpio in the 10th House, we need to first examine the basic meanings of Mercury, Aquarius, and the 1st House, then Saturn, Scorpio, and the 10th House. You might want to make a chart like the illustration below, indicating keywords or key concepts for each of these factors (see Table 8).

Mercury, the energy of communication, is expressed in an inventive, unusual, independent, or eccentric manner (Aquarius) and is directed through the 1st House (personality, how other people see me). This child might need to express himself as an independent thinker. However, there is conflict because of the square from Saturn (restriction, structure, or security needs) which might inhibit this free and independent communication or expression.

How might this be limited? Look to the sign and house in which Saturn is found. The sign Scorpio, which is intense, powerful, and charismatic, is found in the 10th House. For a child, the 10th House and Saturn often reflect the parents. Perhaps there is a powerful and intense father (Saturn in Scorpio in the 10th House) who expects a more structured (Saturn) type of thinking (Mercury) from the child. The 10th House also deals with reputation and honor in one's life. The child may fear (Saturn) a loss (Saturn) of reputation (10th House) if he speaks his mind and shares his independent or eccentric ideas.

All these interpretations result from a very simple step-by-step process of using key concepts and keywords. You might find it helpful in your study of astrology to memorize a few key concepts about each planet, sign, and house. This will help you become more independent of books when interpreting charts.

Aspect Patterns

Closely related to planetary aspects is the study of patterns within the personality. The aspect patterns are sets or aspects which join planets together into a kind of "planetary picture." We'll explore four major aspect patterns which are helpful in delineating the child's chart, although there are also many others. These are the Stellium, the Grand Trine, the T-Square, and the Grand Cross.

The Stellium

The Stellium or Satellium consists of three or more planets which all conjunct one another (see the chart of Shirley Temple Black). These energies are concentrated, and unite to form a powerful bond. A Stellium gives the child a tremendous ability to focus. This can be used positively through constructive, creative effort. A Stellium often indicates a special talent in the area symbolized by the planets, signs, and house.

The primary pitfall of the Stellium is that the child may concentrate too exclusively upon using the energies of these planets and not fully develop other important aspects of herself. This can also indicate a potential to fall into a kind of rut in terms of response and action. The way out of this potential trap is provided by aspects from other planets which will stimulate change or action.

Look at the example in Shirley Temple Black's chart. This Stellium involves the planets Venus in Aries in the 4th House in conjunction to Jupiter and Mercury in Aries in the 4th House. Also, the Sun forms a very wide (10-degree) conjunction to Mercury. Little Shirley Temple's enthusiasm, energy, and charm lifted the spirits of moviegoers in the 1930s at a time when the Great Depression had overtaken the

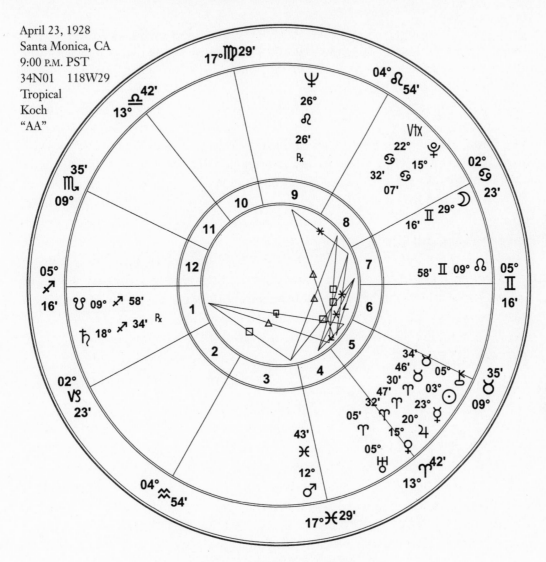

April 23, 1928
Santa Monica, CA
9:00 P.M. PST
34N01   118W29
Tropical
Koch
"AA"

Shirley Temple Black's Natal Chart

United States and the world. It is very noteworthy that not only is Jupiter, the energy of optimism, a strong tie in the Stellium, but she has Sagittarius rising, which is the Jupiter-ruled sign of the zodiac. It's no wonder that her bubbly personality and winning smile raised everyone's hopes in a time of despair and rebuilding.

In the appendix, please note other excellent examples of Stelliums—Jodie Foster, Florence Griffith Joyner, Dorothy Hamill, Scott Hamilton, Christopher Parkening, Tatum O'Neil.

The Grand Trine

The Grand Trine consists of three or more planets or angles (Ascendant or Midheaven) which are in trine aspect to one another (see Jimmy Seals' astrological chart). Generally, planets are in a Grand Trine by element—fire, earth, air, or water (see Illustration 4). The Grand Trine is a circuit of energy which continually flows through an individual's life. This pattern seems to give a sense of divine protection to the person blessed. However, like the trine it represents, it can be easily taken for granted.

Once developed by the child, this powerful circuit of energy will confer a strength and resilience which will be tremendously helpful throughout her life. To interpret this pattern, consider the key concepts of the element involved to basically support the meaning of the planets in their signs and houses. For example, Grand Trines in

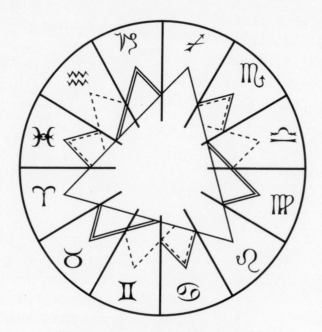

Illustration 4. Elemental Triplicities.

air have a powerful mental and intellectual thrust. In Jimmy Seals' instance, the messages of peace and serenity he delivered through his music as part of the musical duo Seals and Crofts is an excellent example of a Grand Air Trine realized. In water, an emotional support system is easy for the child to access. In fire, an inspirational focus

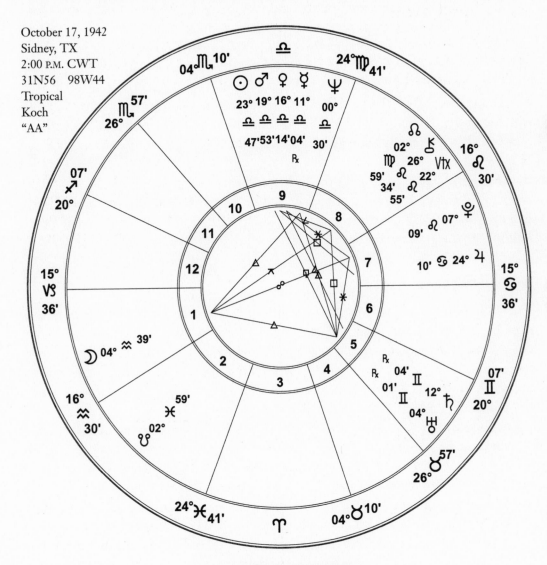

Jimmy Seals' Natal Chart

drives the child. In earth, a practical, sensible approach will be noticeable in personality development.

To help the child use this pattern of energy most effectively, encourage activities which will help the child appreciate this special flow. With the Grand Air Trine, he can develop his intellectual abilities by applying mental energy to creative projects. The child will also benefit from learning to listen to others and their ideas.

The Grand Water Trine sometimes brings a sense of emotional containment to the child. She can benefit from learning how to give of herself and by developing consideration of others' feelings.

With the Grand Fire Trine, a child can sometimes overwhelm others with his dramatic intensity. Directing this fiery energy into philosophical studies and becoming aware of Universal Laws will help him to become a more efficient instrument for the Higher Self as he matures.

The Grand Earth Trine gives the child a keen sense of practicality. She should be encouraged to build things. There may also be a special sense of how to deal with money. The child can benefit from learning how to balance this strong sense of materialism with an appreciation for life's deeper, intangible values.

The T-Square

The T-Square aspect involves three or more planets, and may include the Ascendant and/or Midheaven. This pattern is made up of two squares and an opposition; one planet squares two planets that are in opposition to each other (see Maya Angelou's chart). The planets are usually in the same mode (cardinal, fixed, or mutable). With the T-Square, we see a focus of energy which is continually tense and often frustrating.

By understanding these underlying frustrations in the child, we can offer him support and help find creative ways to release them. The T-Square functions like a perpetual motion machine. As long as continual growth and positive awareness accompanies the energies involved, the child will continuously move forward in his development. If fear, guilt, or too much anxiety accompany the child's approach to life, the T-Square can prove to be the source of much personal aggravation and frustration.

Look to the house opposite the open arm of the T-Square (in Angelou's chart, the 5th House) to find resourceful ways to focus the energy and resolve much of the tension. In our example, the 5th House is the open arm of the T-Square, because it is

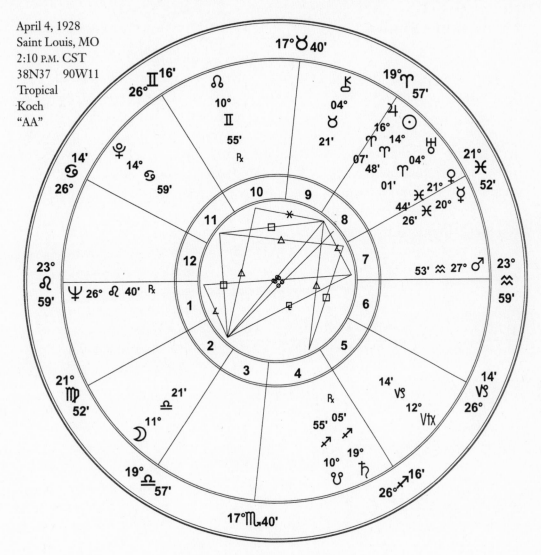

April 4, 1928
Saint Louis, MO
2:10 P.M. CST
38N37   90W11
Tropical
Koch
"AA"

Maya Angelou's Natal Chart

opposite Pluto which is squared by the Moon and the Sun/Jupiter. In Maya Angelou's case, her creative artistry—dance and writing—were her salvation and means of overcoming abusive emotional trauma. The T-Square can be indicative of a child who is strongly motivated. In many instances it is the key to areas of achievement and success. The tension can be used to spur great accomplishment!

The Grand Cross

The Grand Cross involves four or more planets or the Ascendant or Midheaven which are in opposition and square to one another (see Illustrations 5 and 6). This pattern creates continual stress. Children who have Grand Crosses need to learn positive ways to relax and relieve tension. These children are motivated to build, achieve, and succeed, but the obstacles to their goals may sometimes seem insurmountable. Much support is needed from the parents and family to give the child a true sense of purpose in directing these energies. Learning to accept both victory and defeat is paramount. This pattern frequently indicates strong potentials for exceptional success, since it indicates powerful motivation.

Through the application of aspects and chart patterns, we gain deeper insights into the child's astrological chart. In the chapters that follow, we will integrate the concepts of planets, signs and houses in approaching the child's physical, mental, emotional, and spiritual needs. It is of primary importance that we remember to use these astrological insights into childhood responsibly. Each child is born with special gifts and special lessons to learn. As parents, teachers, and guides of children, we have the task of aiding the child's discovery of the Self through love and understanding.

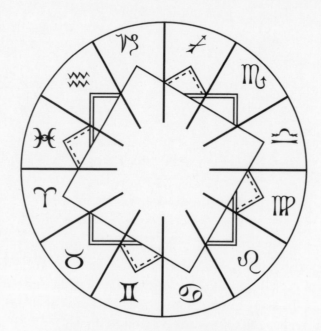

Illustration 5. Modal Quadriplicities.

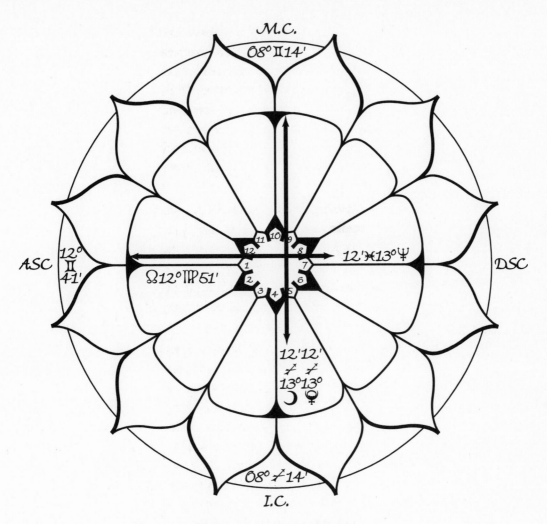

Illustration 6. Grand Cross.

5

Physical Needs and Child Development

The human being must develop four types of bodies—physical, emotional, mental, and spiritual. We mature within these frameworks, and must learn to integrate and balance the needs of each body. No single part seems to exist alone, although it is important to focus on the physical, emotional, mental, and spiritual aspects of life within their own individual framework.

The growing awareness that all of these bodies coexist within each of us has revived interest in holistic approaches to health. *Holistic* implies integration of and harmony between the functions and needs of all the parts. True physical well-being involves harmony between the physical, emotional, mental, and spiritual aspects of the Self, making wholeness and wellness very closely linked!

In approaching the physical needs of the child, therefore, we must keep in mind that this aspect is just one part of a greater whole. One way to study physical health and fitness while maintaining a holistic perspective is through medical astrology. Please realize that this is not an attempt to diagnose or prescribe, just offering suggestions to aid in balancing and harmonizing the body, mind, and spirit.

Each of the planets, signs, and houses has a particular correlation to the physical body. The two houses which relate most directly to physical strength are the 1st and 6th, although all the houses have some impact upon the reasons behind physical wellness or illness. The signs correlate with particular parts of the body, whereas the planets symbolize how these parts are likely to be affected. The following information encompasses some of the simpler approaches to determining a child's physical needs, and covers certain aspects of well-being I find extremely important in the developing child.

Planetary Energies and the Physical Body

Correlating the planetary energies to the child's physical needs provides us with some fascinating information. Each planetary energy most strongly influences a particular part of the physical body.

The Sun and Health

Physically, the Sun represents the child's basic energy level. It is through Sun energy that *prana, ch'i,* or life force, flows, creating vitality in the human body. By maintaining a balanced diet based upon whole, natural foods, we offer this vitality continued renewal. Filling the body with dietary pollutants such as artificial colors, flavors, and preservatives can rob it of its physical vitality.

We can also enhance physical vitality by directly absorbing the rays of the Sun (in moderation, of course!). We are responsible for maintaining a smoothly running physical vehicle. Ignoring fundamental physical needs will diminish the child's capacity to endure the stresses of life.

The Moon and Health

Moon energy corresponds to the basic body cycles and regulates bodily fluids. Eating habits and food preferences are also a function of the Moon. The Moon is our emotional link to physical health, and represents our basic security needs.

It is impossible for a child to be healthy if she does not have her primary emotional needs fulfilled. When they are imbalanced, the bodily cycles are also out of sync. The body has a difficult time fully assimilating the nutrients from food if a child eats while under extreme stress or is emotionally upset at mealtime.

Repressed emotions such as anger, fear, guilt, jealousy, and low self-esteem can also cause physical problems. Medicine is increasingly recognizing the link between physical and emotional well-being. Aspects from the Moon to other planets will indicate the different ways in which the emotional needs are affected. With the Moon aspecting Mars, the child's increased impatience may make it hard for him to express anger positively—especially if the aspect is dynamic. Aspects between the Moon and Saturn frustrate or limit emotional expression, often through feelings of inadequacy or guilt (this will be further discussed in chapter 6). Aspects between the Moon, Saturn, and/or Pluto can be indicative of a child who shuns nurturance or blocks it in some way (anorexia can be a potential problem).

For the girl entering puberty, understanding and coping with the menstrual cycle can initially present problems. This is a lunar function, and the very nature of the menstrual cycle correlates to factors in the chart which are tied to the Moon. Learning about this cycle not only helps the young woman intellectually, but brings a more stable emotional approach to menstruation and the changing hormonal cycle. If the chart shows aspects between the Moon and Saturn, she may have negative feelings about this cyclical process. With Uranus aspecting the Moon, her menstrual cycle may be erratic, and there may be symptoms of premenstrual syndrome (PMS). Increasing vitamin B_6, vitamin E, calcium, and magnesium may be helpful during early adolescence and into adulthood.

Mercury and Health

Mercury corresponds to the nervous pathways in the body—the system within the human which links impulses and responses. Children who have several aspects to Mercury from other planets may experience tremendous amounts of mental and nervous energy, and could have difficulty resting or slowing down. Since mental functioning is strengthened by adequate amounts of B vitamins in the diet, the child's diet needs to be especially rich in this vitamin complex when there are several aspects to the planet Mercury in the chart.

There is an association between Mercury and the thyroid gland, which regulates the metabolic rate. When the thyroid is functioning improperly, the metabolism can be either too slow or too fast. The thyroid, seated in the throat, correlates to the throat chakra of the body. This chakra, or energy center, regulates the mental functioning. When harmony exists between the Divine Flow and personality self, intuitive and logical thought flow in a balanced manner. But if the logical thought processes begin to overrule the intuition, an imbalance in this chakra will result and can create a corresponding imbalance in thyroid functioning. This is often a problem when Mercury is in dynamic or difficult aspect to Uranus or Pluto.

Nourishing the thyroid gland can prove helpful in balancing thyroid function. Adding kelp and dulse (seaweeds) to the diet will provide the thyroid with the iodine, minerals, and vitamins needed for its proper functioning without overloading the body with salt. These can be used directly on foods as seasoning or taken in tablet form as supplements.

Thiamine deficiency is also implicated with Mercury aspecting the outer planets. Some good-tasting fresh sources of thiamine are green vegetables, coconut, pineapple, almonds, peanuts, wheat germ, and nutritional yeast.

In balancing the psychological and physical indicators of poor thyroid functioning, parents can teach children how to positively direct their thoughts. Needless worry can be replaced by creative storytelling or writing. Allowing intuitive thoughts to guide and direct her life is one of the greatest lessons a child can learn. It is especially important to the child whose chart indicates Mercury stress, since the intellect will usually try to overpower the intuition.

Venus and Health

Venus signifies the types of food a child will like, especially his taste for sweets. It also rules the veins of the body, and can indicate possible blood disease and imbalances. Venus is also associated with the kidneys and the throat due to its correspondence with the signs Libra and Taurus.

I have seen children with Venus in dynamic aspect to Saturn who will eat when they do not feel loved. If this type of behavior continues, a structure (Saturn) of fat may result, creating even more overwhelming problems with self-esteem. Also, this aspect and Venus in difficult aspects to Pluto is sometimes seen when anorexia is a problem and self-esteem and body image are problematic. Here, the potentially destructive qualities which can result from this kind of energetic frustration needs to be addressed at a very fundamental level. Even young children can begin to exhibit behavioral clues that she has difficulty feeling good about her body image.

Venus also corresponds to the blood sugar. Aspects from the outer planets to Venus are very often indicators of potential blood sugar problems. This is especially notable when difficult aspects (especially square and quincunx, and sometimes, conjunctions) from Saturn, Uranus, Neptune, and Pluto to Venus are present. The behavioral problems associated with low blood sugar are unpleasant: irritability, hyperactivity or lethargy (sometimes they alternate!), and lack of mental clarity. A parent may think the child is just being difficult, when he is really suffering from a biochemical imbalance!

Balancing the blood sugar can sometimes be accomplished through dietary changes alone. Encourage the child to eat small, frequent, nutritionally rich meals. Avoid too many refined carbohydrates (sugar, white flour, etc.) and processed foods. Adding fresh fruits, nuts, and freshly prepared raw juices is helpful. Supplementing the diet with vitamin B_6 and GTF Chromium can be helpful. Take care when using supplements, however, as you can create new imbalances if you are not properly guided!

Jupiter and Health

Jupiter is the largest planet in our solar system and corresponds to the liver, the largest organ in the human body. I had learned in anatomy class that the liver was large, but I found out just how massive it is when I was in nursing school. During my surgical clerkship, I had the good fortune to scrub for several cholecystectomies (removal of the gallbladder). The gallbladder is just beneath the liver, so someone had to hold the liver up and out of the way to expose it to the surgeon's scalpel.

One morning, I was the one chosen to retract (or pull back) the liver. After holding this organ with a surgical instrument for about twenty minutes, the muscles in my arm were pleading for a rest. Then, when the surgeon told me I would have to hold it for several minutes more, I thought I would collapse. Since that time, I have had a healthy respect for this king-sized organ!

Jupiter is also related to the breakdown of fats and carbohydrates in the body. The liver acts as the body's detoxifying agent. This breakdown of toxic materials also warms the blood, generating most of the body's heat. Children who have dynamic aspects between Jupiter and Saturn could have a sluggishly functioning liver. They will probably be more sensitive to food additives and other chemicals, since the liver may not break down these substances rapidly enough.

Aspects from Jupiter to other planets may also indicate overindulgence. (For example, children with Venus-Jupiter aspects are notorious for their love of sweets, and Moon-Jupiter aspects are likely indicators of overeating in general.) The natural expansiveness of Jupiter needs to be directed *outside* the self through adventure, generosity, and good humor.

The child who compulsively overeats is probably not even aware of this habit, since overeating is often an unconscious act. Help the child become conscious of what, when, and where he is eating. Avoid rewarding these children with goodies like chocolate bars, cake, or ice cream—they will associate the need for reward with negative, self-indulgent behavior. Try rewarding the child with a trip to the zoo, the wild animal park, or some other outing that provides learning, fun, and sharing.

Saturn and Health

Saturn correlates to the framework of the body: the bones, skin, teeth, and nails. It also correlates to collagen, the glue which holds our cells together.

Harmonious aspects between Saturn and Venus generally indicate beautiful, healthy skin, whereas dynamic aspects could indicate skin problems such as eczema, acne, excessive dryness, or psoriasis. Adding vitamins C and E to the diet is helpful when these aspects are present.

Saturn also rules calcium and its absorption in the body. Bioflavonoids and rutin (part of the vitamin C complex) are also keys to building collagen. We all know the importance of calcium in the formation of healthy bones and teeth in children. Children with insufficient calcium in the diet suffer from rickets and often have poorly formed teeth. Another factor in calcium absorption is adequate amounts of vitamin D.

Sun-Saturn aspects in the chart may indicate lowered physical vitality, since Saturn has an inhibiting effect when in dynamic relationship to the Sun. The flowing aspects generally bring a controlled, cautious approach to health. The immune system can be aided by increasing vitamins A and D in the diet. These occur naturally in fish liver oil. Of course, a healthy exposure to sunshine is another source of vitamin D which is absorbed through the skin!

Uranus and Health

Uranus corresponds to the nerve impulses of the body. Contacts from Uranus to other planets can indicate an erratically functioning nervous system, especially in times of extreme stress.

The child whose chart shows a powerfully aspected Uranus, or Uranus conjuncting an angle (ASC, MC, etc.) may display erratic behavior. Mars-Uranus aspects often go hand in hand with hyperactivity, but this should be manageable with a proper diet. There have also been direct correlations between hyperactivity and some food additives.

Uranus sometimes has the effect of creating reversals of energy. Children with aspects between Uranus and the Sun, Moon, or ASC (Ascendant) sometimes have a reversed response to medication. Observe this child carefully when administering any type of medication. If at all possible, try the least intrusive methods of caring for illnesses first! These children usually respond positively to "energy medicine"—acupuncture, Reiki, chakra balancing, and magnetic therapies.

Neptune and Health

Neptune sometimes makes it difficult to assess the child's physical vitality. Children whose Neptune conjuncts the Ascendant or is in the 1st House may be difficult to diagnose because they often present misleading or masking symptoms.

Neptune in aspect to any planet will sensitize that energy. For this reason, children who have aspects from Neptune to the personal planets are likely to be extremely sensitive to drugs and alcohol. They may respond best to smaller than normal dosages of medication since they could experience an extreme reaction or sensitivity to any given drug.

I have seen many correlations between dynamic Moon-Neptune and Sun-Neptune aspects and allergies in the child. The Moon-Neptune aspects seem to be more indicative of food allergies, while Sun-Neptune aspects correspond more to environmental allergies. Sometimes children may have allergies and not present common allergic symptoms such as asthma or hives. Instead, there may be heightened irritability, lethargy, headaches, hyperactivity, or other symptoms.

Parents might be aided by keeping a journal of the foods the child eats and any resulting symptoms (e.g., drinking or eating milk products may give the child headaches). If a correlation seems to be established, the suspected food might be eliminated from the diet for a while. These types of studies are time-consuming, but can ultimately result in a more harmonious and healthful situation.

Pluto and Health

Pluto corresponds to the endocrine glands and cell regeneration in the body. Plutonian energy functions at the deepest level of consciousness and also indicates deep emotional needs. Aspects from any planet to Pluto may indicate psychological distress or a possible breakdown of whichever body system is ruled by that planet.

For example, Sun-Pluto aspects are sometimes found when an individual develops problems with the heart, which is ruled by the Sun. Sometimes this is simply the body reacting to the individual pushing beyond her limits for too long. Teaching the child to recognize the need for rest and relaxation can be important for her long-term vitality. Adequate nourishment is, of course, necessary. Inclusion of vitamin E as a dietary supplement might also be considered.

Mars in the Signs and Recreation

Mars actually energizes the physical body and the vitality of the Sun. It is through Mars that the child expresses physical assertiveness. The adrenal glands and muscles are also associated with Mars, as is the assimilation of many minerals such as iron, phosphorus, chlorine, selenium, and sodium.

Because childhood is a time of heightened activity and physical development, the energy of Mars needs some extra attention. Building a strong body through increased sports or other activities is one way to intensify the development of healthy vitality. This is a function of Mars.

Mars is associated with body temperature. Inflammation is a Martian process, and a child whose chart has a strongly aspected Mars may respond to physical stress with increased body temperatures. This is one indicator that the body is fighting back and regenerating itself. The approach of always bringing down body temperature when a child is ill may ultimately do her more harm than good. If the child is extremely uncomfortable, catnip or chamomile baths are often helpful. Of course, very high fevers should never go unchecked, but we must realize that sometimes fever is a good sign!

Mars Aspects and Health

When Mars is in aspect to Jupiter, a child tends to press limits and can be more accident prone. Any aspect from Mars to Jupiter inclines a child to think confidently, but the dynamic aspects—the semisquare, square, quincunx, and opposition—can be especially frustrating since the child is not interested in honoring limits, but in pushing far past them! These are the kids who seem like speed demons, even on their trikes and bikes. Conversely, the child with Mars in conjunction, sextile, or trine Jupiter can be overly confident and underprepared, since the tendency is to feel a bit lazy.

The child with Mars-Saturn aspects may have a low level of physical energy, and should be encouraged to devote some time to physical activity in order to raise energy levels. This is especially true when Mars is in square, quincunx, or opposition to Saturn, and attitudes which seem a bit defeatist can be part of his personality. Sometimes these kids really do not like sports, but many children go the other way and decide to overcompensate and train until they drop. The flowing aspects between Mars and Saturn add self-discipline and an ability to set limits and work or train carefully toward goals. Mars conjunct Saturn can be directed either way, with much depending upon the sign and house placement of Mars and Saturn and other aspects made with these planets.

Children whose charts show dynamic aspects between Mars and Uranus can often be accident-prone since they tend to take higher risks and may even be fascinated by the idea of doing what seems impossible. While this may mean that a toddler will try to run before she can walk, the six-year-old may think she can fly. During preteen years, there can be an inordinate fascination with activities that test physical possibilities. Sports like skiing might be interesting and breaking boards with karate moves could be the perfect way to resolve this drive. Later, these are the adults who skydive, bungee jump, and are drawn to extreme sports.

Aspects between Mars and Neptune suggest extra physical sensitivity but can also increase the potential for developing grace. Unfortunately, Neptune's effect usually places a damper on Mars' exuberance and vitality or the child might prefer to channel physical energy into creative activities like playing music. When other connections to Mars are supportive, aspects with Neptune can indicate that the child can utilize visualization to improve physical skills. Also, during the teen years these aspects can be indicative of the youngster who harbors powerful dreams about his physical prowess or abilities.

Mars in aspect to Pluto generates a desire to take physical abilities into a different realm. The flowing aspects can be especially helpful in sports activities, since the ability to draw on a deeper strength and also to build energy reserves can be strong. The dynamic aspects—the semisquare, square, quincunx, and opposition—can prompt a child to challenge others in a way which provokes a strong or defensive response. Learning the limits of personal power can be difficult for these children, especially if they are faced with any kind of abuse. Sports can be a plus if properly directed, and particularly if the child is taught to respect the self and others in the process.

Mars in the Signs: Recreation and Sports

To develop a continual reserve of energy, the child needs positive outlets for physical activity. Some kinds of physical recreation which will appeal to the child can be determined by the placement of Mars by sign in the chart. Refer to Table 9 for more information. These activities are intended as suggestions and should not be considered as limiting factors.

Mars in the Houses and Health

The house placement of Mars indicates the types of environment and people a child will enjoy interacting with while participating in sports. I have noticed that children who have Mars placed near the angles of the chart need to express their physical strength to others. A four-year-old boy with Mars opposing his Ascendant and Aries at the Midheaven recently approached me, flexing his muscles. "I'm strong!" he exclaimed. His mother tells me that he will try to lift almost anything. She is having difficulty explaining to him that while he can certainly grow up and have great strength, he will probably not be twelve feet tall or be able to lift a house with one hand!

1st House Mars—Mars in the 1st House will enjoy staying physically active. Babies with this placement may have trouble getting to sleep unless they've had sufficient physical activity to burn off any excess energy. This child may be interested in sports, dance, or other activities which require endurance and strength. With difficult aspects to Mars, this child can be accident-prone.

2nd House Mars—Mars in the 2nd House indicates a more easygoing kind of energy. This child needs to develop endurance.

3rd House Mars—Mars in the 3rd House can indicate high activity and talkativeness. Focus can be a problem for this child, and having opportunities to stay physically and mentally active will provide direction for energy which could be seen as nervous by those who hope to have peace and quiet.

4th House Mars—Mars in the 4th House indicates a quiet competitiveness. While this child may not be excessively active, she will need direction for physical energy. If Mars is square to the ASC from this house, she can be accident-prone, especially at home.

5th House Mars—Mars in the 5th House will enjoy recreational activities and sports as a means to direct physical energy. If he is not particularly competitive, this energy may be positively directed toward hobbies or other creative activities.

SIGN	ACTIVITIES
Aries	Running (especially sprinting), martial arts, baseball, tennis, fencing, free calisthenics (gymnastics), acrobatics, acrobatic skiing, athletic dancing, tap dancing
Taurus	Weightlifting, tai chi, ballroom dancing, discus, gymnastics, football (especially defense positions), table tennis, snorkeling, golf
Gemini	Handball, racquetball, juggling, jump rope, parallel and uneven parallel bars (gymnastics), badminton, tennis, basketball, bicycling, skateboarding, hang-gliding, wind surfing, fencing, pole-vaulting
Cancer	Swimming, surfing, water skiing, scuba diving, tae kwon do, karate, golf, fishing, boating, snorkeling, folk dancing, belly dancing
Leo	Gymnastics, distance running, rodeo, high-diving, surfing, golf, captain and/or quarterback of football team
Virgo	Racquetball, handball, table tennis, tennis, scuba diving, aerobic dancing, yoga, gymnastics, English saddle riding, figure skating, baseball
Libra	Ballroom dancing, yoga, tai chi, ice dancing, balance beam (gymnastics), juggling, ballet
Scorpio	Swimming, diving, most gymnastic events, deep sea diving, high diving, high jumping, hatha yoga, endurance sports, aerobics, body contact sports
Sagittarius	Archery, horseback riding (especially jumping), javelin, high jumping, long jumping, hiking, soccer, cheerleading
Capricorn	Snow skiing, mountain climbing, rock climbing, hiking, running (especially marathons), figure skating, endurance sports, tai chi
Aquarius	Figure skating, roller skating, hang-gliding, skateboarding, gymnastics, basketball, volleyball, baseball, relay races, parachuting, skydiving
Pisces	Swimming, snorkeling, deep sea diving, dancing, English saddle riding, fishing, ice dancing

Table 9. Mars in the Signs: Recreation and Sports.

6th House Mars—Mars in the 6th House is indicative of a child who may not be especially graceful, since she can feel uncomfortable when placed in situations that call on physical prowess or skill. However, this child may enjoy learning the skills necessary to be good at individual sports. When ill, this child is likely to run higher fevers.

7th House Mars—Mars in the 7th House indicates a strong level of competitive energy, although this child will not necessarily be a sports fanatic. Encouraging physical activities which have positive goals and help the child feel more confident about his power will have a positive effect on confrontational behaviors.

8th House Mars—Mars in the 8th House can be indicative of a child who has ample energy reserves. She will enjoy activities which help her build strength, skill, and a sense of control over his/her body.

9th House Mars—Mars in the 9th House functions best in situations which are uplifting. Team sports can be great fun, but he may also enjoy martial arts or other sports which are linked with philosophical values and ideals in some way.

10th House Mars—Mars in the 10th House children enjoy being acknowledged for their physical prowess and accomplishments. Taking on leadership positions in team sports will seem natural, or she may enjoy cheering on her favorite team. Winning is important to her.

11th House Mars—Mars in the 11th House is perfect for team sports activities, since learning to direct his energy toward a common goal with others will be exhilarating for this child.

12th House Mars—Mars in the 12th House can be indicative of a child who prefers to dream instead of risking physical distress. However, she may enjoy dance or swimming (getting this child to feel comfortable in water may be a challenge for some).

The Signs and the Body

The twelve signs of the zodiac correspond to the body parts. If a child has several planets in one sign, that particular system of the body may be easily stressed. Some of the correspondences are noted below.

Aries—Rules the face, the cranium, and the arteries and veins of the head and neck.

Taurus—Rules the neck and its vertebrae along with the muscles, veins, and arteries in this area. The throat is also ruled by Taurus.

Gemini—Rules the shoulders, arms, hands, and lungs as well as the muscles, veins, and arteries of these areas.

Cancer—Rules the stomach, breasts, chest, and diaphragm as well as the muscles, arteries, and veins in these areas.

Leo—Rules the heart and the lower back and the muscles, veins, and arteries of these body parts.

Virgo—Corresponds to the pancreas, spleen, and intestinal tract and the muscles, veins, and arteries of the upper abdominal area.

Libra—Rules the kidneys (renal glands) and lumbar vertebrae and the veins, arteries, and muscles which support these areas.

Scorpio—Rules the reproductive organs, the colon, and the pelvic bones as well as the muscles, veins, and arteries which supply them.

Sagittarius—Rules the thighs, the sciatic nerve, the saphenous vein (the largest vein of the body), the coccyx, ilium, femur, and sacrum as well as the muscles, veins, and arteries associated with these areas.

Capricorn—Rules the knees and their ligaments, the gallbladder, the iliac artery, and the popliteal vein.

Aquarius—Rules the ankles, the tibia and fibula, the calves, blood circulation, and the spinal cord.

Pisces—Rules the feet, the lymphatic system, and the body's mucus level.

The 1st and 6th Houses

The 1st and 6th Houses are the two houses which are primarily related to physical health. The 1st House corresponds to the physical body itself. The sign on the Ascendant indicates the general physical health of the child. Any planets placed in the 1st House will also affect physical strength. The energies which strengthen the physical body are the Sun, Mars, Venus, and Jupiter. The energies of the Moon, Saturn, Neptune, and Pluto often indicate a detriment to overall physical health.

The Moon can tie the child's state of health to his emotional stability. Saturn's influence often leads to excessive levels of physical stress. The child will need to learn holistic relaxation methods such as biofeedback in order to compensate for this contact. Neptune sensitizes the physical body and can indicate allergic reactions or sensitivity in general. Pluto sometimes has an undermining effect on the physical body. If Pluto forms dynamic aspects with other planets, it can indicate potentially self-destructive health problems. These will generally be related to repressed emotional factors.

The 6th House's correlation to health has much to do with the child's health and hygiene habits. A child with planetary energies in this house will pay more attention to health. Developing responsibility for physical well-being will be more crucial for the child with an energized 6th House.

Final Health Considerations

In evaluating the overall health of the child, first consider the Sun, Moon, and Ascendant with their signs and aspects. Then locate those planets which have the greatest number of aspects. The areas occupied or ruled by these planets may require special attention. The sign most influenced also should be noted, and will serve as an indicator of the child's special needs.

The best thing we can do for our children's health is to offer them the highest quality foods, a positive attitude about their bodies and physical well-being, the best possible environment, and abundant love and attention. Helping the child develop a balanced lifestyle is a primary responsibility for the parents. Examples and lessons of this lifestyle in childhood form the dominant framework for habits later in life. To alter a negative habit requires focused attention and great effort. A child whose personal habits are conducive to good health, however, will have more time and energy for other pursuits as she matures.

6

The Emotional Needs
of the Child

Each planet in the chart indicates a level of need, and many of the planetary ener-gies have a profound correlation to emotional development. In the earliest years, a child's emotional security is determined by the relationship with his mother and father. Interactions with siblings or grandparents can also be a factor, although relat-ing beyond the immediate family is usually rare. The child is open to influences from family and will project himself upon them.

In analyzing astrological symbols to understand the developing child's emotional needs, we must also become aware of some of the basic psychological mechanisms operating in her life. The child will be ready to explore and develop varying aspects of the Self at different ages. In the very early months, a baby is struggling to figure out her new body and learn how it works. She is also familiarizing herself with the exter-nal environment and the people within it. We must consider the different phases of a child's development in relation to a child's astrological symbology if we are to success-fully apply astrology to children.

One of the key points to keep in mind when interpreting children's charts is that the planetary energies and their aspect connections symbolize the specific sensibilities and sensitivities of the child. It's like finding a ticklish spot on the body—some people have really sensitive feet, others can't stand to have their knees tickled. When looking to the chart to gain an understanding of emotional needs and psychologically sensitive issues, we see a myriad of possibilities. One child may welcome the challenge of proving himself, while another shies away since his "trigger" mechanism operates differently. It is also important to explore these concepts through a lens of objectivity, since when dealing with psychological and emotional issues with our children we're likely to run into our own issues as part of the process!

The Personal Planets as Indicators of Need

The Sun, Moon, and personal planets (Mercury, Venus, and Mars) symbolize the facets of the personality which are the most readily discernible. The Sun, which represents the sense of Self, may not seem to be manifesting externally in the infant. However, the physical expression of the Sun—basic vitality—is strongly manifested. A limited expression of Sun energy seems to emerge in the preschool years, although the true awareness of the Self will not be complete for many years to come.

Lunar energy encompasses subconscious motivations and the basic instinctual and habitual responses. This level of expression begins to manifest from the moment of birth, since the baby does have a strong inner awareness of what is happening. Our exploration of the emotional needs, then, should begin with the Moon, the indicator of early psychological development.

The Moon

Most of our emotional responses are made without forethought—we simply react to a situation without thinking. These responses are based upon prior experiences in similar situations. This is the subconscious self.

For the developing child, the emotional response patterns may be strongly influenced by the primary caretaker, usually the mother. Although the child does have her own particular needs, it is difficult for a tiny infant to tell Mommy, "I like that color," or "Play more of that music," or "I really feel good when you rub my feet." Mommy will know these things if she opens her intuitive mind, however, since she will be tuning in to the child's subconscious nature.

The Moon in the Signs and Emotional Needs

The child's strongest emotional needs will be symbolized by the Moon's sign and house placement. These needs remain with the child throughout life. The ease or difficulty with which the true needs will be realized can be further delineated by examining the aspects from the Moon to the other planets. The sign placement of the Moon is the basic guideline in determining the child's most pressing needs. This fundamental emotional framework is further altered by house placement and aspects from the Moon to other energies in the chart.

Moon in Aries—This child needs to be independent, and will probably be very direct in expressing wants and desires. The baby with an Aries Moon is likely to be tremendously impatient. Activity is highly important. As the baby grows, he will be more and more active and is likely to explore anything and everything.

The small child retains this impatience, and may express it with bursts of temper. As she matures, the child will find that by becoming mentally inventive instead of throwing temper tantrums, she will not have to wait so long for things to happen. Here, there is a strong sense of creativity. This child needs to be noticed and needs to lead.

Moon in Taurus—This child can be very stubborn, and likes to know what to expect in all situations. The small child with a Taurus Moon will probably not enjoy sudden changes of environment, an alteration in diet, or any unexpected change which has not been previously introduced.

There is often a loving placidity about these children, especially in the early years. The child's parents will appreciate his patience. This child needs to build a strong security base but must watch becoming too emotionally attached to people, places, and things.

Moon in Gemini—This child enjoys diversity and may be easily distracted in the very early months of life. There will be a wide variety of interests and quickly changing moods. As the child grows, she may be uncomfortable with highly charged emotional situations unless they can be explained rationally or expressed verbally.

The highest need here revolves around diversity and continual mental activity. Consistency may equal boredom for the Gemini Moon. These children need to move about and should be provided with all sorts of little transportation toys. They feel a tremendous need to communicate thoughts, which tends to spur early communication skills.

Moon in Cancer—This child is emotionally sensitive, with a strong attachment to the mother, home, and family. These babies do not want to see Mother go anywhere without them. Apron strings were invented for the Cancer Moon!

As these children grow, they may feel a strong need to nurture others. They should have plenty of "babies" in the form of dolls, pets, plants, and, if possible, smaller children. Their need for nurturance and protection is primary, as is their need to learn how to care for others.

Moon in Leo—This child craves attention and will employ highly dramatic means to get it if necessary. Sign this child up for acting lessons as soon as possible so she can get lots of attention by performing on the stage! Leo likes to be in the center of whatever is happening, and children with a Leo Moon demonstrate this even more so than the Leo Sun. The highest need revolves around being that center.

There is sometimes an almost royal luxuriousness and laziness with the Leo Moon. The Leo Moon child also exudes a special warm radiance which is difficult to resist. The proper use of this charismatic power is part of the lesson Leo has to learn.

Moon in Virgo—This child needs to feel appreciated. There is sometimes a sense of not measuring up, since these children expect themselves and everyone else to be perfect. Of course, these standards for perfection are likely to come from the way Mom did it!

These children will have very strong preferences, but those preferences can be changed through reasoning. They feel the need to do something for someone else, and the Virgo Moon child should be given every opportunity to help other people. He has a tremendous curiosity about how things work, especially the workings of the body. These are the children you are likely to find playing "doctor" with the kid next door.

Moon in Libra—This child needs to feel peaceful and wants to feel that they are equal to (or better than) everyone else. Because of this need, these children sometimes spend too much time comparing themselves with others rather than setting goals for their own personal development. Sometimes they feel a sense of inferiority, since the need for perfection and balance in all things is very strong. Emotions tend to vacillate in an attempt to maintain balance.

Consistency in the external environment is important. These children need to relate to someone else, and will feel more secure when they have companions. Refinement is required even in childhood.

Moon in Scorpio—This child is deeply sensitive and has powerful, intense emotions. Because of this, it is often difficult for this child to openly express her feelings. Parents must learn to observe subtle changes in the child in order to understand what is troubling her. Scorpio Moon needs to have some secrets, and should be allowed plenty of privacy—a "secret treasure box" would be perfect.

In infancy, the Scorpio Moon child is tremendously sensitive, even to subtle stimulation. The parents should be alerted to this sensitivity, and should frequently offer the baby soothing, comforting caresses. These children need to learn that the deep feelings they experience are okay. If not, they may develop an emotional coldness in order to hide or repress their natural sensitivity.

Moon in Sagittarius—This child craves the freedom to move about and explore the world. Even small babies with this Moon placement are eager to venture out into the world. The Sagittarius Moon also loves to play games, tell stories, and learn new things. This need to expand may include overindulgence at the dinner table as well! An urge to know the truth will stimulate this child to ask many questions—endlessly.

Moon in Capricorn—This child prefers to control the emotions. The emotional nature is keenly felt, but may be difficult to express. This child needs to feel responsible and respected, and will enjoy the company of mature individuals.

A wry sense of humor may be noticeable, even in childhood. Capricorn Moon children need structure in their lives, and appreciate a carefully scheduled lifestyle. Lax attitudes and irresponsibility from adults will undermine his sense of security. Consistency of behavior reinforcement is needed.

Moon in Aquarius—This child prefers to stay away from excessive emotional expression, and may seem rather detached. Children with this Moon placement often develop strong ties to their friends. It is important that this child finds a way to feel unique and special. If that uniqueness is not appreciated, the child may become even more emotionally detached from those in his personal environment.

A life which is too severely structured may engender a rebellious streak in this child. However, her inventiveness should be channeled in constructive directions. This child may actually need to travel in "outer space" via airplanes and other "spacecraft."

Moon in Pisces—This child is very emotionally sensitive and can easily absorb the moods of others in the environment. This child needs to blend in with others and feel a bond with the significant people in his life. There is also a need to escape from ordinary reality into a world of fantasy and imagination. A primary challenge is to integrate the inner and outer environments. The most pressing need is to feel peaceful tranquillity.

The Moon in the Houses and Emotional Needs

These Moon sign interpretations are basic guidelines which use key concepts of the Moon and the signs. Additional information on the basic security needs of the child is obtained by using the house placement of the Moon. The child with a 10th House Moon, for example, needs recognition and feels the need to achieve. The type of achievement is determined by the qualities of the Moon sign.

Use the house placement to determine the areas which are most important to the child's sense of personal security. The house placement will also show which kinds of people and situations may significantly effect her sense of security.

Moon in the 1st House—This child needs to be noticed and likes to be in the company of others. This child can be self-absorbed, but much depends upon the Moon's aspects. Emotions have a powerful impact on health.

Moon in the 2nd House—This child may be especially sensitive when developing self-esteem, and he needs to address issues of personal worth during the developmental years. Material things can be especially important, and it's easy for the child to become possessive of people and objects.

Moon in the 3rd House—This child needs to communicate and will crave connections to and interaction with others.

Moon in the 4th House—This child needs to feel embraced by home and family and may be especially attached to family traditions and holiday celebrations.

Moon in the 5th House—This child loves to be entertained and may also be entertaining. This child needs plenty of opportunity to develop creative talents and exercise recreational interests.

Moon in the 6th House—This child can be very picky about diet and environment. This child needs to feel that she is aware of and can be in control of her physical body.

Moon in the 7th House—This child usually likes social activities since the emotional need to connect to others is very powerful.

Moon in the 8th House—This child is deeply curious and will be very protective of his most intimate feelings and possessions. This child needs to be allowed to have a few secrets, but should be encouraged to trust others who are part of his intimate life.

Moon in the 9th House—This child needs to be on a quest. This child may enjoy travel, reading, and the parts of school that are inspirational to her. Her spiritual life is a high priority.

Moon in the 10th House—This child needs respect. That may seem strange for a child, but it begins when a child is taught to respect others and himself. He needs room to achieve and celebrate accomplishments. This child may also feel an early impulse about developing career aims or ambitions.

Moon in the 11th House—This child needs to be around friends but also needs to learn and employ goals.

Moon in the 12th House—This child needs to dream and may spend a great deal of time developing imagination and creativity.

Moon Aspects

Moon energy is further altered by aspects to other planets. Think of the Moon as the primary matrix of need, and the aspects from the Moon to planets and points in the chart as the complex pattern woven by those needs. If the Moon makes more than three aspects, you are likely to observe a child who seems to be highly sensitive at an emotional level. But whether or not those emotions are easily expressed will depend upon the nature of the aspects and whether or not other planetary energies like Venus and Mars aid the expression of feeling.

Moon and Mercury

The Moon contacting Mercury harmoniously will aid the child in communicating her needs. Conversely, the Moon in dynamic aspect to Mercury is likely to create difficulty in separating the emotions from rational concepts. The child's need to communicate is heightened, giving a thrust to this aspect of development. Interactions with others become an important focus.

Moon conjunct Mercury—This aspect strengthens a child's ability to talk about feelings. However, emotions can get in the way of objectivity some of the time. Learning to separate "how I feel" from "what I think" will require patient guidance. Encourage this child to write, tell stories, and develop communication skills like public speaking.

Moon semisextile Mercury—This aspect stimulates a desire to bring feelings into a level of rational understanding. Learning to reach out to others through the emotions is important, and asking for needs to be met can bring positive results in establishing emotional security.

Moon semisquare Mercury—This child can be overly sensitive when learning how to express herself. Until she reaches an age when developing social skills is appropriate, she may tend to blurt out thoughts or ideas before realizing the impact of her words. There are still likely to be times when she can be somewhat disarming with her tendency toward frankness, even after lessons are illustrated!

Moon sextile Mercury—This aspect adds an ease and comfort to sharing inner feelings and thoughts. This child may feel especially close to his mother, and is likely to look to Mother as the primary line of confirmation that he is right. Mother's influence upon learning can be profound.

Moon square Mercury—This aspect brings frustration into expressing feelings. What she deeply feels may conflict with what the child actually says. This child is very sensitive about whether or not others understand her, and if misunderstood can become emotionally upset. Rational arguments may be virtually impossible, since separating how she feels is difficult.

Moon trine Mercury—This aspect stimulates a strong desire to be sure that others really know and understand what the child wants and needs. While there may be some sensitivity to the way others react to his words, developing understanding is so important that he can be rather flexible. There can be a real talent in writing, public speaking, or public relations ability.

Moon quincunx Mercury—This aspect can stimulate a tendency to ask for the wrong things at the wrong time. There can be a general lack of cooperation with others, especially if she feels that "nobody really cares what I want." Learning to speak up with confidence is a powerful lesson, and with the right guidance, this child can become quite adept at communication and facilitation.

Moon opposite Mercury—This aspect can indicate real conflicts between what the child feels and thinks. It's like a tug of war between mind and emotion, and in early years, emotion usually wins. Personal feelings have a dramatic impact on thinking processes, and separating feelings enough to be objective is likely to require only the maturation that comes with time and experience.

Moon and Venus

The Moon and Venus bring the need for relationships and artistic expression into focus. With flowing aspects, artistic expression may emerge easily. If the aspect is dynamic, there can be an increased sense of vulnerability if the child is asked to perform or share his artistic talents in public. Supportive parents and teachers can help him overcome reticence and shyness. Regardless of the nature of the aspect, Moon-Venus contacts bring a sweetness to the personality. This sweetness is usually less negatively manipulative with the flowing aspects than with the dynamic ones.

Moon conjunct Venus—This child may be quite tender and caring. Expressing affection is easy and she may enjoy feeling physically close. Hugs at storytime, open displays of affection, and giving to others feels good. This aspect frequently indicates a healthy, supportive relationship with the mother and good feelings about her.

Moon semisextile Venus—This aspect provokes an urge to connect and become more closely attached to others. Early relationships may be very changeable, although this aspect can indicate an ability to develop some flexibility when situations, playmates, or environments change. Expressing needs and feelings in the most appropriate manner may require practice—but everything in its time is an important lesson here. Learning what is socially appropriate will be important to this child, but only when it is appropriate!

Moon semisquare Venus—This aspect stimulates a kind of emotional vulnerability that stems from wanting to be liked or accepted. Personal relationships can be a challenge, even during the elementary school years, since self-esteem is sensitive and he may make choices to please others instead of doing what feels best for himself.

Moon sextile Venus—This aspect indicates the potential for developing true grace. However, this child may not seem extremely ambitious, since this aspect tends to confer a "take it easy" kind of attitude toward life. Emotionally sensitive to others, this child may enjoy the effects of expressing real feelings of affection and care. Artistic expression may be indicated if other aspects support it. The Moon-Venus contact helps to assure that a kind of genuine artistry flows in everything she does and says.

Moon square Venus—This child may display an increased emotional vulnerability. While he can be very affectionate and caring, he may be afraid to risk leaving one situation and going on to another. This is the "having my cake and eating it, too" aspect. Emotional manipulation of others can result, but usually as a mechanism to assure that he will be safe. Learning to be honest about feelings can be difficult, since needs for immediate gratification can become a substitute for developing truly close bonds and fulfilling needs in a more healthy manner.

Moon trine Venus—With this aspect, the flow of emotions seems natural and unencumbered. There is a natural charm inherent in the personality that can prove to be a fabulous asset. Trusting inner impulses and needs aids a sense of security and inner peace. She may adore music, the arts, and even have an early appreciation for literature and should be encouraged to put effort into developing her particular skills. There can be a lazy attitude, since these things come easily and the child may not feel motivated to go the extra mile.

Moon quincunx Venus—This aspect adds a strong desire to be liked and may also stimulate a kind of emotional want list that is difficult to fulfill. Being attracted to people and situations that are not really good for or in harmony with this child's real needs is a good possibility. In early social development this can manifest as choosing friends for the wrong reasons and then complaining that he does not fit in. He may also feel that Mother does not fulfill his needs, and the resulting insecurity can lead to relationship problems later. The remedy to this aspect seems to center upon learning how to give love without the expectation that it has to be returned. Ultimately, it will be, but not always, in the manner which is most anticipated.

Moon opposite Venus—With this aspect there can be a great hunger for love and affection. However, the ability to express great emotional depth is definitely there. Overdoing emotional expression is the primary lesson of this aspect, since this child may not know when to stop or how to limit emotional outpours. A protective quality can be positively developed, and the need to take care of others may take precedence over taking care of herself. There can be a great changeability in the way she feels in regard to self-worth, especially in elementary school and the early adolescent years. Objectivity can be a difficult lesson, especially if and when hurts happen. Finding someone to trust (like a positive relationship with Mother or a female friend or relative) can provide a positive anchor for the emotions.

Moon and Mars

Moon to Mars aspects are almost always stressful and during the childhood years spur impatience and, often, a strong sense of inner turmoil. All Moon-Mars aspects seem to be emotionally manipulative, with the dynamic aspects indicating a more devious use of the energy. This is the aspect my friend Stephane calls, "Let's you and him fight!"—an actual need for some sort of conflict. It is as though crisis propels the individual into action. During childhood, these crises will probably revolve around the child's circle of friends, although you may also observe attempted manipulation of Mom and Dad. Generally, these children operate well in crisis situations— they're on home turf!

Moon conjunct Mars—This is a high-impact aspect in a child's chart. He can be emotionally volatile and is certainly likely to express feelings with a degree of assertiveness. This child needs positive challenges for his competitive nature and may show a kind of daring and courage that is admirable. Sports may be suitable, but depending upon the other factors in the chart, some of this can also be played out through learning experiences, games, and setting personal goals. When learning about setting limits, this child is likely to push pretty hard against anything that seems to inhibit his self-expression. Lessons of cause and effect are worthwhile and not likely to be forgotten.

Moon semisextile Mars—With this aspect, expressing feelings can be a positive tension-reliever. During infancy, if physical tension is not relieved, extreme fussiness can result. This baby needs to move and will be likely to respond positively to infant massage. As mobility increases, fussiness is likely to decrease. While a competitive edge may be noticeable, it is likely that she will seek comfortable outlets for expressing it.

Moon semisquare Mars—This aspect can stimulate a kind of awkwardness. There can be hesitation about self-assertion which stems from a desire to avoid being hurt or hurting others, and the end result can be frustrating. However, avoiding competitive situations altogether is not advisable, since learning how to deal with challenges during childhood is the best preparation for real life! The task rests in finding the right challenge at the right time. Since he may think he is ready when adequate preparation, skills, or maturity is not present, teaching preparedness can go a long way toward creating balance.

Moon sextile Mars—This aspect stimulates a degree of positive self-assertiveness. It may be easy for her to ask for what she wants or needs, although the nature of the sign placement will be strongly influential in this regard. There's an easy flow between inner feelings and self-expression, and she can also exhibit a strong sensitivity to the way others react to her.

Moon square Mars—With this aspect there can be huge levels of frustration when dealing with the development of assertiveness and courage. In essence, this aspect indicates strong levels of emotional sensitivity, but it's a hair-trigger kind of sensitivity. Helping this child stay in touch with deeper feelings and needs and finding healthy ways to meet or express those needs is absolutely crucial. Bottling up anger is never a good idea, but for this child, it can create a potential powder-keg. He can also be very manipulative, and seems to know how to push everybody else's buttons. There are positive outlets for this, but emotional blackmail is not one of them. Vestiges of this kind of behavior need to be addressed early and with some gentility. If this child receives hostile responses, he may accelerate the hostility instead of containing it. Positive affirmations of this child's strength and security are the core remedies for the more volatile side of this energy pattern.

Moon trine Mars—With this aspect, the flow between inner feelings, emotional sensitivity, and self-assertiveness is natural. She can be at ease in most situations since there's a sense that she is strong. While personal courage can be easily mustered, she may not be especially interested in pushing it. Why rock the boat? You may also observe that she rises to most occasions in the nick of time, but for the impatient parent or teacher, questions may arise exactly when she will take action. Outside motivation is sometimes necessary for this child to forge ahead toward challenging goals.

Moon quincunx Mars—This aspect can lead to inner feelings of agitation, especially if this child is uncomfortable or uncertain and does not know exactly how to change a situation to suit his needs. Digestion can be upset when he is under stress, even if that stress is just a change in routine. He can seem very uncomfortable in competitive situations, but if prepared or well trained, can become a worthy adversary! However, it's not a good idea to push him into anything which produces too much anxiety. When anxiety does arise, sensitivity to these feelings will go a long way toward helping this child determine the best course of action.

Moon opposite Mars—With this aspect there's a tendency to feel at war with the self. This child needs positive outlets for her feelings, and will benefit from learning good sportsmanship as she matures. The toddler years can be filled with outbursts of temper, since frustration levels can reach a peak very quickly. Patience will be a trying lesson. As this child grows into early social relationships, she may stir up trouble between friends if she has been hurt or feels insecure.

Moon and Jupiter

Moon-Jupiter contacts create a sense of optimism. The pitfalls of these contacts, especially in the dynamic aspects, involve having great expectations of the self and of others. Carly Simon's 1970s hit song "Anticipation" captures the feeling of Moon-Jupiter contacts rather well: "Anticipation is making me late. It's keepin' me waitin'."

By continually projecting one's hopes into the future, it is difficult to be happy with situations in the present. This lesson is reluctantly learned in childhood. This is the "I want all of it NOW!" syndrome. Another facet of Moon-Jupiter contacts deals with overindulgence. These children may have difficulty knowing when to quit, especially at mealtime.

Moon conjunct Jupiter—With this aspect the idea of limits will be almost unfathomable. Teaching the toddler that he cannot do something can be frustrating for the parents, since he is likely to feel that just because he wants it, he can and should have it! While this aspect does confer high levels of confidence, it also indicates the potential for getting in over one's head.

Moon semisextile Jupiter—With this aspect, pushing limits is as natural as waking up in the morning. However, learning how to judge whether or not wants are good for her can be difficult. It's also important that parents make realistic promises to this child, since disappointments from others can lead her to follow suit.

Moon semisquare Jupiter—This aspect presents a strange puzzle for a child. He can feel especially confident and optimistic, but may jump into situations too soon or want things that are inappropriate. As a result, he may become a procrastinator, deciding that it's safer to make a promise and not follow through, thereby frustrating himself and everyone else, too! This is a toddler who needs to be carefully watched since he can wander off in search of adventure at a moment's notice. That tendency does continue, and learning to judge whether or not a choice is good for him will take patience and consistency.

Moon sextile Jupiter—This aspect adds a positive sense of optimism and confidence, but can also indicate a kind of lax attitude about meeting challenges. It's easier for this child to do the minimum or rely on talents than to do hard work, and learning that applied effort may be necessary to excel can be especially valuable. It may take maturity and life lessons before this makes any sense, however.

Moon square Jupiter—The frustrations from this aspect are usually seen as a kind of ravenous appetite—it's difficult for this child to get enough of anything! Teaching her to be satisfied with things as they are can be challenging for parents, since she has a sense that the grass is greener on the other side. While the positive elements of a sense of adventure are part of this energy dynamic, the tendency to go into situations unprepared or expecting that the reinforcements will arrive in the nick of time can lead her to make promises which are difficult to fulfill or to hold unrealistic expectations of the self or others.

Moon trine Jupiter—This child may seem especially content. This planetary combination adds a kind of pleasantness to the personality and heightens this child's sense of faith and confidence that things will always work out. This can be an indication that the relationship with the mother is comfortable and that she seems to be readily available to the child. The primary pitfall of this aspect is the potential for low-motivation and a tendency to rely on things to fall into place instead of feeling that he needs to make an effort.

Moon quincunx Jupiter—With this aspect there can be a feeling that things are just beyond this child's reach. While there is some confidence and optimism suggested by this aspect, there is also a tendency for that confidence to be somewhat misguided. Parents and teachers can help her understand her strengths and limitations, since otherwise she can tend to target goals which can be untimely or ultimately lacking in fulfillment. In health, this aspect sometimes indicates potential problems with weight gain.

Moon opposite Jupiter—This aspect stimulates a strong sense of "I want" but does not necessarily confer a powerful drive to pursue those wants! Learning to bring expectations in line with possibility may require several attempts. During the toddler years, this child can be especially demanding or may have difficulty settling for a glass of juice when he sees the size of the carton from which it is poured. Throughout childhood, this child can have the tendency to push past limits and then collapse at the end of the day from exhaustion. Learning that there are other options can provide important clues to managing commitments later in life.

Moon and Saturn

Moon-Saturn aspects indicate inner frustrations and difficulty expressing emotions. Even the flowing aspects may have a strong measure of emotional control. The need for consistency, structure and reliability is paramount with these children.

With a Moon-Saturn aspect, the child's need for nurturance may be so overwhelming that she seems depressed and melancholy much of the time. This can be alleviated somewhat by offering the child a sense of responsibility and purpose. Ignoring the signs of depression can create a block which will be difficult to overcome in the adult years.

Any dynamic aspect between the Moon and Saturn can indicate insecurity, giving the child an especially strong need for approval from the parents. The parents should be encouraged to offer special positive input to the child. Sometimes a parent is simply unable to give much energy to the child, due to a divorce, strong commitments to work, or other situations involving absence or limitation. When this is the case, the child has a special need for a stable emotional base. The expression of feelings may be inhibited. Positive methods of dealing with fear and anxiety should be taught early. The fearfulness he experiences is often due to feeling too alone and alienated from much needed support.

Moon conjunct Saturn—This aspect indicates a powerful need for security, consistency, and confirmation. There can be a serious nature to this child's personality, and adults may tend to think that she is capable of taking on more responsibility than her years would indicate. While she may rise to the occasion, saddling the child with too much too soon can result in a feeling that her childhood has been lost. However, this aspect can also indicate a very powerful bond with the family and especially Mother. It's important that this child knows that it's okay to be a child and that she is not responsible for everything that happens around her.

Moon semisextile Saturn—This aspect indicates that a child may be very enthralled with the idea of growing up and that there is some impatience with the limitations of childhood. Assuring that the developmental challenges are appropriate to age and maturity is important, since doing things beyond his capability can be emotionally stifling. He may show uncertainty in the face of new experiences, but given adequate preparation he can probably adapt to changes rather well.

Moon semisquare Saturn—This child tends to feel disappointments very keenly and seems to be a magnet for guilt. It's quite likely that Mother may be involved in her career or other experiences which limit her availability to the child, and as the child matures it's important for the child to distinguish between the things she can and cannot control. If she exhibits emotional withdrawal, it could be a reflection of a basic fear that emotional support is limited, unreliable, or frustrated in some way. While this child can become self-reliant, emotional resilience may not be easy to develop. It is helpful if parents and teachers positively reinforce basic security needs whenever possible, and aid this child in learning self-discipline and trust.

Moon sextile Saturn—This child is likely to seek out positive role models and welcome situations which reinforce a sense of personal responsibility. Trusting authority figures may come easily, which can be helpful throughout life, but is especially important during early educational experiences. Helping him clarify priorities and manage time can aid the child in putting this energy dynamic to good use.

Moon square Saturn—Accepting emotional support can be difficult for this child. Early changes, such as alterations in family dynamics or moves, can have a powerful impact on her sense of security. For this reason, parents aware of this energy connection in a child's chart may need to go the extra mile to help her feel safe and secure if these kinds of changes do occur. What the child experiences at a subconscious level can be difficult to ascertain, but symptoms such as emotional withdrawal or refusal of food may be indicators of needs for extra careful and loving support. Pushing this child into new learning situations before she feels ready can have a strong effect in undermining security. For this reason, it's important to determine why she exhibits fear or resistance and to help her determine if that fear is justified. Abandonment fears may be a key issue.

Moon trine Saturn—This aspect indicates good emotional resilience and a generally strong feeling of personal security and safety. It's quite conceivable that he will show a strong tendency toward self-discipline and that he will enjoy being around adults. Getting through the different developmental stages of childhood may be a breeze, although other dynamics can challenge this assumption. At the very least, the sense of inner strength suggested by this aspect will be helpful. Even in the elementary school years he may seem to be the friend others seek when they need support.

Moon quincunx Saturn—This aspect presents a dynamic of emotional complexity. While this child may exhibit a desire to tackle new situations, she may get into things before she is ready or may procrastinate due to underestimating what is required from a situation. Inconsistencies or mixed messages from parents and teachers can have a devastating effect on self-confidence. Although all children need consistency when it comes to rules, discipline and support, this dynamic can indicate that circumstances will test the merits of that consistency. Unanticipated changes may throw her off balance, but with understanding and open support, she will learn that life is filled with things that are difficult to anticipate and that she is capable of handling them.

Moon opposite Saturn—This aspect presents a challenge to a child's emotional stability and sense of security. In some respects, you may observe a kind of stubborn resistance from him and may feel that he does not like to be close. However, he needs cuddling, support, and care just as any other child does, but may resist if he feels inhibited or smothered in some way. Learning to overcome a fear of abandonment may require considerable re-education, since once he has experienced a loss, the fear of repeating it can be huge. His response to change can be "resist first, change only if necessary."

Moon and Uranus

Moon aspecting Uranus brings a powerful need for independent thought and action. Rapidly shifting emotions are likely. Rebelliousness is also quite probable with the dynamic aspects. A sense of emotional insecurity could come from a feeling that Mother is inconsistent and changes too rapidly. (This may be the actual situation, or just the child's perception of it.) The child with Moon-Uranus aspects will require a strong measure of independence. She will definitely feel different from most of her friends. These feelings can bring a sense of alienation if they are not dealt with positively.

> **Moon conjunct Uranus**—Expect to see consistently changing moods and attitudes. This child seems to invite change and will appreciate a chance to experience different environments and unusual people. However, he also tests limits, and during each developmental stage when limits are being established, he can exhibit behaviors which try the patience of parents and teachers. Focus can also be a problem when attention and quiet are necessary. Drawn to people and things which are unique, he may seek confirmation and appreciation for the fact that he feels different, too. Many times this aspect echoes the potential that the mother is unusually or highly independent.

> **Moon semisextile Uranus**—This child needs to reach for newness and change, but may not understand or appreciate the importance of limits first, changes next. She may be attracted to situations which are just beyond her grasp. The motivation to be there first can be stimulated, and maintaining or regaining concentration can be challenging if she loses interest.

> **Moon semisquare Uranus**— stimulates a desire to break away from existing situations in favor of experiencing something completely different. This aspect is often an indicator that home or parental relationships are nontraditional or extraordinary in some way. If other factors in the chart do not support consistency, the emotional repercussions of this synergy can be of a rebellious nature when he does not get what he wants. Waiting is definitely not easy, and distractions can be a problem in learning. However, there is sometimes a kind of genius indicated by this aspect, since the child is willing to explore things in a unique manner.

> **Moon sextile Uranus**—This aspect can be an indicator of special abilities, but at an emotional level denotes an ability to feel confident when independence is

necessary and/or important. Trying new things and adapting to changes in environments and relationships can be easily accomplished and may even be sought after by this child once she has more control over her actions and choices.

Moon square Uranus—This child can feel emotionally unsettled much of the time. There is a rebellious streak but mostly there's a need to integrate change into his life in a manner which induces a sense of security instead of a feeling that all control and stability have been lost. If the home circumstances are unstable or relationships with the parents, especially the mother, are inconsistent, then feelings of rebellion can increase. While he may resist restraints and fight against authority, reasonable restrictions which strengthen a feeling that he can exercise his independence can bring balance. However, discipline can be a problem if the child feels unfairly treated or negatively singled out in some way.

Moon trine Uranus—This aspect stimulates a feeling of confidence in a child's sense of uniqueness. She may invite change and look forward to moving into the next stage of development by showing an eagerness for the new. Friends are likely to become especially important even in the elementary school years, and she can exhibit leadership tendencies which spark others to follow her unique ideas or suggestions.

Moon quincunx Uranus—This child may feel that things are never quite settled. The emotional profile is that of disruption in the face of boredom; therefore, learning situations need to be consistently challenging to his unique abilities to encourage the ultimate in personal development. Unanticipated or disruptive changes in environment or family dynamics early on can leave the mark of uncertainty, even if things seem settled afterward. Keeping commitments can be difficult unless this child learns that honoring obligations ultimately leads to greater freedom. This can be best illustrated by parents who exhibit stability in their own emotional lives and who present images of consistency to him while honoring their own and the child's individuality.

Moon opposite Uranus—This aspect can stimulate a powerful rebellious streak! She can seem a bit untamed, and it is that wildness that is part of this child's special genius. When properly nurtured, she can learn to take risks and create changes which lead to positive transformations instead of destruction. She will not respond well to unnecessary restraint and may need situations which seem a bit risky in order to feel satisfied. Physical activities like gymnastics classes at an early age may satisfy some of these needs. If family situations remain unsettled, this child may fail to learn trust and may feel that the only constant *is* change. While this is true to some extent, emotional scarring can result if nurturance is kept at bay as a means of remaining independent.

Moon and Neptune

Moon-Neptune aspects bring real emotional responses to imaginary situations. The consciousness is tremendously impressionable, and external stimuli should be screened for excessive harshness or too many negative vibrations. Vibrations are quite real to these psychically sensitive children. They can feel when something is wrong; it is impossible to hide feelings from them.

These children need to integrate their inner world with the outer reality. If the parents are continually telling the child, "It's only your imagination," the child will not only begin to mistrust his inner feelings, but will also tend to trust the parents less. The child may be flowing easily into an altered level of awareness and just not know how to deal with it. The parents need to exhibit special sensitivity when dealing with this child.

Moon conjunct Neptune—The key factor in this child's emotional profile is high impressionability. Encouraging her to use imagination in creative ways can be helpful, since learning how to bring dreams into reality is an important challenge. She may also be more sensitive to the emotions of others, so being surrounded by negativity is likely to reflect negativity. Likewise, being surrounded by harmony will reflect more peaceful qualities. There can be a mystical or dreamy quality about this child and some tendency toward escape or emotional denial. However, much will depend upon the child's life circumstances, since positively directed energy can aid a child in developing true compassion for others.

Moon semisextile Neptune—This aspect stimulates a need to express tenderness and sensitivity. He may seem in his own world much of the time and needs to be encouraged to develop creative or artistic outlets. Sometimes this child can feel that others do not really understand what he needs, and learning how to identify and ask for these needs can be a challenging lesson.

Moon semisquare Neptune—This child may be overly sensitive to the emotional and environmental climates. Others can feel as though their own emotions are reflected by the child in some way. However, she can also be especially gentle and caring and will enjoy opportunities to extend herself to others.

Moon sextile Neptune—This aspect confers a tenderhearted quality and may stimulate a deep desire to yield to imaginative and creative impulses. He may feel an especially powerful tie to Mother.

Moon square Neptune—This aspect can stimulate a sense of confusion, since distinguishing between the real and imaginary realms is difficult—especially in the early years. She needs experiences that have tangible and grounding influences like plenty of hugs, loving caresses, or even quality time in the garden or kitchen with Mom. Even if Mother tries to make herself accessible to this child, the child may feel that she is never quite there. This projection may result from actual circumstances ranging from the rather innocuous experience of waking in the night and feeling alone to actual periods of physical separation. Creating a touchstone with her can be helpful. Allowing security blankets or other hands-on devices can be positively confirming.

Moon quincunx Neptune—With this aspect the emotional security base can feel unstable or uncertain. Mother may have to go overboard to assure this child that she is really there for him, although this aspect can be an indicator that circumstances like work could take Mother away part of the time. The challenge of this aspect is difficult for a small child, since he may feel reticent to express his needs or may misjudge them. Creative and artistic expressions can help him objectify some deeper feelings. Learning the difference between his feelings about things and his response to others who have strong feelings of their own can be challenging, since it's easy for him to be overwhelmed by the emotions of others.

Moon opposite Neptune—This aspect adds a tremendous emotional sensibility, and this child may seem delicate. A healthful, nurturing environment is especially important, and consistent and available energy from Mother is a necessity. If other planetary aspects support her sense of emotional security, then this aspect could indicate a tendency to feel somewhat distant from Mother, but reasonably okay otherwise. Extra care needs to be taken with music, movies, videos, and other experiences which change the vibrational nature of this child's life. Artistic expression can be encouraged and may become a mainstay of her life. Establishing emotional boundaries can be a lifelong challenge, although she will be uncomfortable cutting off connections to significant individuals and needs to learn how to distinguish between what someone else feels or wants and what she feels or wants.

Moon and Pluto

The child with Moon-Pluto aspects is emotionally intense, and may feel that his emotions overtake him too readily. With dynamic aspects, the Moon-Pluto child may repress emotions too easily, and can be too open to extreme feelings or fear. Sometimes this aspect indicates a perceptive connection to the emotions of others—especially Mother.

Many of my adult clients who have difficult Moon-Pluto aspects have shared extremely painful situations with me. The message they often received from the parents was "Don't be," or "Don't feel." Many actually began to feel that being alive was somehow wrong, and several of them often wondered exactly why they had to remain among the living!

Yet the life force is tremendously powerful with this aspect. The real fears may arise from having a strong, magnetic power and not understanding how to use it. There is sometimes a denial of personal needs with Moon-Pluto aspects. This can result in feeling extreme loss of contact with the sensitive and receptive parts of the self. These children need to develop their own personal power and may struggle to feel okay about having it. They need to be given permission not only to have their feelings, but to express them freely.

Moon conjunct Pluto—This child can feel overwhelmed by her own emotions and even more so by the strong emotions of others. Even as an infant, she can be intense and may seem to go to extremes, especially if upset. It's almost as though the emotions take on a life of their own. In many ways, this aspect suggests that a child absorbs experiences more deeply, but that expressing or clearing what has been absorbed or felt is more difficult. Urging a young child with Moon conjunct Pluto to share feelings will help build trust and comfort with expression. If this child is discouraged from expressing feelings in appropriate ways, the tendency to bottle up emotions ranging from passion to hurt can be huge. Creative, musical, or artistic endeavors can be positive forms to keep emotions flowing. Celebrating life changes can also be helpful, and dealing with the mysteries of life in creative ways can be especially important.

Moon semisextile Pluto—This aspect suggests the tendency to be more emotionally sensitive, but the child may be able to deal with things at a deeper level than others realize. There may be a personal magnetism evident even in infancy and others may be drawn to the child. However, he may not be comfortable as the center of attention or may resist letting others into his personal space. Playing with other children may be difficult at first, and then later, when early friendships develop, there can be a tendency to become deeply attached to those friendships. Parents can do this child a favor by using illustrations from nature which help to explain the continual renewal of life processes.

Moon semisquare Pluto—With this aspect there may be a denial of needs and feelings present. This can be especially notable if early life experiences encompass losses, moves, or significant changes in the family. However, this child can handle these changes if other elements in her support system provide emotional stability and a place for healing. Ultimately, one of the major lessons she will face entails coming to grips with the difference between the power that heals and the power that hurts. Her fascination with power will be evident early, but few children know what to do with it! Expressing needs directly can be difficult, too, and if she uses emotional blackmail to get what she wants and succeeds, then these tendencies are very likely to continue into later life. Letting her know that she can have these needs and wants fulfilled without doing or saying things that make others feel badly can be sweet relief.

Moon sextile Pluto—There is potential for a great emotional capacity which can be healing initially to family and ultimately extended to others in some way. This may seem a strange thing to say about a child, but comments from family may illustrate the point. These are the babies who spark comments like, "When he arrived, everything in my life changed!" While such feelings may be true of the effect any child has in the life of parents or family, the impact from this child's presence may seem especially noteworthy. There is a potential downfall to this connection, since it is possible that this child will feel much more than he expresses. However, he somehow seems to have the capacity to deal with this strong emotional intensity.

Moon square Pluto—This aspect suggests a high-stress emotional profile for a child. Abandonment or abuse issues may seem more prominent, although sometimes this is a suggestion that such things exist in the child's environment and that the child takes in the experience in a very personal way. For example, divorce may seem to have a more deeply felt impact. The reasons for this stem from the fact that this combination adds a tendency for a child to take in everything that's happening in the emotional climate as part of the self. If those feelings are hurtful, then the deeper emotional impression can be that she somehow caused this. It can become a rather vicious circle, and the only way to break that can be to form a true bond of trust and understanding with someone. This can be a huge risk (or seem that way) for this child, but having honest and tender emotional support which can withstand the ravages of time and life tests brings the healing this child craves and deserves.

Moon trine Pluto—This child has emotional resilience. The inevitable changes that accompany life experiences are more likely to be felt as natural alterations, much like the loss of baby teeth. The bond with Mother can be especially powerful and may be a true life-sustaining force (it may even eventually become a mutual support system). While emotional expression can be intense, there's rarely any doubt about what he truly feels or needs.

Moon quincunx Pluto—This aspect brings emotional complexity. There is a potential that this child will learn to sense that her needs are constantly being compromised by changes she cannot control. If family circumstances limit this child's ability to feel that her needs are being met, then the resulting lack of fulfillment can lead to resentment or guilt. However, there can be a kind of resilience present which allows the child the capacity to cope with changes more effectively, and her bounce-back ability can be good. The key to finding the positive outlet is to help this child learn to trust her feelings and to know that it is okay for her to have needs and to be in touch with those needs.

Moon opposite Pluto—This aspect brings one of the most intensive challenges to a child's sense of emotional security, safety, and stability. This child may respond to alterations in home and family life with feelings of resentment or hurt and he may not know how to express that hurt. If parents or family are insensitive to or unaware of the child's frustrations, fears, or anxieties, then it's not likely that the child will feel confident about being open with his feelings since the tendency to hold in emotions can be powerful. Yet others may feel that there's something happening beneath the surface that's not showing on the outside. That could be an understatement! If parents, teachers, or care-givers take actions which lead to guilty feelings, shame, or disappointment, this child can feel especially hurt and may hold onto that hurt indefinitely. More than anything, he needs to know that his needs are important and that he deserves to have those needs fulfilled.

The Psychology of the Sun

The energy of the Sun is tied to emotional security and the sense of Self. The individuality of the Sun energy begins to emerge once the child has developed enough mastery over basic bodily functions so that she can start paying more attention to the outside world. The Sun is a major factor in determining "Who am I?" This radiance of Self really becomes focused once the child is relating to others on a more frequent basis, especially in the school years.

Although the full power of the Sun's energy does not mature until the early adult years, its formative stages and early expressions begin in childhood. The sign in which the Sun is found gives clues to the qualities the child will focus upon in developing a self-image. House placement indicates where the child needs special recognition. Aspects to other planets will further define the areas having and lacking support in the development of self-image. The more difficult aspects involve contacts from the Sun to Saturn and the outer planets Uranus, Neptune, and Pluto. Interpretations for specific aspects are noted in the following paragraphs. I have not, however, included the minor aspects (semisextile, semisquare, and quincunx) from the Sun to Saturn and the outer planets. My observations have led me to conclude that these aspects tend to operate on a very deep level throughout childhood and often indicate factors that only surface later in the early adult years as the personality becomes more finely developed. Aspects between the Sun and Mercury and Sun and Venus are interpreted in chapters 7 and 8.

Sun and Mars

When the Sun and Mars are in aspect, a child will feel a stronger need to assert himself. All Sun-Mars aspects add energy.

   Sun conjunct Mars—This aspect can indicate a highly competitive nature. This child likes to win, and learning that meeting a challenge can be just as important as coming out in first place can be a difficult concept to handle. Impatience and a fiery temperament are key qualities in the emotional self, and it may take a number of years before she figures out the relationship between impulsive action and potential destructive results. Parents need to encourage sports or other arenas where she can exercise and develop a positive competitive spirit.

Sun sextile Mars—This aspect can indicate boldness and this child may seem to have no fear when it comes to trying new things. The early years may be especially active ones, although he is likely to respond well to lessons which include cause and effect.

Sun square Mars—Outbursts of temper may be a trademark of this aspect, especially during the temperamental twos and threes. This aspect can confer a kind of wildness, and telling this child "no" when she really wants something may result in a challenge—even from a toddler! Providing positive arenas for proving herself can make a huge difference in this child's life. Whether sports or academics, the desire to compete is easy to identify. However, it can be difficult for this child to learn discipline unless there is consistency within an environment of strong role models.

Sun trine Mars—This aspect indicates a strong need to stay active and busy, and there can be a kind of restless energy present if this child becomes bored. Fortunately, he may be willing to find things to occupy his time and energy, although ample opportunities to excel will be appreciated. This can indicate talent in utilizing physical abilities, although motivation may have to come from the outside if that talent is to reach excellence.

Sun opposite Mars—This child has little patience for anything that even resembles waiting. Healthy outlets for physical expression are absolutely necessary, and helping this child find the best possible ways to achieve goals will lead to a potentially high self-confidence. Yet if the environment or family situation reflects hostility, this is the child who will give it right back, and she may seem to have an uncanny ability to trigger angry responses from others. Learning how to direct anger may be among her most challenging life lessons, and it begins in the very early years.

Sun and Jupiter

When the Sun and Jupiter are in contact, the child may have an exaggerated sense of self-importance. This is especially true with the dynamic aspects. Frankly, I do not see huge differences between specific aspects with the Sun and Jupiter contacts except for the nature of flow or friction (harmonious versus dynamic aspects). Sometimes the child is overindulged by the parents (usually the father). These children usually feel that the father or the parents expect a great deal from them. With the flowing aspects, these expectations may be more easily integrated and the child may be able to identify specifics more readily. However, any child with Sun and Jupiter connected wants to be more important or desires to reach beyond his current situation or capacities. The dynamic aspects can indicate more difficulty defining limits—knowing when to stop is a problem. The flowing aspects can indicate laziness, so they are not necessarily a bonus unless the child is taught how to express gratitude for his good fortune.

Sometimes, the difficult aspects between the Sun and Jupiter indicate that the child may experience difficulty simply accepting herself as she really is. These are the children who excel at stretching the truth. If the child is applauded for her honest efforts, the need to stretch her own importance will not be so great.

Sometimes, because limitations are hard to assess, the child cannot learn to say "no" and will overobligate himself. This can result in damage to his self-esteem if all those obligations cannot be met. When the child learns to honestly accept himself, it is easier for him to assess his limitations as well as realize the ultimate possibilities for growth and expansion.

Sun and Saturn

Sun-Saturn aspects may inhibit the exercise of willpower and self-projection. Saturn's energy confers the need to gain permission or to satisfy a sense that actions and attitudes have gained approval. As a result, all aspects between the Sun and Saturn are indicative of restraint in self-expression. However, the child with dynamic aspects between the Sun and Saturn may sense that she is somehow inadequate. Potential feelings of inferiority can be altered if the parents positively reinforce the child's sense of self, and especially her achievements. In any case, this child will crave approval and needs well-defined structure in her life. Also, dynamic Sun-Saturn aspects indicate a need for the child to have an especially secure relationship with the father. If the father is absent or inaccessible, the child needs some other grounding male influence.

Sun conjunct Saturn—This child's need for consistency is very powerful, but just as important is his need to learn and experience real respect for himself and others. He also likes to feel in control of things, and even at an early age you may observe behavior that would indicate a desire to keep everything as he wants it. There may be more comfort going from one logical step to the next, and when faced with new circumstances he will be much more confident with some preparation or warning. Once a sense of a situation is established or trust is developed in a relationship, much of his hesitancy is likely to dissipate. This child will also be more comfortable in circumstances that seem to be most socially acceptable, since going against what is perceived as the norm can undermine confidence. However, other factors in the chart may indicate rebellious attitudes, and if coupled with this aspect a child can be comfortable adapting to social norms while exercising his individuality.

Sun sextile Saturn—This aspect suggests a quality of self-control and enhances a child's comfort with the adult world. Learning and educational experiences may be enjoyable, since accomplishing some mastery over information and over the physical plane will be positively self-confirming. Identifying positive role models can be especially helpful to this child, since she may be more comfortable following in the footsteps of accomplished individuals until she establishes a sense of personal identity. She may respond well to positive forms of discipline and may be capable of accepting personal responsibility at an earlier age.

Sun square Saturn—This child tends to be more sensitive to criticism and may have an inhibited sense of self-confidence. Seeking permission can create hesitation, delays, or inhibition, especially if life circumstances dictate undue restraint or lack. If he suffers unreasonable limitation or is fostered in an environment lacking in positive support, the results can be highly damaging to the development of a healthy and positive personal identity. Relationships with the father and men can be difficult, especially if the child experiences primary male influences as lacking or negative. This aspect suggests possible feelings that approval from parents or others from whom he needs approval is deficient in some way. You may also observe strong levels of self-criticism which, in the later childhood years, are projected as excessive criticism of or attempts to control others. Scapegoating can also become a feature of his behavior, especially if he feels others (like the parents) are not fully responsible. Why should he take responsibility when everyone else is not? Rewards for embracing personal responsibilities can go a long way toward healing these feelings. If this child learns and adopts codependent behaviors, it's quite likely that he will continue these models into his adult relationships and may never feel comfortable being himself without going overboard to please others in order to gain acceptance. There can be a continuing sense of lacking support or fears that actually being what he wants to be will have negative results. Self-forgiveness can be an important and necessary step in healing these painful feelings and releasing shame or guilt.

Sun trine Saturn—This child may feel safe and supported. Family structures tend to be more sound and respect for social rules and mores will be easier to develop. Following the established order will always be more comfortable than changing the status quo, especially if others or an existing situation clearly provide real security. Taking risks may be difficult, and when confronted with new situations she may first resist as an automatic response. Conservative attitudes may almost always prevail unless other factors in the chart suggest otherwise. While this aspect can indicate an ability to form a positive sense of self, it can reinforce a feeling that keeping things as they are is always the best choice.

Sun opposite Saturn—This aspect can suggest that a child feels continually confronted by roadblocks. Self-criticism can be exaggerated, and if others reinforce that he is lacking or deficient in some way, the child is more likely to accept this as truth. The fortunate quality of this aspect is that it does provide a stimulus for goal-setting. The challenge is to learn how to set realistic goals which are within the scope of the child's ability to achieve them. Learning to accept personal responsibility and being rewarded for this achievement will greatly aid this child, and this can begin in the preschool years. Identifying the circumstances or reasons behind his fearfulness can be especially helpful to this child. Then, from a realistic perspective he can begin to tackle the situation at hand. The need for positive role models is especially important, since the desire to feel respect is best answered when there is a target!

Sun and Uranus

Sun-Uranus aspects are indicators of unique qualities. With the flowing aspects, this uniqueness is more readily accepted by the child and by society. The dynamic aspects, however, are a different story! With these aspects, the child may often feel like a fifth wheel and out of place in the world.

Helping the child appreciate her uniqueness is paramount when Sun-Uranus aspects are present. Sometimes a desire to rebel against authority or to be different from Dad will spur the child to create disruptions in her environment. These children need to learn how to use their unique qualities to inspire positive changes in the world around them. Freedom always entails responsibility—a lesson which may be a challenge for the Sun-Uranus child to learn.

Sun conjunct Uranus—This child will be eager to experiment with new possibilities. In fact, he may seem to invite situations which are unusual in some way. Frequently this aspect suggests that the father is independent or free-spirited, and if that is the case, this child is certainly likely to model that image until he finds his own sense of identity. This child will appreciate the room and opportunity to exercise inventiveness and independence, but may need to learn how to balance his tendency toward revolutionary attitudes and actions with the need to be personally responsible. While this aspect can suggest some insurgency against authority, other elements in the chart will indicate how powerful this particular quality will be.

Sun sextile Uranus—This aspect suggests that this child has a positive potential for harmoniously marching to the beat of her own drum. The ability to attract environments and relationships that support this independent spirit is strong, and she also can readily adapt to changes that arise beyond her control.

Sun square Uranus—A rebellious spirit resides, restlessly, within the heart of this child. Excessive restraints are likely to provoke outbursts of frustration, and balancing personal responsibility with a need to be free can be difficult. Settling for the status quo can be difficult, and even in the toddler years it's easy to observe that this child is most attracted to unusual things and innovative people. This aspect does suggest some dissatisfaction with the father and can be an indicator that Dad and he do not see eye to eye as this child grows. This child is not really interested in conforming, although supportive aspects from Saturn or Jupiter to the Sun can indicate that he may be able to exercise his need for independence within existing structures.

Sun trine Uranus—This aspect indicates a real potential for this child to develop her special qualities and abilities and to feel good about standing out against the crowd. An environment which caters to these abilities will likely be appreciated, although there can be a tendency to take for granted unusual or special supports. There can be a kind of ingenious quality about the child or her personality, and her ability to put a unique stamp on creative endeavors is usually noticeable as early as the elementary school years. During the teen years, she may not feel the need to overturn all structures in order to accomplish breaking free from the parents psychologically.

Sun opposite Uranus—The unsettled energy represented by this aspect can be expressed as a lack of focus or disruptive actions and attitudes. This child can be easily bored, especially during the school years if the material is not interesting or he has already grasped the meaning and is ready to move on. For this reason, it's a good idea to give this child some special attention and to carefully evaluate his needs on a regular basis. Disruptions in family circumstances can be more unsettling than expected, and although it might be assumed that this child would welcome the changes, these changes can spark rebellion if he wants to keep things as they are! Appropriately involving the child in creating or accommodating changes can be a positive lesson. Simply displacing him undermines his sense of security and may result in a feeling that he does not fit in with the new circumstances.

Sun and Neptune

Sun-Neptune aspects in the chart confer a mystical quality about the child. These children often have difficulty being noticed and may feel invisible, especially if the aspects are conjunction, square, or opposition. It is hard for anyone with Sun-Neptune aspects to see themselves clearly, and this can be especially confusing for a child. Sense of self as separate from others is part of later developmental changes, and with these contacts, the experience of separation can be very difficult and especially painful. It is very important with these children that the adult clearly distinguishes between what is real and what is imaginary. Movies, television, and other forms of entertainment should be carefully screened, or at least shared with the child so that realistic feedback will be immediately available.

Sun conjunct Neptune—This aspect suggests strong levels of impressionability. Others may feel that this child lives in a world of her own, and in early childhood it's very easy for this child to become completely involved in play-acting or imaginary experiences. There may be a strong connection spiritually to the etheric planes, and the resulting mystical quality is usually a hallmark of the personality. This aspect is indicative of a tendency to avoid confrontation and may add a shy quality to the child's personality. While encouraging her to develop creative or artistic interests can provide an excellent way to objectify this energy, it's important that parents and others recognize that she may be especially sensitive to criticism and can be reluctant to show the results of her efforts if critical remarks are anticipated.

Sun sextile Neptune—This child may seek out peaceful people and situations and will be happiest when surroundings and relationships seem to flow. Creative, musical, and artistic interests may be abound, although he may not be especially ambitious or interested in recognition. However, when placed in circumstances which are comfortable to the child, expressing special talents can be very rewarding. Doing things that seem to make a difference or to help others can add life-affirming messages to his existence.

Sun square Neptune—This child tends to feel out of touch with reality or may have difficulty developing her personal identity. In the early years, this aspect tends to manifest as a feeling that she is not strongly connected to the father. Perhaps Dad's work takes him away for long hours or days, or he may be absent in other ways. There's also a tendency to overidealize the father, especially if Dad's psychology plays into this theme. The identity-confirming messages a child seeks through the father are somehow missing or incomplete. As a result, when individual identity is emerging in the preadolescent and teen years, this child may be more of a follower than a leader and may tend to emulate others rather than finding her special self-expression. Falling victim to the illusions generated by others who seem more magnetic, popular, or influential can act to delay the child's realization of her identity.

Sun trine Neptune—This aspect can indicate positive uses of imagination and creativity during childhood and throughout life. However, this aspect is notorious for indicating laziness and lack of motivation. This child may find it so comfortable to escape or to allow others to take the lead that he sees no reason to risk himself and step out or engage in other growth-oriented risks. Positive, enthusiastic feedback from parents and teachers can help to motivate this child.

Sun opposite Neptune—This child tends to feel a bit lost. That sense of disorientation can come from the fact that what she imagines as real can stand in sharp contrast to her actual reality. In some respects, this aspect suggests strong creative capacities, but there may be little motivation to share that creativity or to complete things. There's a vulnerability of Self—a feeling that she is unimportant—which can be devastating if it is not countered by positive, life-affirming messages and supports. If the father is absent or emotionally distant, the child's need to identify with the masculine is in jeopardy unless some effective substitute arises. Objectifying the self through creative endeavors can be very helpful, and it's important that her efforts do not go unnoticed.

Sun and Pluto

Sun-Pluto aspects are among the most difficult in childhood, since the child must deal with power issues from the beginning. With the flowing, harmonious aspects, the power of the self may be more easily acceptable. But with the dynamic aspects, his power is likely to either be undermined or felt as some monstrous beast.

The child with Sun-Pluto aspects will be attracted to the superhero—the ordinary human who transforms herself into a superpowered being. Learning that she is also superpowered is hard for these youngsters. This child must be given ample opportunities to express personal power, but without becoming overbearing. I have talked with many mothers of children with Sun-Pluto aspects who often have trouble saying "no" to their child. Teaching this child a right and wrong use of personal power can be a challenge for everyone—from family to teachers! Otherwise, the pattern of overbearing behavior and the extreme desire to control others could become intense in the adult years. If the child is continually struggling to have power over someone else, the real issue is probably that the child does not feel she has permission to simply "be," or to exercise any real control in her life.

The child with Sun-Pluto aspects can be profoundly in touch with the Source of All Knowledge and can feel this Higher Power intimately. In the early years, this feeling is projected onto the parents. The child does this in order to identify and find a frame of reference for this level of power. With the conjunction and the dynamic aspects, the child may feel threatened by this powerful energy, especially if the environment is not supportive of the child's need to integrate his personal power with that of the Higher Self. The child may feel that if he cannot be more than human, he has no reason to exist. What he needs to learn is that he is more than just a personality, and that this personality is connected with a Higher Source.

> **Sun conjunct Pluto**—Personal power is a real fascination for this child. Father may be very magnetic or influential, and if he allows the child to develop and exercise her own power during the formative years, this could provide exactly what is needed to endorse this child's sense of self. If the father is absent, he may exist as larger than life in some way. Nonetheless, it can still be difficult for this child to understand limits, and she can test these limits severely during developmental crises. The charisma of her personality can also become quite strong, and if other aspects indicate healthy self-expression, she can be a truly influential leader, even during the early years.

Sun sextile Pluto—This personality invites affirmative changes and can be excited about growing through the different periods of maturation and development. Parents and authorities may be seen in a positive light, and this child will be likely to seek role models who project an air of control and creativity. Goals are important, but he may need assistance in developing workable goal-setting techniques.

Sun square Pluto—This can be one of the most challenging aspects during childhood, although most children whose environments are supportive ultimately learn to deal with the frustrations indicated by their desire to be in control before they're ready. In some instances, the child may feel continually stripped of her power. Family situations such as the separation from or the loss of a parent can further enhance these feelings. The relationship with the father is especially critical in this case, and if for some reason the father is absent or unavailable, she may develop a strong fear of abandonment and basic lack of trust, especially with males.

The potential for self-destructive attitudes and actions is very strong, since he is likely to excessively push the limits of authority. Even during the toddler years, resistance to feeling controlled by others can be evidenced. However, it is in the preteen years when this dynamic begins to awaken more fully. It is crucial that parents and teachers be aware of the fact that the child needs to feel powerful, but also needs to understand that others can be powerful, too. Practical studies in fields like science which illustrate transformational change can be helpful to him, since he is also learning that everything is subject to change, including himself. These children should not be degraded. If they are, they will just fight back harder, and perhaps get themselves into situations which are personally toxic. The parents, teachers, and guides of these children need to find ways to allow the child to continually assess his own worth without becoming ruthless or harsh with himself or others. Provocation of guilt feelings can lead to self-destructive behaviors, and parents or teachers who utilize guilt as a motivator will not be doing this child a favor! However, accepting responsibility for the results of his actions is a necessary part of the learning process.

During the teen years when she is experiencing a need to emotionally break free from the parents, this child can become exceptionally self-destructive, especially if her own needs for power seem to be continually challenged. It's important that Mom and Dad respect the needs of this young person while holding firm to reasonable boundaries and safeguards. This young person may also be fascinated by healing and life's ultimate experiences of birth, sexuality, and death. Discovering the beneficial alterations which can accompany these experiences can spark a desire to become a true catalyst for positive change within the self and the world.

Sun trine Pluto—This child may experience more positive and uplifting circumstances in regard to power, healing, and change. The different stages of personal growth and development may feel more natural. Even when adolescence can seem disconcerting with its hormonal rushes and strange new feelings, he has a greater capacity to integrate the experience into his sense of self. Relationships with parents and authorities may still require the usual adaptations, but the ability to feel comfortable dealing with demands and expectations of parents and other authorities can be easygoing. While there may be a strong charisma present in this child, he may not always be comfortable taking risks.

Sun opposite Pluto—This aspect provides a particular challenge during childhood. There may be a feeling that she is somehow unwanted, even if this is not the case. Deep within, the impulse is to prove that she deserves to exist, and behaviors which test this premise are likely to be exhibited. Dealing with developmental and educational challenges can be tough, and although there is a fascination with becoming powerful, she may not know how to go about gaining that power without setting a potentially destructive course. There can be an inability to deal with defeats. Things that may appear small to adults (like problems with grades in school) may feel overwhelming to the child. The child wants to feel worthy of her own power, and part of that worth is determined by the quality of the child's performance in the external world. Activities that allow the child to see that she is getting better or making progress can be positively self-confirming. Learning to set goals and objectives that are within the child's grasp is extremely important.

Parents and authorities may be viewed as adversaries by this child, especially if traumatic circumstances or losses have occurred in the early years. It's also quite common for children with Sun-Pluto oppositions to place those they care about in a kind of adversarial position in order to test their commitment. In many ways, the child is testing his own abilities to maintain commitments and proving that he has reason to trust himself. Since he can be a magnet for guilt, it is crucial that parents be aware of how deeply this child is likely to feel shame and guilt and help him release destructive thoughts and attitudes. Ultimately, this child has the potential to learn how to identify and develop transformation and healing within the self and the world in which he lives.

Dynamics Between the Sun and the Moon

Now that we have a clearer understanding of the basic emotional needs indicated by the Sun and the Moon, we need to examine how these energies work together in the chart. The external, assertive Sun aspected by the receptive, subconscious Moon is a primary determining factor in a child's emotional security. The Sun represents the masculine side of the self, while the Moon is the feminine side (called the *animus* and *anima*, respectively). Aspects between the Moon and Sun in the chart indicate a significant need for the child to deal with these primary elements of the personality in a more direct manner. Many women who have friction-producing aspects between the Moon and Sun have struggled with their own femininity, since the need to satisfy the masculine part of the psyche (Sun) can overwhelm the more sensitive subconscious self (Moon). The drive to achieve or to exercise will power can overcome the inner receptive needs of the self. When dealing with young children who have difficult or dynamic Moon-Sun aspects, we need to give positive feedback about both the feeling nature and the assertive part of the Self. The child whose chart does not indicate a Sun-Moon aspect may not need to focus on these dynamics so intensely or may have distinctive impressions of the father-mother archetypes represented by these energies.

Moon conjunct Sun—This aspect indicates a union of the conscious and subconscious aspects of the self. This child may perceive the parents as a powerful unit in her life. Usually, this aspect brings an easy integration of the emotional needs and the ego self. The masculine and feminine aspects of the self seem to be well-balanced in this child's psyche. Other aspects may challenge this assumption or complicate the picture, but, in general, the subconscious and conscious sense of self are in sync with one another and operate in a unified capacity.

Moon sextile Sun—This aspect indicates the potential for a well-integrated personality. The parental support system is likely to be harmonious, with parents presenting a complimentary influence in the child's life.

Moon square Sun—There is a conflict between the subconscious needs and the external self. The child may feel pressured to act in a way he does not feel good about. Usually, this pressure results from wanting something he does not really need. If Mom and Dad come from different approaches, the child can feel caught in the middle of these parental disputes or differences, and may feel that it's impossible to please both parents. It's also conceivable that he can learn early on how to manipulate both parents, so that if one does not give him what is wanted, he will play one against the other in some way! If parents cooperate with this kind of behavior, the child may ultimately have difficulty integrating the masculine and feminine aspects of his psyche, since one always seems to be pitted against the other. Additionally, this can lead to problematic relationships later in life.

Moon trine Sun—This aspect indicates a supportive relationship from family and parents and suggests that learning has the potential to positively integrate what a child needs with what she wants. Self-awareness may develop comfortably, with good confirmation and a sense that she is an integral part of her family. A sound external support system is still necessary, although this aspect does indicate a great deal of emotional and personal resilience.

Moon quincunx Sun—This child may feel that he is constantly having to make adjustments in his needs in order to get even part of them fulfilled. Satisfying both parents can be difficult, especially if they seem to have different approaches to dealing with the child. It's easy for this child to feel caught in family struggles, feeling that ultimately his needs are less important than the needs or demands of others.

Moon opposite Sun—This child may be overly sensitive and can display strong emotional reactions to everything that's happening in the world around her. There can be a kind of seesaw effect, with the child vacillating between wanting to be noticed and wanting to be nurtured. Integrating masculine and feminine aspects of the psyche can be a trial, and one part of the self can suffer in favor of the other.

Mercury and Emotional Expression

Mercury is not traditionally considered an emotional expression. However, Mercury's role in the expression of feelings is highly important. Mercury represents the function of articulating ideas and feelings and influences how we communicate them.

Most human beings are more comfortable if they can talk about their emotional experiences to someone special. A child needs to feel that he can talk about anything with his parents, and that it is okay to share feelings and ideas. When a child is not given opportunities to communicate his emotional needs, he will have problems communicating almost anything else! Mercury's function in our lives is to link internal processes to the external world, and one of the most important inner processes is the experience of emotion.

Another way Mercury plays a part in the emotional life of the child is through the child's ability to distinguish between a feeling and a thought. Children who have Mercury placed in water signs tend to think with their feelings! Aspects from Mercury to the Moon and Venus also indicate an entanglement of thought and feeling. These aspects bring the sensitive, feeling part of the Self in contact with the rational, cognitive part.

> **Mercury and the Moon/Venus**—With the conjunction and the dynamic aspects between Mercury and the Moon or Venus, the child may become emotionally upset if she is not understood intellectually. If an error in judgment is made, the emotions may be unsettled. Certainly, these aspects will give the child an especially sensitive ability to "feel" another person's thoughts, but there can be some confusion tied in with these energies.

> **Mercury and the Sun**—When the Sun and Mercury are conjunct at birth, the child may be especially sensitive if someone criticizes or challenges his ideas. This is because the ego self (Sun) and the communicative abilities (Mercury) are united. It is difficult for the child to separate communication of thoughts and ideas from the ego or sense of Self. This is an intimate connection of the two processes.

> The conjunction of Sun and Mercury can add a tremendous force to the child's mental energy, but it can also be a problem if she does not learn to distinguish between her ideas and her identity. In her mind, she *is* what she says and thinks! In classroom situations, this could create a problem when the child makes a mistake. The child may feel that the intellectual error reflects badly upon her and her self-esteem could suffer. The child needs and wants to be thought of as intelligent. Sun-Mercury conjunctions can have a positive impact if the child learns to channel this need to have her ideas recognized. Such mediums as public speaking, debate, or creative writing would all be good outlets.

Mercury and Jupiter—Another way in which Mercury can create emotional problems is seen with Mercury-Jupiter contacts. Here, the child tends to stretch the truth. The expansive quality of Jupiter adds just a few more inches to the size of that fish! This is usually more marked with the dynamic aspects between Mercury and Jupiter. There may be a feeling from the child that the plain reality of a situation is not enough.

To positively deal with this potential, encourage the child to tell or write stories, both fiction and nonfiction. Offer positive feedback and deal honestly with the child about what is true and what is not. Encourage him to allow his enthusiasm for an idea to bring it into greater focus, and with drama. One thing that is sure with Mercury-Jupiter contacts—this kid can sell anything!

Mercury and Saturn—When Mercury and Saturn are together in dynamic aspect, the child may worry excessively. Saturn can have a burdening effect upon the mind energy. These children can benefit from learning how to focus upon positive thoughts.

The child with the conjunction and dynamic aspects between Mercury and Uranus may have very different ideas and ways of communicating than most of her friends. Sometimes these unusual thoughts can be alienating. She may have the impression that she is "weird." If parents and teachers can show the child how to use these original thoughts creatively, she will have more confidence in her creative ideas. Reinforcing trust of the intuitive mind is also helpful to these children.

Mercury and Neptune—When Mercury and Neptune are connected, especially in dynamic aspect, a child may tell imaginative stories or fabricate information. This can definitely have emotional repercussions! A child who is taught the ability to distinguish between fact and fiction will be better able to deal with these types of aspects. Parents can listen attentively to the tall tales, appreciating the child's imaginings, but need to encourage the child to tell the truth when relating actual events! Parents also need to be aware that the cute little stories told at age five, if left uncorrected, can give the child the impression that he can lie without being caught. This could lead to sociopathic behavior later on.

Mercury and Pluto—With Mercury and Pluto in conjunction or dynamic aspect, thoughts and ideas have a compelling sense of urgency. The child may be secretive with her thoughts in order to seem mysterious or enigmatic. This is helpful when solving mysteries or doing scientific research, but it can make honest emotional communication difficult. Parents and friends may often be met with silence if the child simply does not want to communicate. If there is communication, it can be irritatingly manipulative. She may fear that telling it all would undermine her power in certain situations.

The child will be greatly helped if parents can work with him to understand that sharing ideas and feelings can enhance his command of a situation. The Mercury-Pluto child may be intellectually ruthless toward the self, and can feel assaulted if the ideas or thoughts he expresses are harshly criticized. Accepting changes in attitudes and ideas is absolutely necessary for these children, and learning to allow others to have different ideas from their own will go a long way toward assuring that they will be much more positively influential as adults.

Venus and Emotional Needs

A child feels a greater sense of worth when she is given love and appreciation. In many ways, this allows a child to more positively express herself. The energy of Venus involves the expression of what we value, what we love, and who is important in our lives.

Another facet of Venusian energy is self-love. By allowing ourselves to love another person, we are fulfilling a personal need within ourselves. Small children are notoriously selfish, and usually have to be taught to share their energy, their possessions, and their time. Part of this is pure developmental process, since in the very early years a child considers everything a part of himself. Much of any child's behavior will, of course, be conditioned by the parents and society. Each child, however, will have his own particular needs and style in the expression of love.

Artistic expression is another Venusian manifestation, and is a wonderful way of sharing and opening a part of the inner self to the world outside. Children have creative needs which should be allowed to blossom.

Observing children's behavior one will note that crawling babies and very young toddlers are reluctant to share. They tend to play by themselves and rarely interact with other babies (even though they may enjoy being near them). These babies are slowly unfolding their identity, which is still rather amorphous. They are likely to believe, "My toy is part of me."

Venusian expression seems to be easier for the child after about age four, when the child may finally want to give something to another person. But children are more fully involved in the Venusian stage of development during the teen years, when "falling in love" becomes a reality. But, regardless of the child's age, she needs to feel love from others.

Venus is also one of the most sexually expressive energies of the chart. Children begin to deal with sexuality very early in life, although it awakens much more powerfully when the hormones become active during puberty. During the last years of the twentieth century, society had finally begun to express the awareness that children do have a sense of sexuality, but this does not mean that their sexuality operates on the same level as procreative adults!

Venus is also one of the archetypes of feminine energy in the individual. Its sign and house placement along with its aspects will indicate how comfortable the child is with the feminine aspects of the Self. Additionally, Venus stimulates an individual's sense of beauty, and even in childhood will indicate how a child wants to present his image to the world.

The sign placement of Venus offers insights into the way a child wants to love and be loved. Its placement by house will tell us what the child appreciates, the type of environment in which a child feels most creative, and the directions in which love energy is likely to flow. Venus in the 11th House, for example, is strongly attached to relationships with friends—much love is given and received through friendships. Aspects from Venus to other planets indicate not only of the expression of love, but also how the child's self-worth is affected. More specific definitions of Venus aspects are found in chapter 8, since during childhood it is largely through creative efforts that a child realizes her value.

Venus and Jupiter—Venus-Jupiter aspects often confer a sense of generosity and a very strong need to relate to others. The expectations of others may be a problem, and the child will benefit by practicing the art of unconditional love. This child may have great difficulty setting limits on what he wants. The tendency to be disappointed if his wants are not fulfilled can lead to frustrated behaviors. Ultimately, parents need to teach him that it's unlikely anyone will have everything he wants all at once!

Venus and Saturn—Venus-Saturn aspects can inhibit the expression of love. Even the flowing aspects are restrictive (Saturn being Saturn), and the dynamic aspects are harder still to deal with. Dynamic aspects between Venus and Saturn can be indicators of low self-esteem in the child. The child may feel that she must do certain things, or do things in a particular way, to be loved. These self-imposed restrictions on receiving love can be tremendously detrimental to the open expression of love.

Sometimes there is fear associated with love when these aspects are present: the fear that the love may not be there, or the fear that love will cause pain. The parents can help the child by becoming sensitive to the barriers the child builds against intimacy. Developing trust in his own feelings can be very hard for this child. Once the sexual self begins to develop, it is important for the child with Venus-Saturn contacts to be able to cope with these feelings without fear and guilt.

Since Venus also deals with the concept of beauty, sometimes children with Venus-Saturn contacts are too focused on whether or not they are pretty. This can be important to little boys as well as little girls. Whether fortunate or unfortunate, our society places a strong value on the way someone looks. Given the media exposure children receive today, they, too, are being bombarded by images that they will try to emulate. If this child receives messages from parents or teachers that indicate there is a problem with her looks, then she will take it more seriously and worry about it. It is crucial, especially for the child with Venus-Saturn connections, to understand the many layers of beauty and to learn how to accept herself with love—even with a few flaws that challenge the popular ideals.

Venus and Uranus—Venus aspects to Uranus can bring the need for a highly unusual form of love. This love is definitely an expression of and need for unconditional acceptance. An urge for free emotional expression is powerful, since spontaneous emotion is a definite reality. These kids are often the champions of the underdog. Parents may wonder why Samantha brings home the weirdest kids in the school—it's because she can relate to them!

Children with Venus-Uranus aspects may enjoy group associations, team activities, and things they can do with others. However, there is also a need to stand out in the crowd. You may find the child with Venus-Uranus aspects beginning a new fashion revolution or setting trends. The need is to be different and to let others know that being different is fantastic!

Venus and Neptune—Venus-Neptune aspects can confer a tremendous emotional sensitivity to the child. The emotional expression is linked with divine love, offering the child an opportunity to be a vehicle for divine compassion. The creative energies are extraordinarily responsive, with a strong attraction to music, dance, and other flowing art forms.

Because there is such a potent sensibility, these children can easily be hurt by the insensitivity of others. Emotional expression may be difficult because this aspect, with its elusive feelings, sometimes makes it hard for the child to know exactly how he feels. He may have trouble distinguishing between his sense of what another feels and his own feelings—it's as though the emotional boundaries are very loose. Sometimes this child can be a crybaby.

Consequently, the child may be too easily influenced by others, especially when the dynamic aspects are present. Venus-Neptune is boundless love. Forgiveness and compassion are easily understood and expressed, especially with the flowing aspects. Give this child an opportunity to help others, and encourage as many forms of creative expression as possible.

Venus and Pluto—Intense, and sometimes overwhelming, emotional expression is the key to Venus-Pluto energy. Attachment can become a real problem with Venus-Pluto contacts, because once love feelings are there, they become deeply ingrained. With the flowing aspects, the ability to transform and continually alter the sense of self-worth is present. Growth and change are seen as part of life's natural course of events. Positive self-transformation is relatively easy to develop.

However, with the dynamic aspects between Venus and Pluto, the child may sense that love is self-destructive. A strong association between love and pain may be present. We know that Neptune sensitizes. Pluto deepens, and opens us up to the most vulnerable parts of ourselves.

When Venus and Pluto interact dynamically, opening up to the depths of emotion may hurt. Vulnerability can be guarded against to such an extent that the child can shut herself away from love entirely.

To change this, the parents, guides, and teachers of these children must patiently show him how to outwardly express feelings. Art and other creative activities can be good tools. It must be understood that the art is not being negatively judged. However, the child is likely to feel mistrustful of others, and must learn to trust his own feelings before others can be trusted.

When sexual feelings begin to be aroused, the child needs to have an outlet for her expression without guilt. Sometimes teens with Venus-Pluto contacts will begin to have sexual feelings and then feel so guilty that they cannot deal with them. If the young person can learn that this is just another part of the Self emerging, the guilt will be less overwhelming.

The parents can help by being supportive, empathizing with and talking about these "weird new feelings." What a difference this will make for the teenager or child! This aspect, when positively developed, confers upon the individual the ability to heal through love.

Mars and Emotional Needs

The emotional energy of Mars is expressed through assertiveness, anger, strength, and sexuality. For the small child, angry feelings will be one of the early expressions of pure Martian force. We all have feelings of anger, and must learn to express them without being self-destructive. Parents need to allow the child to have his angry feelings, but they also have a responsibility to teach him that anger needs to be directed in ways which will not destroy.

Positive assertiveness is also directed through Martian thrust. This masculine energy is sometimes difficult for female children to embrace, but they must accept and direct it too! The sign and house placement of Mars will indicate the areas in which the child needs to be assertive and show how the assertiveness will be directed. Mars in water signs is often a difficult expression, especially the frustratingly indirect flow of Mars in Cancer. The child with Mars in an air sign may dissipate the energy too rapidly by shouting angry words. When dealing with anger, the child with Mars in a fire sign will be the most direct, while those with Mars in earth or water signs tend to repress angry feelings.

The key to Mars energy is that it needs to be either released or transmuted. Children will have difficulty transmuting energy, though, since this requires inner awareness. Besides that, children are purists when it comes to energy expression! When a child becomes angry, she can learn to direct the anger in nondestructive ways. Parents can provide an outlet such as a punching ball or pillows on the bed so that the child has a physical release when necessary. The child needs to learn that anger is normal, but destruction through anger will create problems. To punish a child for expressing anger will only cause the child to repress angry feelings and become even more destructive! The task at hand is to teach the child that the negative expressions of anger directed at others will result in pain, whereas diffusing the anger nondestructively will open a doorway to change.

Since the ability to direct Mars energy in the most appropriate ways requires some maturity, I do not see a huge difference in the operation of specific Mars aspects until early adulthood. However, there are definite differences in the flowing and dynamic aspects, and differentiating between these qualities is important. For this reason, I will maintain more general categories: Mars in flowing aspect or dynamic (difficult) aspect to other planets.

Mars and Jupiter—Combinations of Mars and Jupiter by aspect provide an interesting dynamic in childhood. Identifying and setting limits can be a huge challenge for the child with a Mars-Jupiter aspect, since the assertive vitality of Mars is amplified by the expansive quality of Jupiter. While any Mars-Jupiter contact can increase a child's sense of confidence, the dynamic aspects can ultimately lead to an undermining of confidence unless a child learns about his specific limitations in different situations. This child is likely to be competitive and may even welcome any challenge that allows him to prove himself. But how does a parent or teacher teach this child to know when to stop?

It is helpful if a child with Mars-Jupiter contacts also has evidence in her chart of a good response to discipline and reality—supportive Saturn aspects or strong Mercurial qualities. These concrete (Saturn) and logical (Mercury) additives can be invaluable. However, even if the chart does not suggest that these qualities are easy for the child to attract or experience, parents and teachers can help to instill them nonetheless! It may simply be more challenging for them.

When Mars and Jupiter are in flowing aspect to one another, there is a tendency to fall into the assumption "If I really want it, then I can have it." While that may be true, putting forth the effort is another story! This child may learn to put forth only minimal effort and expect that someone or something will come along to make up the difference if it is needed. Strangely enough, if this child can learn to couple discipline and focus with consistency of effort, his abilities can quickly take him to the top.

Mars and Jupiter in conjunction or in dynamic (frustrating) aspect to one another suggest great difficulty in establishing personal limitations. This child may not have a natural sense of how to budget her energy. She is the one who will play until she collapses in the middle of the playroom floor, or later in the teen years will stay up all night with friends and then wonder why she can't wake up to finish a school project in time. It's almost as though she needs to push past limits before she figures out that they exist at all! This child may resist efforts on the part of parents and teachers to learn about prioritizing unless there are other factors present which would invite that kind of lesson. Illustrating that she can accomplish more by setting priorities is an excellent beginning. Sports can be helpful, but working in tandem with others in mutually supportive circumstances also builds continuity—a much needed commodity for this child.

Mars and Saturn—All Mars aspects to Saturn are likely to restrict feelings of anger, causing the child to feel trapped inside his anger. This inhibited energy may then be released in cruel ways. The harmonious aspects between Mars and Saturn often aid in the constructive use of assertive energy. These children can be very good builders. The child with Mars-Saturn aspects will feel a strong desire to be in control and to direct things *and* people.

The dynamic aspects will often indicate more extreme inhibition of the expression of anger, which can create both physical and emotional difficulty. Sometimes these children have parents who bridle their self-assertiveness, which tends to create anger toward the parents. This can become self-destructive and will block an easy flow of understanding between parent and child.

Sexual assertiveness is often uncomfortable for this child to develop, since there is frequently a restrictive attitude toward sexual expression from the parents. Healthy caution is one thing, but guilt about the feelings of sexuality is damaging to the young person. The teenager with difficult Mars-Saturn aspects is especially susceptible to these feelings. She may feel that the permission to even have these feelings does not exist, and the frustrations can lead to violent or destructive outbursts.

Teaching him that sexual feelings are a normal part of growing up will alleviate much of this turmoil. Replacing guilt with an awareness of the possible consequences of his sexual actions will give the young person a choice and is a much clearer use of the dynamics between Mars and Saturn. The ability to make choices strengthens his sense of personal power, whereas guilt feelings will simply be frustrating.

Mars and Uranus—Mars-Uranus is usually quick tempered. Any aspect between these two planets confers a need to generate lots of excitement. The child should be given ample opportunity to express herself freely, but could benefit from the lessons of positive caution as well. In fact, teaching reasonable caution may be absolutely necessary, particularly when dynamic aspects are present! (For example, these children may be fascinated with high-risk activities such as skydiving or ski jumping, and should be encouraged to explore these activities after adequate instruction and when maturity allows it.)

The dynamic aspects often bring an explosive temper, especially when the child feels he has been too inhibited by someone or a situation. Sexual interests may develop early. These impulsive youngsters may act first, then think about consequences later—if at all. Learning to consider the results of his actions will give this child a sense of personal confidence. He must learn that responsibility goes hand in hand with freedom. Part of that responsibility comes from understanding that every action has a consequence.

Mars and Neptune—Mars-Neptune aspects dissipate assertiveness and anger. It can be difficult for this child to feel confident about putting herself into situations which require confrontation, even when the aspect is a flowing or supportive one. Neptune sensitizes, and the sensitivity to pain (or fear of it) can be increased with Mars-Neptune aspects.

With the dynamic aspects, a child may have angry feelings, but will have difficulty finding an outlet for them. Anger is not an easy emotion with Mars-Neptune contacts because it can cause so much confusion. Also, expressing anger can ultimately leave him with a feeling of emotional exhaustion. Teenage males with dynamic Mars-Neptune contacts often overcompensate for assertiveness by becoming the superathlete or the model male. Surrender is frustrating to these children. Teenage girls with Mars-Neptune contacts often overidealize the "macho" male image, or may have problems dealing with boys in a realistic manner. Because a realistic assessment of others is blocked by idealism, the child may either feel powerless or victimized. This can lead to escapist forms of behavior or tendencies toward addictive behaviors.

This is the child who may get into trouble playing too many video games, especially if the games have violent content, since her impressionability can lead her to live in the fantasy of the experience. The reality base may be limited or inhibited in some way and, if prompted by a situation, she could carry it too far before she realizes what has actually happened. Linking cause and effect can be very difficult for this child to learn.

On the other hand, this child may also feel a profound need to rescue others from painful situations—he can identify with the pain! This can create a trap for the preteen and teenage child, however, who may develop a tendency to be drawn into codependent relationships filled with addictive behavior patterns. Certainly helping others is admirable, but the other person must learn how to help himself. Most children do not have the objectivity to understand this, and will simply identify with the other person. Parents may need to help this child identify when it is constructive to help and when he needs to keep a reasonable distance. Teaching him to cope with feelings of despair by using his natural talent of positive visualization can help. Encourage this child to bring this positive vision into action, to see that the hope for a better tomorrow is valid. Dramatic arts can be a good resource for external expression, as can music. Children with Mars-Neptune aspects are often rather charismatic, and can have a positive influence in the lives of others.

Mars and Pluto—Mars-Pluto connections suggest a strong need to feel personal power. A sense of omnipotence may be present, even in young children. With the harmonious aspects, the child is likely to have a magnetic personality. Assertiveness can be quite intense. She can express anger creatively through sports or other activities. The child with dynamic aspects between Mars and Pluto may feel powerless because she has a powerful father or others who usurp her personal power. Anger is likely to be repressed when difficult Mars-Pluto contacts exist, causing angry feelings to work against the child. Negative self-concepts and improper use of personal power can result.

This child must be given permission to express both his power and anger. He needs to learn that ventilating angry feelings when they surface is better than letting them build up and then explode like a volcano! Positive expressions of personal power can come by supporting the child's need to influence or bring change into the lives of others. Help the child target ways in which he could help someone else—perhaps by helping an ailing friend or relative, or even taking in an injured bird and nursing it back to health and freedom. Teens can volunteer to work in hospitals or veterinary clinics.

This child needs to see transformation in action. This happens around us all the time, especially in situations in which a person is becoming whole following an illness. She needs to change things, and can be shown ways to bring about positive change in the world. Working on projects to improve or renovate the house or yard is also a helpful way to teach these lessons.

The child with Mars-Pluto may be most drawn to early sexual experimentation. Sometimes, when the harsh aspects are present, the early sexual experiences are traumatic. While these aspects may be indicative of sexual or psychological abuse, they do not guarantee it. What is suggested is that the balance of power that exists in sexual situations can be truly difficult. If sexual abuse does occur in the early years, the impression upon the child's psyche can be highly destructive. The potential with Mars-Pluto contacts is that the ability to heal and regenerate is good, since the ability to take action (Mars) can help the child objectify the trauma. The key issues represented by this aspect revolve around the acceptance and positive directions of personal power, and learning not to allow others to absorb or steal that power from him.

Jupiter, Saturn, and the Outer Planets in Emotional Expression

The personal planets form the foundation of a child's emotional sense of self. Their energies are those which are most accessible in terms of awareness. Aspects from Jupiter, Saturn, and the outer planets will either strengthen or weaken this emotional profile. However, these energies also have their own indications in terms of the emotional matrix.

Each of the planets typifies an expression of need. Jupiter represents the need for confidence and optimism; Saturn, the need for structure and discipline; Uranus, the need to feel special; Neptune, the need to reach inside the Self; and Pluto, the need to express power.

As we have explored in the preceding material, these planets can have a powerful influence in the child's emerging personality. The energies of Jupiter and Saturn seem to be experienced as social influences, and are indicative of the social climate, rules, and mores that surround the child and influence her life. The individual often senses the operation of the outer planets—Uranus, Neptune, and Pluto—as "circumstances beyond my control," at least until a significant level of self-understanding has been achieved. Children may feel especially powerless in their early years, but, with encouragement from aware parents, can begin to harmonize more readily with themselves and their true needs.

Jupiter and Emotions

Jupiter inspires growth through conferring a sense of hope and confidence. For the child, Jupiter is the bright promise of tomorrow. The sign in which Jupiter is placed will indicate the dominant theme that emerges in the child's overall philosophy of life. His belief system may revolve around the qualities of Jupiter's sign. The house placement of Jupiter will indicate where the child feels a sense of openness and enthusiasm.

Jupiter indicates attitudes toward generosity and sharing as well. If a child believes that sharing will in some way diminish what she has, she will be reluctant to do it. The parents can teach the child that sharing is a constantly flowing cycle—the more we give, the more we receive. This is the Law of Abundance. However, before it is recognized spiritually, it must be experienced emotionally!

Self-indulgence can be a negative form of Jupiterian need, and will surface when the child feels a lack of confidence. Aware parents can be alerted to this type of behavior and help the child avoid negative patterns of indulgent behavior.

Saturn and Emotions

Saturn provides the basic structure of our lives and without it, there would be little security or stability. It is a positive and necessary quality. It also represents the lessons we must learn and the steps we must follow to grow. The structured, restrictive energy of Saturn is uncomfortable to many adults. After all, Saturn tells the story of growing up and becoming a responsible adult—how many adults do you know resist growing up? During the childhood years this energy often feels binding, thus creating a sense of lack or loss. A child's conditioning toward Saturnian energy will be directly related to how the adults in his life express it. Parents need to provide a sound and consistent framework that feels trustworthy to the child. If the adult has problems dealing with positive restraints and responsibility, the child is also likely to have difficulties!

Saturn remains in a sign for a little more than two years, and the sign placement of Saturn describes the kind of structure that will be most natural for the child to experience and accept. The house placement of Saturn shows where a child may experience greater restraint, or, better yet, may need to develop greater restraint and personal responsibility!

As parents, we are learning more profound approaches to dealing with our children. When I am counseling adults, I often see problems that are direct results of the difficult aspects between the personal energies and Saturn. Feelings of loss, rejection, and undue restriction are common.

In dealing with children whose charts indicate harsh Saturn contacts, I work directly with the child's Saturn element: the parents. If the child is of school age, we can usually see some of the self-critical elements of these contacts already surfacing. Saturn also is represented by teachers, since they provide the lessons during most of the child's formative years!

One mother relayed to me that her young teenage daughter, through her continual need for perfect structures in her life, projected a wall between the two of them. She described situations in which her daughter would deny her own abilities. The mother would feel compelled to point out how her daughter was limiting herself. The daughter would then withdraw and create even stronger barriers between her mother and herself. I suggested that this mother focus upon her daughter's strengths for a while. The two of them also began a yoga class together, something the mother had previously criticized. This sharing provided a link for them. Now the daughter is opening up more to her mother, asking for ways to improve some of her negative attitudes.

Many times, astrologers and students of astrology will see difficult Saturn aspects in the chart and jump to the conclusion that the parents are the problem. We should not blame the parents when we see difficult Saturn aspects. Rather, the parents need to be encouraged to project as much unconditional love and understanding as possible toward their child. It is, after all, the child's chart we are examining.

What we do see with many Saturn aspects, however, is the child's own sense of limitation, frustration, or loss. This is often projected upon the parents, society, or teachers. In the adult years, the projection is on the government, the boss, and so on. Children must learn to deal with the realities of life, and embracing Saturn will require time and maturity. This is the primary symbol of Saturn—the necessities of life and the real world.

This real world does not have to be negative, but can provide a secure and powerful base of operations. The difference comes when the child develops an attitude of positive abundance through integrating the energy of Jupiter. If there is an antidote to Saturn, it's Jupiter! However, all factors must work in balance with one another. Saturn requires balance in order to be useful.

If this need for structure and discipline within the self is not developed by the child, it will generally be provided by the external environment in the form of denials and limited opportunities. This need for balance is one of the reasons why Saturn's placement in Libra (where it is considered to be exalted) is a natural plus. The energy itself is continually seeking that balance.

Astrologers have finally developed a positive respect for Saturn energy, but we still understand its restrictive influence in our lives. If we are to live on a more harmonious plane, each individual must recognize the need for personal responsibility. This is a positive use of Saturn. These responses begin in childhood, and are conditioned by the parents.

Saturn has been described as the "shadow of the self," a concept Dr. Liz Greene introduced in the 1970s which confers part of the power of this energy. The shadow does not have to be feared, only recognized. In helping a child deal with her feelings of fear, guilt, or jealousy, we are nurturing a positive attitude toward Saturn. Often, the fear is just a reflex. Sometimes, by working with a child's negative feelings, the parents can begin to deal openly with theirs. This kind of family healing is wonderful to watch.

Ultimately, the structures Saturn provides will be found within the Self. They are not houses or bank accounts or even parents. The real structure is a reliance upon our own inner strength and the willingness to take responsibility for every action, thought, and feeling we have. To begin learning this in childhood will build a tremendous foundation of personal trust in one's own abilities. It will help the child become a more complete expression of the Self.

The Transpersonal Planets: Uranus, Neptune, and Pluto

These planets move very slowly and remain in a sign for long periods of time. Generally, personal awareness of these energies is not illustrated in early childhood. In fact, there is a generational influence suggested by the sign in which these planets are placed. We see the child coping with these planetary energies through their contacts to the personal planets (as described earlier). However, the house placement of these planets will indicate where within the Self the child experiences these higher needs.

Uranus and the Need to Be Different

Uranus in the Houses

The need to feel special is strong for every child, and Uranus' house placement will give you ideas of how to encourage the child to develop that sense of uniqueness.

Uranus in the 1st House—This child expresses an unusual and independent personality. He needs plenty of room to exercise his individuality, and should be given ample opportunities to interject his preferences for clothes and other image related items. During the teen years, watch for surprise hair colors at the very least!

Uranus in the 2nd House—This child may be attracted to unusual things, including technological and electronic items. She may have very little practical sense when it comes to money, and may need to take extra care in order to keep track of material things. However, her value of friendships is very strong.

Uranus in the 3rd House—This placement adds a restless quality to the personality. He can be a quick learner, and may have difficulty paying attention to subject matter which is uninteresting. His desire to drive or use whatever vehicles are available to get somewhere more quickly can try the patience of the parent who prefers a more leisurely pace.

Uranus in the 4th House—This placement frequently indicates several changes in home environment and/or family structure. This child may always feel a bit like an outsider when it comes to family relations, and is rather likely to assume that she was secretly adopted! Ultimately, she may be the one to break up family fate or challenge family traditions.

Uranus in the 5th House—This child will need to express a unique form of creativity. Unusual art forms, innovative music, and inventive games will be part of the child's needs. Relationships with unusual people ultimately follow, especially during the teen and early adult years.

Uranus in the 6th House—This child will enjoy using whatever innovations are available to become more proficient at anything. He may also have a very sensitive nervous system and in healing methodologies may respond very readily to energy-altering techniques like acupuncture, Reiki, or shiatsu.

Uranus in the 7th House—This child may seek out social situations which involve friends whose interests are ground-breaking in some way. She is likely to resist being put in any sort of mold, and may seek out opportunities to make changes in the world around her as she matures. Sometimes these children are social activists at an early age!

Uranus in the 8th House—This placement suggests a powerful connection to the inner realms and strong intuitive abilities, especially involving others who are close to him. Curiosity about what makes things work may be present, and studying nature can be enjoyable. Expect questions about birth, death, and sexuality.

Uranus in the 9th House—This child has a keen interest in learning but very little patience with the process. Traditional learning methodologies may not suit this child's learning style, although other elements in the chart will suggest whether or not this is necessarily the case.

Uranus in the 10th House—This placement stimulates a desire to gain public notice. Not just anything will do: this child needs to stand out as unusual or her accomplishments need to be ground-breaking.

Uranus in the 11th House—This child has a strong desire to try different things. While goal-setting can be important, those goals are likely to change, and learning to develop short-term goals will help assure a sense of completion. Friendships are highlighted, although childhood friends are not likely to be the friends of adulthood.

Uranus in the 12th House—This child has a powerful imagination and creativity. However, he may not be able to actualize that creativity without some outside stimulus, especially if he feels shy or uncertain about it.

Neptune and Pluto

Neptune's need to reach inside the self and Pluto's need to express power can be interpreted by studying the house placements of these planets as well. Recognize, however, that the child may not exhibit a personal awareness of these energies as part of the self until she reaches maturity since they operate on a very unconscious level. I describe Neptune's house placements in chapter 7 in the context of creative self-expression. However, Pluto's dynamics in terms of unconscious emotional drives may be seen during the early years, even though a child may not be able to objectify the energy. Pluto's position can be indicative of deep-seated anxieties or fears that are, for lack of a better description, absorbed into the psyche.

Pluto in the Houses

Pluto in the 1st House—This child can overreact to situations with high emotional impact and may develop a kind of mistrust of new situations or people. He can present a kind of intensity that can be disarming to some observers.

Pluto in the 2nd House—This placement can suggest a fear of not being good enough. This child needs additional reinforcement of her self-worth.

Pluto in the 3rd House—The energy in this placement can suggest a display of anxiety over communication, and this child may feel reluctant to voice his opinions or ideas unless he knows that it's safe.

Pluto in the 4th House—This energy can produce a fear of abandonment and a sense that the security base can be destroyed at any moment. Major changes in family in the early years will have a deep impact on this child's psyche.

Pluto in the 5th House—This child needs reassurance that love is a good thing. This child may be sorely disappointed if she has shared tender feelings with someone and does not feel reciprocation.

Pluto in the 6th House—This child can be fearful of falling ill or may be insecure around doctors. Sometimes a child with Pluto in the 6th House is afraid of dogs or cats, especially if he has been in an unsupported situation when an animal scratched or bit him.

Pluto in the 7th House—This child may not trust commitments from others. For this reason, it's necessary that parents keep their promises to her. Breaking a date to go to the zoo could feel completely awful to this child.

Pluto in the 8th House—This child needs to understand why things happen as they do. He may be naturally insightful about what motivates others, and because of this awareness may be mistrustful until situations prove otherwise.

Pluto in the 9th House—This placement stimulates a need to feel deeply connected to the truth. This child may test the limits of truth if there are difficult aspects to Pluto. Early spiritual teaching will have a profound effect on her life. Dogmatic beliefs can be dangerously provocative.

Pluto in the 10th House—This placement can indicate a need to be in charge. This child may not do well as a follower, simply because the emotional drive is to be in control. However, aspects to Pluto will determine how this is played out or tested in the child's life.

Pluto in the 11th House—This child needs to learn to trust friends. He may choose friends because they are influential, not realizing that he can be just as strong and that others are likely to see him as a leader.

Pluto in the 12th House—This child may not trust that her dreams are okay, and will need validation that bringing her imaginings into the world can be a good thing. Give this child plenty of space for secrets and ample opportunities for time alone.

The Ascendant in Emotional Expression

The Ascendant (ASC) is a highly sensitive point in the chart. This is the mask an individual wears before the world. Sometimes that mask is easily removed; at other times, the mask becomes the Self.

Understanding how we project ourselves to the world aids in personal integration. In truth, the Ascendant represents how our attitudes are reflected into the world, which is why this is how others are likely to see us! A child begins developing this mask through observing, feeling, and experiencing the reactions of others to himself. The sign on the Ascendant and the planets in the 1st House are indicators of this part of the personality projection.

Using the key concepts for the qualities of the sign, you can determine how the child will project herself to the world. If Leo is rising, the child will project a proud, dramatic, and powerful image of the Self. With Pisces rising, she would project a more tranquil, mystical image. Any planets conjuncting the Ascendant, whether in the 12th or 1st House, will further alter this projection and gain significance in the emotional and personality profile of the child.

Sun on the Ascendant—This conjunction gives a sunny disposition. These children tend to be highly noticeable, and like to shine above the crowd.

Moon on the Ascendant—This conjunction adds a receptive quality to the personality. The child may feel self-protective. His emotions are more noticeable.

Mercury on the Ascendant—This conjunction connects the personality to the intellect. The child may be very talkative and communicative. The mental abilities will provide part of the mask for this child, and will be a sensitive area of the self.

Venus on the Ascendant—This conjunction can bring physical beauty. This planet may create a need within the child to present the most beautiful image possible. This is a two-edged sword, because the child may feel a need to be perfectly beautiful. If her beauty does not meet these exacting standards, the child could feel insecure.

Mars on the Ascendant—This conjunction confers a need to project strength and energy. These children will often be highly active. Assertiveness is a key factor in personality projection, and physical activity is a must. Many times this indicates a strong interest in sports.

Jupiter on the Ascendant—This conjunction projects a sense of confidence, optimism, and enthusiasm. However, it can also exaggerate the personality. Sometimes overindulgence is noticeable, causing the body to expand. Here is the image of the jolly fat person. Which part of the image is the mask?

Saturn on the Ascendant—This conjunction projects seriousness. The child may seem to be more responsible and mature than his years might indicate. Taking things too seriously can be a problem. This child often wants to project an adult image.

Uranus on the Ascendant—This conjunction indicates the need to be different. These children might be trend setters. Their mask is the desire to be unique.

Neptune on the Ascendant—This is the actor. These children can be like chameleons, changing their personalities to fit their environment. They also can project a mystical beauty.

Pluto on the Ascendant—This conjunction projects a powerful vibration. This mask is often very heavy for the child. These children go through tremendous personality changes during life, although they sometimes happen gradually. Reactions to the child can be extreme. Generally, these children know where they stand with others.

Planets in the 1st House will have similar effects to planets conjuncting the Ascendant. Planets which aspect the Ascendant (by trine, square, etc.) will further alter the personality projection.

The Child's Emotional Profile

We have examined the astrological energies as they specifically relate to a child's emotional needs. The first six years of a child's life are ruled by the energy of the Moon, the primary emotional need. During these years, a child will receive thousands of messages about who she is, and will be matching those messages to her needs. These are critical years, when the strengths and weaknesses indicated by the planetary profile are most impressionable.

The child who is strongly supported emotionally by parents and family may find it easier to balance some of the difficult factors of the personality. If the support and understanding are not present, these factors seem to loom larger for the child.

One way to begin understanding the child's basic needs is to blend together the meanings of the Sun, Moon, and Ascendant. These three factors indicate the child's fundamental personality needs. Next, examine the personal planets along with their signs, houses, and aspects. You may find a theme emerging in the chart which indicates the child's primary weaknesses and strengths.

For example, if the chart shows several aspects from Saturn to the Sun, Moon, and personal planets, the child will need to work through his fears and guilt feelings. Learning that mental attitudes can make the difference in happiness or sorrow is critical.

If Uranus is heavily aspected, the child will need to appreciate her uniqueness and learn to channel it in a productive manner. Balancing intuitive and rational thinking is necessary. Should the chart contain several aspects between Neptune and the personal energies, the child may have difficulty relating to the real world. Encouraging her to develop creative talents will help integrate her personality profile. The child with strong Plutonian influences needs to accept her intensity. Learning to channel personal power could create conflicts with others until she feels a strong measure of self-worth.

Through patience, love, and understanding, we can guide the children on our planet to a more complete expression of themselves. This truly offers hope for a brighter tomorrow as we continue through the doorway into the Aquarian Age.

7

Nurturing Intellectual Needs in Childhood

One of the most fascinating aspects of child development is the child's mental unfolding. Parents and grandparents track all the signals that a child is progressing, especially that he is learning to communicate. From the first smile to spoken words to learning how to read, each step is likely to be a topic of conversation. Parents seek ways to assure that a child will have the best opportunities to learn, and in today's world, cherish signs that the intellect is blossoming. There are many factors involved in intellect—the ability to conceptualize, the communication of concepts and thoughts, memory, creative ideas, the application of rational thought, judicial thinking, decision-making, speculative thought, and more.

Intellect carries us beyond emotion into a more objective frame of reference. A child is not initially an intellectual creature, although a few prodigious children seem to have high capacities for intellectual development. These are the ones you find orating memorized Shakespearean soliloquies at age four while other children are just beginning to speak coherent sentences!

Most parents want their child to have an excellent mind, since we live in an age when intellectual gifts are highly esteemed. But sometimes this focus on the development of a

187

powerful intellect overpowers other needs a child may have. In order to be whole, the child must achieve a balance between the mental, emotional, physical, and spiritual parts of the Self; only then can the power of the intellect be used to its utmost. Otherwise, the mental capacities are likely to be overemphasized or misdirected in order to compensate for underdevelopment in some other area.

Through astrology, we can determine many facets of the flowering mental energy. We become acquainted with a basic spiritual law: "What you think, you become." Astrological factors that have strong intellectual connotations are the Moon, Mercury, Jupiter, Saturn, and Uranus. The houses with strong intellectual focus are Houses 3, 9, and 11. Air is the element of the intellect, with fire signifying inspiration.

The Moon and Mercury

A small baby begins to explore her personal environment through the five senses, which are interpreted through the energy of Mercury. When the baby sees Mother's familiar face, her mind sends signals of recognition. These senses are also used in learning. The concept of "hot" is too often learned by being burned. The sense of taste is one of the first senses a baby uses to learn - she tries to put almost everything into her mouth!

As a child grows, environmental exploration becomes more refined. No longer does he put everything into his mouth—the child can now begin to identify objects by their shapes, colors, and textures. The mind gains the ability to integrate more and more information. The placements of the Moon and Mercury by sign are strong indicators of how the child perceives his environment.

The Moon signifies our *thought patterns*, with her sign and aspects symbolizing their basic nature. The Moon in air signs is likely to generate abstract thinking. In earth signs, the thoughts are focused on the physical plane. In water signs, they are impressionable and may even be photographic. And in fire signs, the thoughts are highly active and creative.

Through the Moon, we experience the uniqueness of our lives, then hold those experiences in the subconscious vaults of the mind. Aspects from the Moon to the other planets alter the basic flow of thought patterns. Saturn disciplines thinking, while Uranus electrifies and sometimes scatters it.

Mercury shows how the child *communicates* these thought patterns. Mercury's sign, house, and aspects are primary indicators of the intellect's outward expression. Mercury's developmental cycle occurs from age seven to thirteen. During this cycle of growth, a child focuses on understanding herself and the world in which she lives. Language is mastered; communication skills are refined. During these years, the child will project the qualities of Mercurial energy more strongly.

Mercury in the Signs

Mercury in Aries—This child may be very direct in communication and highly creative mentally. His basic approach may be to get the facts, then go on to something new.

Mercury in Taurus—This child may be reticent to communicate until she has the facts. She will want to be certain before speaking or committing herself to an idea. These are children who observe, then speak.

Mercury in Gemini—This child is quick, witty, and easily distracted. These trivia gatherers like to learn a little about a lot. I think of Mercury in Gemini as the "butterfly mind."

Mercury in Cancer—This child may have a photographic memory, and is often indirect in communication. These children are mentally protective, and are likely to hold back information until they are certain that it is safe to speak.

Mercury in Leo—This child wants to speak with authority and presence, and is usually interested in discussing something he already knows about. The mind becomes easily attached to concepts and ideas. This child may be difficult to persuade once he has made up his mind!

Mercury in Virgo—This child tends to analyze situations before communicating anything and feels the need to speak clearly, distinctly, and properly. Mercury in Virgo sometimes has a mental fence-sitting posture, since the child definitely wants to be right.

Mercury in Libra—This child can communicate beautifully, with flowing images and word-pictures. However, she may be highly indecisive, since much time can be spent weighing options. Therefore, the opinions of others or authoritative sources may be consulted before making commitments.

Mercury in Scorpio—This child will usually probe deeply into subjects and will communicate only when necessary. His mind is fascinated by the mysterious.

Mercury in Sagittarius—This child is prone to blurting out her thoughts. She likes to speak profound truths (as she sees them) and is often interested in learning things which have moral messages. There is an adventurous quality to the mind and distractions can be a problem.

Mercury in Capricorn—This child is disciplined and focused. The child's communication is likely to be concerned with things that have practical value. These children often have common sense in abundance.

Mercury in Aquarius—This child is blessed with an original and abstract mind, and will prefer learning things which can benefit humanity. This child will find communication by electronic means fascinating, and his ideas will likely be rather unusual. One thing you may often hear from the child with Mercury in Aquarius is, "I know." This know-it-all attitude can become very irritating to others at almost any age!

Mercury in Pisces—This child is imaginative, impressionable, and usually quiet. These children will often just answer "yes" or "no" rather than elaborating on ideas so they can get back into their own personal world more quickly.

Mercury's Aspects and Intellectual Development

These basic ideas about Mercury in the signs should give you a concept of how different children communicate their mental energies. A child will talk about things that interest her. The signs of the Moon and Mercury indicate some of these interests, but the planetary aspects and house positions of these energies tell us even more.

Mercury and the Sun

Because Mercury is so close to the Sun in its orbit, the only major aspect possible between these two bodies is the conjunction. When the Sun and Mercury are conjunct in the chart, generally the child will have strong ties between the ego self and the intellect. This can give a powerful boost to the mental energy. Powerful oratorical abilities may be present. Words are expressed dramatically and with authority.

There can be difficulties with this aspect, however, since the child may have problems accepting other's ideas. Teaching him how to listen effectively will prove highly beneficial. Criticism of the child's ideas may make him defensive. In classroom situations, this can create a difficult situation for the teacher. Parents can help the child by teaching him that differences of opinion do not mean that his ideas are not okay.

Mercury and the Moon

Specific aspects between the Moon and Mercury were explored in chapter 6. However, it's important to distinguish the effects between psychological and intellectual expressions. Harmonious, flowing aspects between the Moon and Mercury in the chart will indicate an easy flow with the perceptive, intuitive self and the ability to relate thoughts that are easily understood. Communicating and learning blend easily and harmoniously. Listening is a large part of learning, and harmonious aspects between the Moon and Mercury often enhance listening abilities. This child is aware of the need to relate to both the inside and outside worlds. The feeling nature supports the thinking nature. Changes in the subconscious habit patterns might be easy to bring about, which can facilitate learning about new subjects.

Dynamic aspects between the child's Moon and Mercury are likely to indicate perceptual problems, since emotions tend to get in the way of the thinking process. It may be difficult for the child to share her innermost thoughts without losing something in the translation; hence, a feeling of being misunderstood may arise. Parents need to offer increased support to the child in any new learning situations. These aspects are also likely to create reluctance in learning new subjects. Problems could result if the child changes schools or teachers, and may be notable as learning styles change during milestone years, like going from single teachers and one classroom to changing teachers and classrooms in middle school.

Mercury and Venus

When these two planets contact one another, the child will be drawn to the artistic expression of ideas. The only possible major aspects are the conjunction and sextile. Even the dynamic minor aspect (the semisquare) will enhance the child's artistic abilities, but there may be some frustration in achieving his desired result when this aspect is present.

The child often enjoys listening to or reading poetry or prose. Creative writing should be encouraged at an early age by playing storytelling games with the child. Once in school, she may be especially interested in studying literature. This aspect can be a plus for public speaking skills, and when relating to friends, the child with Mercury-Venus connections may be the one who is the peacemaker.

Developing a genteel manner of speech will be easy for the child with the sextile between Mercury and Venus. In fact, coarse speech may be offensive to this child! He may also give special attention to his handwriting, which could turn out to be quite beautiful. An interest in drawing or calligraphy may be present for those with Mercury conjunct or sextile Venus.

Mercury and Mars

When Mercury and Mars contact one another, the intellect is strongly energized. There is a certain degree of impatience, even with the flowing aspects. Ideas and concepts have to be presented in a concise manner if the child's attention is to be maintained.

Mercury conjunct Mars—With this aspect the mental curiosity is sharpened. The child wants to learn, explore, and experience, and may have trouble with directions like "Wait a minute!" Sometimes she will argue just to keep the mind moving. This argumentative attitude can be quite irritating until the parents realize that the child is simply exercising her mind. For her, an argument is better than no conversation at all! These children usually love to tease.

Mercury semisextile Mars—This aspect suggests a desire to explore new ideas and situations directly and boldly. Ideas which can be grasped quickly will be more interesting than those which require studious effort, unless other aspects to Mercury suggest a tendency toward study.

Mercury semisquare Mars—This child presents a picture of impatience with learning and a desire to explore new things rather than concentrating on something already known. This is fine if he actually has grasped other knowledge, but there may be a tendency to leap ahead into subject material before adequate preparation has been accomplished.

Mercury sextile Mars—With this aspect there can be a pioneering attitude toward learning and an increased enthusiasm for material that is interesting to the child. While this connection can suggest a bright intellect, there can be a lazy attitude toward study—this child may feel that since she seems to grasp ideas rather quickly, study is not necessary. This can work well through the early years in school but can be problematic if she is not motivated to achieve through concentrated efforts in the later school years.

Mercury square Mars—This aspect promotes tremendous mental activity bordering on the hyperactive. Sitting still and focusing for long periods can be frustrating. It's important to allow this child to take a few breaks when studying, as long as he returns to the material after a set period of time. Assuring that the child has adequate time for exercise and physical activity can also be helpful and may actually aid in concentration during the day.

Mercury trine Mars—This aspect adds sharp mentality. A quick learner eager to explore new ideas and concepts, this child may need to be encouraged to push herself, since she may not have to work too hard to achieve in school. This child can, however, show excellent efforts when she is really interested in a subject and may excel in school.

Mercury quincunx Mars—This aspect can indicate problems with hyperactivity. As with other dynamic aspects, a balance between physical exercise, proper diet, and good study habits may require extra efforts on the parts of parent and child. This child may also have little patience with himself in learning situations. If material is not quickly understood, he may lose interest, become frustrated, or simply abandon the material in favor of something else.

Mercury opposite Mars—This aspect will indicate an active mentality and tendency to jump to conclusions. There can be an impatience with learning and she can actually become belligerent or boisterous when bored. Encourage physical activity to burn off unexpressed mental energy.

Mercury and Jupiter

Aspects between Mercury and Jupiter influence the child's intellectual maturation. Jupiter's influence helps the mind assimilate information. Although much of Jupiter's influence is in the social realms of culture and religion, it is also the process by which we integrate larger concepts. The concept of sharing, for example, cannot really be understood as an abstract idea; the child must personally experience how his society views it. Even a child with a sharp mind will be severely limited in attaining a sense of personal identity if he cannot appropriately integrate his thoughts into society.

Jupiter brings expansion of the mind, and when Mercury and Jupiter make a connection in the chart, curiosity, communication, and education may be more important to a child. Regardless of the aspect, these two energy connections can be indicators of a child who talks a blue streak. In fact, keeping the mind (and the voice!) quiet can be quite a challenge.

Mercury conjunct Jupiter—This aspect can signify strong confidence in sharing ideas, and may be an indicator that a child will want to explore communicative skills earlier. She may love to talk and interact with others, and reading can become a favorite pastime. Travel can also be especially rewarding. Many times learning is a passion, and if this child is taught to appreciate learning and is given positive confirmation that knowledge is power, she may choose to make education a high priority.

Mercury sextile Jupiter—This aspect increases confidence in learning abilities and may indicate that he can grasp new subject material quite readily. However, there can be a kind of loafing, since he may not be interested in exerting a lot of effort when confronting new or challenging material. Here, the typical model is the overconfident underachiever—the child who assumes that he knows enough and therefore does not make sufficient effort. If mastering certain material comes easily, then excellence may follow. Applied effort will require careful guidance, and establishing good study habits can add just the right ingredients to allow a child to make the best use of his intellectual abilities.

Mercury square Jupiter—This aspect creates a need to expand personal knowledge, but the child may feel that her mental attributes are somehow falling short of the mark. This can be a signature of the underconfident overachiever. This child may also do or say things which stretch the truth in order to assure that she is reaching or exceeding a benchmark. Sometimes she may feel that unless she excels, something is wrong. This aspect also can be a signal that concentration may be a problem, and the child may be too easily distracted, therefore diluting her efforts and undermining her confidence.

Mercury trine Jupiter—This aspect can be a double-edged sword. While this can be a powerful indicator of intellectual brilliance or a strong mind, there is a danger involved. During the early years, he may speak and read early and may excel remarkably in elementary learning. These things come easily. He may love story-time and can become a marvelous teller of tales or a gifted writer. However, when subject materials begin to demand more concentration and require extra effort, he may fall short of the mark. After all, things have been easy before—why not now? Even more so than with the sextile, the psychological potential behind this learning mode is the overconfident underachiever. The problem and danger lies in the fact that if failures follow, this child can have trouble forgiving himself, since expectations have been shattered. If self-worth is strong, recovery is more easily accomplished. In either case, parents and teachers need to create positive incentives for this child to do his best.

Mercury opposite Jupiter—This aspect shows a strong desire to learn and a restless mind. The feeling that "I don't know enough" can arise early in educational experiences. This attitude or feeling of inferiority can create a situation in which the child is continually enhancing everything she says. Learning to accept any type of personal mediocrity may be very difficult for this child. Distractions can be a problem, since the child may try to learn a little about everything rather than focusing on a limited number of interests. Finishing things can be difficult if she has lost interest. However, there is also the potential of feeling that life is a learning challenge and that as long as there's something to know about, there's a reason for a quest. One would hope that parents and teachers would encourage the quest, but only after adequate preparation for the journey!

Mercury and Saturn

With Mercury aspecting Saturn, mental concentration can be enhanced. The harmonious aspects confer a strong sense of mental discipline and a sharp, reliable memory. The thought processes are more readily accessible and tend to center around areas that are practical and sensible. With dynamic aspects between Mercury and Saturn, the child may not trust his mental abilities. He may feel a sense of severe mental limitation, even if that limitation is not actually present! Sometimes the child may be reluctant to speak or share information for fear that what he says may be inadequate, wrong, or otherwise incomplete.

Mercury conjunct Saturn—This child's ability to focus on a subject or idea can be strengthened. Discipline in learning may be easier, but only if the child is presented with a good model for study and learning. Parents and teachers play a powerful role, and the child may have a strong desire to please these authorities by performing up to their standards.

Mercury sextile Saturn—This child will enjoy the experience of building knowledge and training the mind. Memory can be a talent, and the ability to interrelate concepts and ideas is excellent. Even at a young age, this child may enjoy sharing what she has learned with others and can be an excellent teacher.

Mercury square Saturn—This aspect can prove to be very frustrating for a child. He may sometimes feel that his thoughts and ideas are met with undue criticism. The desire to be right and to gain endorsement by parents and teachers can be especially strong, and when he makes a mistake it can be hurtful and may undermine his confidence. Ultimately, the type of criticism the child receives will largely determine how much he trusts his intellectual abilities. Supportive, constructive criticism can build confidence, but harsh critiques that demand more from the child than he is capable of producing are destructive. This child's esteem and motivation will be damaged by statements like, "You're not meeting your potential." Affirm his potential by rewarding him with praise when efforts command it.

Mercury trine Saturn—This child is likely to take learning very seriously and may take great pride in performing well in school. Writing and communication can flow easily, and learning in a reasonably structured environment may seem more natural than a setting with too much flexibility. However, even in open classroom settings, this child can develop the self-discipline necessary to accomplish the tasks at hand. Practical knowledge may be more interesting than abstracts, but other chart factors may be more indicative of subject preference, like Mercury's sign placement.

Mercury opposite Saturn—This aspect can indicate potentially strong abilities of concentration and mental discipline. However, criticism is likely to feel too harsh, even if it comes as an opportunity to learn. If teachers and parents seem to be excessively critical of this child, she may grow to resent the idea of education or may feel defeated or stupid. Whatever the child's inherent intellectual ability, it can be enhanced by the cultivation of positive mental attitudes. Learning through experience, however, is probably the most appropriate method for her.

Mercury and Uranus

Mercury-Uranus aspects confer brilliance and add an ingenious quality to the intellect. Inventiveness is a dominant trait of these aspects. With flowing aspects, the intuition enhances the mental abilities, inspiring and guiding original thought. The dynamic aspects confer the same qualities, but on a more erratic basis.

Mercury conjunct Uranus—Staying with a subject long enough to master it can be a real challenge. This child loves delving into something new, different, and experimental, but will not enjoy repetition. Easily stimulated, thoughts can scatter like the wind. However, he may be exceptionally sharp and capable of grasping even complex information very quickly. Giving this child every opportunity to progress at his own rate will reap its own rewards, but holding this child back just to satisfy a traditional structure could be frustrating to all concerned.

Mercury sextile Uranus—This aspect is indicative of a clear, sharp intellect and the ability to enjoy a wide variety of learning experiences. There may be a fascination with science and technology and a natural mathematical ability. However, study is not a favorite pastime for this child, since anything that cannot be learned quickly may not garner much attention. Therefore, teaching good study habits early on will be especially helpful in the long run.

Mercury square Uranus—With this aspect a kind of mental hyperactivity is present. While learning can be pure joy, moving quickly is important. For this reason, she may seem to skip through the more tedious subjects, simply content to arrive at the right answer. Unusual subjects will be fascinating, and ultimately a desire to learn about anything may develop. In the early years, provide ample reading material, but also give this child early access to computers. Meanwhile, encouraging organized study habits will provide the kind of structure for this likely brilliant child to shine. Sometimes there are learning disorders suggested by the Mercury-Uranus square, and if a parent or teacher is concerned that a child is displaying keen intellect but not doing well with school, testing for these processing aberrations could be the child's saving grace.

Mercury trine Uranus—This aspect suggests a very quick mind and a good ability to grasp material. Retention is dependent upon other factors. The child will be easily stimulated mentally, but may have some problems focusing the mind. Step-by-step rational thought may not be the way he thinks. The mind assimilates data so quickly that the child may not be aware of all the steps involved— he just has the answer! When asked to explain the reasons behind his thinking, the child may be stumped. Learning mathematical theorems in the later school years will be helpful, although not always enjoyed!

Mercury quincunx Uranus—This aspect is notorious for diverting mental concentration. This child may be working perfectly well in one medium and then suddenly throw all her concentration into something entirely different, just because she was distracted by a different possibility. There can be a kind of genius with this aspect, but determining how to take the impulse to move into a different mental track without undermining ability, agility, or focus requires time and conscious adjustments.

Mercury opposite Uranus—This aspect functions much like a laser-beam thought process. This child has the ability to get right to the heart of material, and will prefer to learn quickly. This aspect also indicates a high potential for losing concentration to distractions, although he may ultimately get back to the material which was the primary focus. Speaking before he has had a chance to think through something is one characteristic of this aspect, and the same is true of answering test questions. It's good for this child to learn to review material before turning it in, and since he will probably be done before most people have gotten halfway through a test, there should be plenty of time to take it twice!

Mercury and Neptune

Mercury-Neptune aspects enhance the use of creative imagery and fantasy. Neptune adds a permeable, highly impressionable quality to the mind. With harmonious aspects between Mercury and Neptune, the intuition can be highly developed and psychic sensitivity is enhanced. The mind is tremendously responsive, and can easily attune itself to inner levels of thought. These children may have imaginary playmates—nonphysical beings who are only imaginary to those who can't see them. I would caution those who would be critical of this awareness to recognize that children have fewer conditioned barriers which would inhibit an awareness of such beings who may indeed exist on other planes!

Once the child begins to relate to others frequently, the ability to link her thoughts with others may be very powerful. These are the kids who can "psych" the teacher in classroom situations and know exactly what to expect on examinations. (It's no problem when you can tune into the teacher's thoughts!) However, the dynamic aspects indicate that the child can tend to imagine a connection which may not be there and is more difficult to define.

Mercury conjunct Neptune—This aspect presents an amazing potential for a child to develop his imagination. The need to exercise this capacity through activities like storytelling, writing, photography, music, drama, or art can be strong, even at a very early age. This child is exceptionally sensitive to the words and energy involved in communication from others, and in the face of positive, loving support will shine. However, when faced with harsh, brutal, or wounding words or negative attitudes, he can shrink away, finding fantasy much more palatable than the real world. With encouragement, he can become a messenger for peace, compassion, and spiritual truth. These things radiate more purely within the consciousness of this child, and need a space to grow. In school, he may enjoy literature and the arts, and interactive, experiential learning situations can be especially helpful.

Mercury sextile Neptune—With this aspect, imaginative thinking can enhance learning. Relating to others may be comfortable, since this child can readily identify with the essence of what is being said, even if the details are not yet clear. Abstract learning and foreign languages can be easily grasped. While there is an indicator that developing communicative skills may seem very natural, this aspect does not add enthusiasm for learning. In fact, there can be a lazy attitude when it comes to applying herself. Unless other factors provide stimulation, this child may try to get by on minimal effort in school!

Mercury square Neptune—This aspect confers the imaginative qualities and sensibilities expected from these two planets in connection, but the square adds an element of tension between the logical thought processes and imaginative or artistic sensibilities. In some instances, this manifests as a child who actually resists his need to fantasize, especially if other factors in the chart would indicate that logic is more comfortable. However, in most cases, this aspect is indicative of the overly imaginative child who may have difficulty with clarity of thinking. There can be a feeling that mental energy is drained, lost, or dissipated in some way. This can be indicative of learning disorders or confusing sensory input. Motivation to learn can be inhibited, especially if there is an organic or other process which makes it difficult for the child to learn and he feels uncertain about his abilities to get things right. Sharing ideas and information in a coherent manner can also be difficult, and there is a potential that the child will withdraw and space out, leaving parents and teachers to wonder how to get through. The doorway may be through the arts, music, or other stimuli.

Mercury trine Neptune—This aspect indicates an easy flow between the logical and fanciful thought processes. Linking the left and right brain hemispheres can be easier, since there is little resistance to the experiential or to the rational levels of learning and expression. The only downfall to this aspect is a quality if low motivation, since the child may prefer the easiest possible route to learning and may do best in situations where she can simply follow a pattern set by others. However, given proper motivation and the development of good study skills, this connection can bring a definite enhancement to learning and ingenuity.

Mercury quincunx Neptune—This aspect adds a desire to think creatively and may indicate a keen interest in music and the arts. However, this aspect is frequently an indicator that a child is likely to miss important details or that he is lacking in motivation if a subject requires extra effort. With time and patience, he can develop a keen mind, and there may simply be some adjustments to make. I often see this aspect present in children who require glasses at an earlier age, but who do not necessarily give an indication to parents or teachers that they are not seeing well. After all, sight is subjective, and if one's vision is compromised it's sometimes difficult to tell since the points of reference are fuzzy!

Mercury opposite Neptune—This aspect suggests a powerful dynamic, with a child's impressionability in overdrive, tending to overwhelm her own ability to think for herself. While there is likely to be a powerful interest in stories, movies, music, and the arts, the desire to escape the harsher realities of life can impede learning since she may spend too much time within herself. Artistic expression should be encouraged, and some structure can be helpful. The level of impact others can make on this child simply cannot be overstated. Careful attention to what she sees, hears, and experiences is absolutely necessary to avoid circumstances that could lead to potentially destructive or unrealistic thinking. Spending time in an earthy, natural environment is often helpful in grounding this child's mental energies. Playing instruments or singing vocal music can help this child confirm her own originality and the fact that she does have a mind of her own!

Mercury and Pluto

Mercury-Pluto contacts indicate mental intensity. The mind probes persistently below the surface, seeking to find the secrets hidden there. With flowing aspects between Mercury and Pluto, the drive to do empirical scientific research may be strong. There is a strong drive to find the root cause, to understand the ultimate who, what, where, when, how, and why. There is a forceful, concentrated learning ability. The dynamic aspects frequently indicate the potential of difficulties in learning which result from biological problems, such as learning disabilities like dyslexia.

Mercury conjunct Pluto—This aspect can add tremendous potential for developing in-depth thinking and persistent mental energy. This child will be the one to turn over the rock to see what's underneath, instead of just walking around or over it! The sciences can be fascinating, and an interest in investigating causes can be present even in the toddler. Parents and teachers should be prepared for the questions which may be difficult or uncomfortable to answer, and when he wants to know something, there's little that can be done to dissuade him. Compulsiveness can be a problem if carried too far, and, if anything, this child may need to learn when to give something a rest. It's also important to give this child permission to hold secrets or to continue thinking through something when he has any uncertainty, since when he feels rushed or pressured there will be a tendency to withhold simply out of stubbornness.

Mercury sextile Pluto—This aspect is indicative of a need to think through things very thoroughly and may also indicate a strengthening of intellectual capacity. Parents and teachers who give her plenty of room to question, probe, and carefully consider ideas while encouraging her to trust the strength of intuitive guidance will aid this child immensely.

Mercury square Pluto—With this aspect, mental persistence can be exceptionally strong. When this child wants to know something, very little will stop the quest. However, there is a tendency toward developing dogmatic and compulsive thinking, and if teachers or parents instruct him in prejudicial thinking or instill ideas which are destructive, this child may carry them too far. I have seen this aspect present in children who have some learning disabilities or sensory impairment, but the capacity to overcome such deficiencies is amazing with this dynamic.

Mercury trine Pluto—This aspect adds significant depth to a child's thinking capacities. Parents and teachers may be surprised at the multidimensional capabilities to the child's thinking, and should encourage her to expand or explore a subject as fully or thoroughly as possible. The ability to link material can be excellent, and studies in history and science alike may provide an excellent opportunity for this child to increase her intellect. Writing and communicative abilities can be exceptional, although it may be later in her education before the full extent of these abilities is realized.

Mercury quincunx Pluto—With this aspect thought processes are more intensified, but there can also be a tendency for the child to divert attention at the wrong times. For example, if his interest in another subject is interfering with the current learning focus, it can be a chore for him to get back on track. There is some potential for learning disabilities or sensory disorders, and the child with this aspect who shows problems with school, reading, or learning may need to be tested. The gift of this aspect is that if there are problems with sensory perception or thought processes, the child has great capacity to make the necessary adjustments and then leap ahead. The life sciences and mysteries may be especially interesting to this child.

Mercury opposite Pluto—This aspect adds strength to the intellectual capacities, but comes with the potential for excessive compulsive qualities to thought processes. If this child is on track with a certain line of thinking and is challenged to change it, the challenger may very well run into strong resistance. This child is not a light thinker! She may also go out of her way to prove someone wrong if they go too far in challenging what she thinks to be correct. Dogged persistence is a good description of the opposition. There is also a suggestion that teachers or parents may present highly opinionated concepts and ideas to this child. But ultimately, if she discovers that these concepts do not fit with her ideas or ideals, there is likely to be a significant break in the mental connection to that individual or school of thought.

House Placement of Mercury

The house placement of Mercury indicates the facets of life and personal development which the child may find most interesting. A child with two or more planets in the 3rd or 9th House will feel a stronger motivation to develop the intellect, regardless of which planetary energies are there. If Saturn is present, there will be a need to learn in order to feel secure. Saturn may also bring a reticence in the approach to learning if placed in the 3rd or 9th house.

We use the house placement of Mercury to determine a child's intellectual curiosities.

Mercury in the 1st House—This placement stimulates an interest in communicating. Also, learning about the self is a strong tendency. This child will enjoy participating in choices about clothing, daily activities, and so on, and will also want to read his baby book or share his picture album with Mom or others, telling stories along the way about himself.

Mercury in the 2nd House—This child likes learning about the world around her. She may also show an interest in learning about the physical environment, nature, and money. An allowance and managing money are an important part of this child's necessary education.

Mercury in the 3rd House—This child will be eager to communicate and share what he knows. Writing skills, storytelling, and reading should be encouraged as early as possible. An interest in sign language and developing manual dexterity may be present.

Mercury in the 4th House—This child will mimic family communication models very strongly. If Mom or Dad use certain gestures, expect to see them from this child quite early in development. She may also enjoy learning crafts and domestic skills like cooking. Invite her to share in projects around home. History may become an interest as she matures in the educational process. She may respond especially well to home schooling.

Mercury in the 5th House—This child needs to make a game of learning. He expresses himself dramatically and will enjoy play-acting. This child can be very witty and may also have an interest in being the center of attention, but only when his confidence is high. While home schooling could be a reasonable option for this child, he will want the company of others when expressing his particular talents. For this reason, if home schooling is the parent's choice, it's crucial to enroll this child in art, music, or dance classes to further these particular abilities.

Mercury in the 6th House—This child can be studious. This child may be more willing to put forth the work necessary to develop the mind, and is more likely to be the one who engages in school projects with some level of interest and a desire to do a good job. Practical subject material may be intriguing, and learning to use tools to increase efficiency will be of interest.

Mercury in the 7th House—This child will show an interest in learning how to effectively communicate, and may enjoy learning in the company of others rather than tackling material on her own. In school, the social aspects of education may be more important to her than learning what the teacher assigns. It's important when this child is assigned working partners at school to develop an ability to understand the nature of the project and each person's responsibilities. If she is coupled with someone who does not do her part or who takes over too much, the child will lose confidence in agreements. This child may be adept at public speaking and debate, and should be encouraged to develop these interests if at all possible.

Mercury in the 8th House—This child is interested in how things work and may enjoy research and mysteries. However, he may not want to tell everything he knows, since the idea of knowing something that others do not confers a sense of personal power. Changing subjects can be a problem if he is deeply interested in one thing and is asked to alter his focus. The manner in which the transition is made can require imagination and patience on the part of teachers and parents.

Mercury in the 9th House—This child may show an early interest in self-expression and communication skills. Exploring and learning foreign languages can be a boost to her intellectual growth. Writing, public speaking, debate, and philosophy can be of special interest. Travel may also be fascinating, as can the study of history. In fact, travel may increase her learning capacity, and cultural interests can be an especially important way to increase intellectual diversity.

Mercury in the 10th House—This child who will want to be recognized for his intellectual abilities. He can also be strongly opinionated, although in the early years he will echo the opinions of those influencing him. For this reason, it's crucial that parents and teachers take clear responsibility for their ideas and methods of sharing them!

Mercury in the 11th House—This child shows an interest in forward-thinking ideas and innovative developments. This child may also enjoy the social aspects of school, and will appreciate the stimulus friends provide. When seeking out confirmation for her ideas, friends will be the logical source, and may ultimately be trusted over parents and teachers!

Mercury in the 12th House—This child can be highly imaginative and artistically inclined. He may prefer a private, closed room for study and will enjoy some serenity when composing ideas or developing thoughts. Meditative practices may seem natural, even in the elementary school years. This placement suggests an impressionable mind, although the sign and aspects of Mercury will indicate how the child responds and uses that impressionability.

Approaches to Learning

Education is a primary feature of childhood, and parents now have more choices in the education of their children. They can choose open classrooms, Montessori methods, Waldorf schools, magnet schools, home schooling, vocational training, and more. Some parents are even teaching their babies to read before they are two years old!

Some children will be better suited to one learning experience, while others will learn more easily in a different situation. Exploring the energies of the Moon, Mercury, Jupiter, and Saturn will illuminate which approach would best suit a particular child. If the indicators are that a child needs more structure (such as Mercury in Capricorn or in aspect to Saturn), then more traditional methods may be suitable. Applying the concepts found in the chart to the learning situations being considered can be rather easy when you get right down to it. Simply remember that it's important that the situation, philosophy, and teachers reflect the kinds of attitudes and structures that will best support the child's learning style, interests, and intellectual potentials.

Moon Speed

The Moon's speed in the chart fundamentally affects the child's approach to learning. The Moon moves at variable speeds in her rotation around the Earth. If you have a computer-calculated chart, the speed of the Moon is probably indicated. If you calculated your own chart by traditional calculation methods, you determined the Moon's speed before you could calculate the exact placement by degree and sign of the zodiac.

Astrologer Marc Edmund Jones first introduced me to the idea of Moon speed as a variable in learning during one of the workshops I attended with him in the 1970s. He suggested that speeds above thirteen degrees ten minutes (13:10) should be considered as fast, whereas Moon speeds below this demarcation would be considered slow. The individual with a fast Moon seems to be eager to confront the experiences of life. These children are the ones who may jump into new situations, often spontaneously.

With the slower Moon speeds (less than 13:10), the child may be somewhat reluctant to approach new situations. These children tend to be observers who only enter into new situations after a period of cautious consideration. After that, they may do just fine with their learning, but if forced to move too quickly may lose confidence.

Moon speeds which are extremely fast (above fourteen and one-half degrees: 14:30) seem to be associated with steel-trap minds, and suggest the ability to learn extremely quickly and retain practically forever. If a learning situation allows this child to get bogged down, for example, if the child has to slow down to wait for others to catch up, she can become very frustrated with the experience.

Coupling this information with the placement and aspects of Mercury, parents may gain a clearer understanding of why their child performs well in school or basically dislikes it.

Jupiter and Learning

While Jupiter's placement indicates of basic confidence and optimism, it also can be helpful when determining learning styles and needs. The sign and house placement of Jupiter will show where and how a child expresses confidence and what types of stimulation will build his learning skills. Jupiter's house placement is described in chapter 9. However, since sign placement can influence the kinds of situations which help a child develop enthusiasm for learning, they are noted below.

Jupiter in the Signs and Learning Styles

Jupiter in Aries—This child needs plenty of independence when learning and will appreciate challenging games as part of the learning process. He needs a place to stand out and show leadership abilities.

Jupiter in Taurus—This child will appreciate an educational experience which blends practical values into learning. She may enjoy more one-on-one contact from teachers.

Jupiter in Gemini—Jupiter in Gemini stimulates a need to learn through developing the rational mind and may indicate little tolerance for subjects which call on or stimulate emotional response. However, this child can be open to a wide variety of information, and if he can see the logical value, may even learn to appreciate the arts.

Jupiter in Cancer—This child learns best in a situation which seems to be based on traditional values. Teachers are likely to seem like a natural extension of the child's personal support system, and sentimental ties may result to favorite teachers.

Jupiter in Leo—Jupiter in Leo will stimulate a strong respect and admiration for others who seem to possess knowledge, culture, and status. Subjects that allow development of leadership abilities may be interesting.

Jupiter in Virgo—Jupiter in Virgo can suggest that a child will be able to adapt well to the work involved in completing her educational endeavors. She may actually be interested in developing good study habits!

Jupiter in Libra—This child loves the social aspect of school, and later on may enjoy subjects like law, the arts, and literature. His sense of justice can be strongly developed.

Jupiter in Scorpio—Jupiter in Scorpio suggests an approach to learning which is based on how deeply the child is connected to the material. Those subjects which are interesting may hold her focus with great intensity. However, the things she does not like may be disliked with a passion!

Jupiter in Sagittarius—This child just likes to learn. The idea that knowledge is power is no mystery to this child, and he will also appreciate having every opportunity to develop his intellectual abilities to their fullest extent.

Jupiter in Capricorn—Jupiter in Capricorn confers a need for well-defined structure in educational experiences. Subjects that have practical value may garner the greatest enthusiasm, and those things which seem too abstract may be virtually ignored.

Jupiter in Aquarius—This child is enthusiastic about developing independence as quickly as possible, and if education seems to be the way to do it, then she may throw tremendous energy behind accelerating her learning. Alternative, open school situations may work best, as long as some reasonable and logical steps are involved to help her maintain a sense of priorities and progress.

Jupiter in Pisces—This child can be very idealistic, and that idealism can extend to teachers and to the educational process itself. The learning atmosphere will have a significant impact on this child's ability to grasp and retain information.

In Conclusion

By blending the needs of the Moon, Mercury, Saturn, and Jupiter in the chart, we can determine some excellent approaches to a child's education. The child with Saturn positively contacted by the Moon and/or Mercury would probably do well in open classroom situations, since self-discipline would be easily expressed. The child with Mercury-Uranus aspects might enjoy some structure, but would not want to be held back by slower students. These children might do well in accelerated classes which allow the child to move at his own pace while still receiving adequate supervision and guidance from his teachers.

If a child shows a great deal of fear about learning (harsh aspects from Saturn or Pluto to the Moon and/or Mercury), the parents would do well to arrange loving, nonjudgmental guidance for the child. This might be easily accomplished through a counselor or aide who works with learning problems. Many learning problems have their roots in emotional, not intellectual, difficulties. Some learning problems may also have their roots in physical disturbances.

Parents often judge the child by her performance in school. Even preschool children can feel pressured by the parents to perform ("Say your ABCs." "Can you count to one hundred?").

Encouragement and testing are two different things. Small children do not like to be tested—life is enough of a test for them! They do enjoy learning, but need to be encouraged to learn at their own pace. Finding that pace is one of the primary tasks of parents and teachers. Allowing the child to feel comfortable with his strengths and limitations is important in aiding the optimum development of the child's intellect.

8

Creative Self-Expression and Talents

Defining Creativity

Most parents hope that their children develop some sort of special talent. Every child has the potential to develop her strengths, and whether the strongest talents lie in the arena of the arts, sciences, practical applications of ideas, healing, or human relations, the experience of awakening creativity in childhood is usually centered on things that are enjoyable for the child. Of course, special interests do not always lead to careers, but are, more importantly, expressions which allow the spirit to fly freely, opening the heart to joy! On a practical level, many of these things require instruction or other means to exercise the interests. For the parents, this usually means a sizable outlay of cash for the integral instruction, in addition to the encouragement and patience necessary to foster a child's curiosities. For the child, it means discipline, time, and energy.

Most people find it difficult to determine exactly which creative talents their child possesses, especially when she offers no overt signals. Under these circumstances, it is easiest for the parents to push the child toward the creative directions most attractive to them personally. They may not even consider whether or not the child has any real talent or interest in these areas. However, in some instances a child will have a particular interest or desire that she expresses with some passion. Still, it's very likely that a child will alter these passions—sometimes as quickly as the wind changes!

The child's astrological profile is an excellent guide to his special interests and abilities. Using this informative tool can help eliminate an extended, and potentially expensive, "talent search" by the parents. It can help offer a child several alternatives that will not only provide creative outlets, but enhance his psychological strengths as well.

Among other things, I studied piano as a young girl. The studio was one of the most respected in our city, and the program was rigorous. Our teacher, a grande dame in her sixties, was very demanding. To attend a lesson unprepared was to be met with a reprimand, no lesson, and a harsh phone call to Mother or Dad. In our music theory classes, my fellow students and I shared horror stories of what happened "the time I forgot a Bach invention halfway through."

While I was persistent in my desires to study music and piano, most of my compatriots were not really excited about studying music—it was just "something Mom and Dad wanted me to do." I remember one young boy, about age ten, who said he really wanted to study ballet. His dad "freaked," however, and said that if he was going to have anything moving to music, it would be his fingers! This example illustrates how easy it is for parents to limit their children's natural development without even intending to do so.

If we are to give our children the opportunity to become whole, powerful beings, then creative self-expression must be a free-flowing part of their personal power. Through the astrological chart, we gain a sense of the child's multilevel needs. We can understand the basic qualities that make up the personality, and can better guide the child in the blossoming of his creative potential.

Creativity involves attunement to the inner realm through imagination and intuition. A child's fantasies must be expressed through her natural abilities, whether they are manifested through the voice, the hands, the entire body, or other means. I find that most people I ask about creative talents or artistic interests think that they don't have any! They categorize "creative people" as artists, musicians, actors, or others who make their living in the fine arts.

However, creativity can take many forms outside this narrow definition. The key is tuning in to the imagination, then expressing it physically. Creativity requires receptivity to our Higher Selves and the surrender of our physical selves to our particular creative flow. To dance with the Muse can be exhilarating and allows an individual to merge with elements of the Self which are truly magical. This brings a completeness that balances the body, mind, and spirit.

A child needs energy to execute his talents, the discipline to learn the necessary skills and, hopefully, some type of reward for his accomplishments. Developing the creative flow helps us reach for the best within ourselves. This instills confidence, personal power, and inner strength. It is not necessary to think that a child will become a world-class artist, but it is important to give him a sense of the connection to his inner being which can bring balance to his life throughout his days.

The primary areas to examine when determining creative talents are the 5th House, any planets in this house, and the sign on the 5th House cusp. Venus, her sign, house placement, and aspects will also indicate child's particular artistry. (Venusian qualities and interests are explored in depth later in this chapter.) Mars shows the type of available drive and energy the child has to execute these talents. Saturn adds discipline and focus to the creative efforts. Uranus, Neptune, and Pluto represent the ability to develop the inner awareness necessary for the tasks.

Creativity and the Planets

All of the planetary energies are involved to some extent in the creative process. The factors noted above, however, are the best indicators of creative artistry within the individual. The basic creative impulse suggested by each planetary energy is defined below.

The Sun—The Sun, which is the Divine Spark, confers the drive to create. It gives the ego its unique creative identity.

The Moon—The Moon's receptivity is also part of the creative flow. It is through the conscious conditioning of the subconscious processes that we connect ourselves with the inner and Higher Self. The Moon also indicates the thought forms of the individual. Study the sign in which the Moon is placed to understand where the child is when she goes inside herself.

Mercury—Mercury is involved in the creation of ideas and the communication of creative concepts. If Mercury is placed on the angles of the chart, the child will be likely to communicate his creative ideas to others with greater urgency and ease. Mercury's creative impulse can be seen through writing, public speaking, and use of manual dexterity.

If Mercury and Jupiter are in aspect to each other, the child may be interested in journalism. Inspirational writing and speaking could also be good creative outlets.

Mercury's connection to Saturn adds a more practical quality and can provide a kind of restraint. However, sometimes Mercury-Saturn flowing aspects show an interest in crafts.

Connections to the transpersonal planets give Mercury's energy a link to the collective unconscious. This may confer an ability to tune into the masses. If writing skills are developed by the child who has Mercury contacting the outer planets, she could become a translator of people's unconscious needs. These types of skills are necessary for the creative writer. This attunement is also helpful if the individual is interested in mass media or advertising.

Linked by aspect to Uranus, Mercury translates intuitive impulses into rational thought. This is the "original thinker," the inventive, ingenious mind. These children may be drawn to creative areas of television, radio, or other electronic media. Computer programming may be a form of creative expression.

Aspecting Neptune, Mercury's creativity is more transcendent. Poetry and prose are likely creative expressions, along with photography and music. Acting is also a strong possibility.

With Mercury aspecting Pluto, the mind probes deeply. Creativity could involve transformational thought, introspection, and regeneration. Mystery writing, science fiction, and psychological dramas could probably prove intriguing for this child.

Jupiter—Jupiter instills confidence in the Self. The child with strong, supportive Jupiter aspects will instinctively want to share his creative expression with the world. There is a natural enthusiasm that can be quite contagious!

Jupiter strengthens a child most when found in flowing aspects to the Sun, Moon, and Venus. She will probably trust in a Higher Power to provide for her needs.

The 5th House

The 5th House is called the house of creative self-expression. It is below the horizon, which indicates that it involves internalized energy. The 5th House is also the area of the chart which signifies the giving of love, which can be expressed through creative activities.

The polar opposite of the 5th House, the 11th House, tells us about receiving love. It balances the 5th House by bringing in feedback from the outside world. This is the house of friends, who applaud us when we succeed, encourage us when we are down, and inspire us to continue. This is also where we create our goals.

Most of all, the 5th House represents one's potential to have fun, and here we learn to develop a playful facet of the self. Creativity flows most easily and is most beneficial when the child is doing something he really loves to do. Through the creative process, the child opens to greater self-love. This increases any child's sense of personal worth and gives more power to the creative efforts. While this facet of the self can indicate artistic leanings, it is also the place where hobbies are explored and exercised.

When examining the 5th House to understand the underlying creative expression of the child, first look to the sign on the 5th House cusp. Consider the qualities of that sign. Aquarius, for example, is inventive, futuristic, and avant-garde. These qualities would permeate the creative self. Then, study the planets in the 5th House, along with their signs and aspects. If there are no planets there, look to the planet that rules the sign on the cusp. Find that planet in the chart, along with its house, sign, and aspects. This indicates the child's underlying theme in creative expression.

The Chart of Mozart

As an example, let's explore the chart of a person whose creativity is well known and still influential in our lives today. In the chart of Wolfgang Amadeus Mozart, the 5th House contains the Sun, Mercury, and Saturn in Aquarius. His sense of individuality (Sun) was strongly tied to creative expression in a unique and original form (Aquarius). We know that Mozart was a prodigy, and frequently these types of patterns that show a focus of energy in a Stellium indicate prodigious abilities.

The planets in his 5th House are all conjunct, uniting willpower (Sun), communication (Mercury), and discipline (Saturn) in his creative self-expression. These form a Stellium in the sign of Aquarius, and it was the strength of these Aquarian qualities that prompted his ability to tune in to the collective consciousness of humanity.

Aspecting these planets is Neptune in Leo in the 11th House, which opposes the Sun, Mercury, and Saturn. This opposition challenged the tendency of these three energies to become overly structured, encouraging Mozart to surrender his artistry to the flow of his Higher Self. Through Neptune's realm, he was able to become a channel for divine energy. When listening to much of Mozart's music, it is easy to flow into a space of heightened consciousness—to let go and feel spirits lifting.

January 27, 1756
Salzburg, Austria
8:00 P.M. LMT
47N48   13E02
Tropical
Koch
"AA"

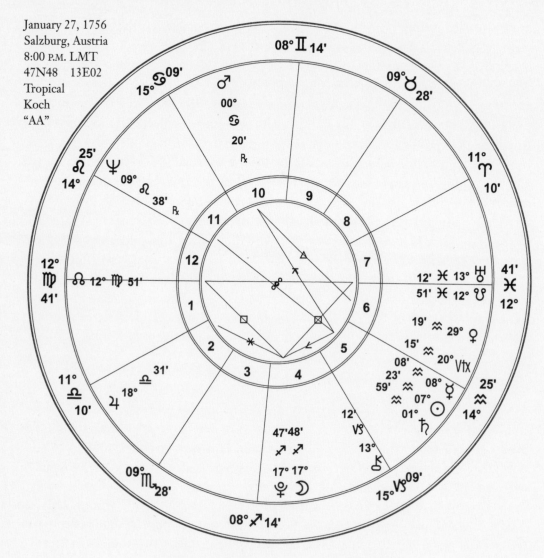

Wolfgang Amadeus Mozart's Natal Chart

To further delineate the planets in the 5th House, it's important to follow the other aspects to the planetary energies in this house. Mars in the 10th House in Cancer forms a quincunx (150 degrees) aspect to Saturn in the 5th House. This aspect proved to be frustrating to the Saturn elements in Mozart's life. His assertiveness (Mars) was irritating to his need for structure (Saturn), impelling him to try different outlets for his creativity. While his father may have taught him that discipline and proper behaviors would be a necessary part of his success, he may have resisted the inhibitions he felt from his father's attitudes. Their relationship was a difficult one, although an integral part to Mozart's artistic development. Yet later, when he was on his own, Mozart found that the constraints of society were a highly frustrating element to the kinds of music he wanted to compose and play. Necessity (Saturn) frustrated his personal drive (Mars).

Finally, the Sun, Mercury, and Saturn form a trine (120 degrees) aspect to the Midheaven in Mozart's chart. This is a powerful support system for creative expression and vocation. It made recognition for his talents easy to achieve.

On the cusp of the 5th House in Mozart's chart is Capricorn. This lends discipline, structure, and consistency to his artistry. This theme is further emphasized by the conjunction of Saturn to the Sun and Mercury. Both Capricorn and Saturn prefer to do things perfectly, and Mozart was known to have produced entire musical scores written note perfect on the first draft!

There are, of course, many other factors in Mozart's chart which had bearing upon his life and creativity, but his life is an excellent example of how the 5th House can be indicative of talents and their development.

When No Planets Are in the 5th House

In our next example, we find a chart which contains no planets in the 5th House. This does not infer that this individual was not creatively expressive, though! Scorpio is on the cusp of this house, adding transformation and intensity to the creative flow. Scorpio is an exceptionally creative sign.

Scorpio's planetary ruler is Pluto, which is found in the 12th House in Cancer. Pluto's energy comes from the depths of the psyche and can be profoundly effective in stimulating reactions from others. The placement of Scorpio on the 5th indicates a strong attunement to the collective unconscious, an ability to reach people in the deepest recesses of themselves. Her energy could also bring about transformational change in others.

Pluto's aspects are numerous. First, Pluto conjuncts the Ascendant in Cancer, and also makes a wide conjunction to Venus in the 1st House. Additionally, Pluto trines Uranus in Pisces in the 10th House and the Pisces Midheaven. Finally, Pluto squares Jupiter in Libra in the 4th House. Not only is the intensity of emotional expression strong, but the essence of the Self-projection (1st House) as the artist (Venus) is enhanced.

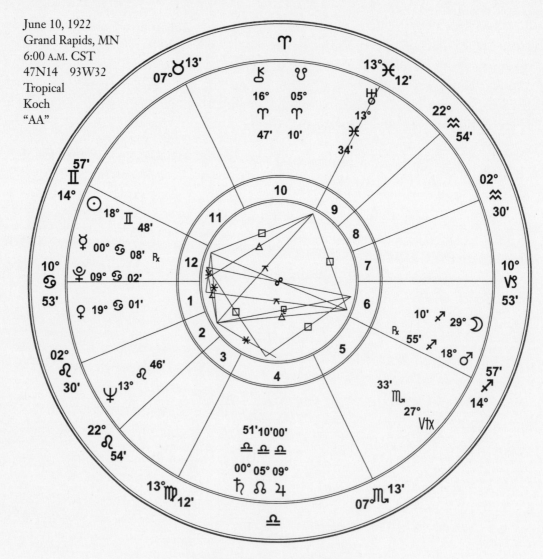

June 10, 1922
Grand Rapids, MN
6:00 A.M. CST
47N14   93W32
Tropical
Koch
"AA"

Judy Garland's Natal Chart

With the T-Square between Mercury in Cancer, Saturn in Libra, and the Moon at 29 degrees Sagittarius, there is frustration expressing the highest needs. But this is overcome by the willingness to take a chance on asserting her uniqueness, illustrated by a second T-Square between the Sun, Mars, and Uranus.

The personality expression (Ascendant), vocation (Midheaven), and basic security system (IC) are all involved in a need to be creatively expressive. The powerful, vital energy with which these needs are expressed is enhanced by the Sun, Mars, and Uranus T-Square.

The Chart of Judy Garland

The example described above is the chart of Judy Garland. Garland played the role of Dorothy in *The Wizard of Oz*. In this role, she carried humanity's consciousness into a magically transformed world. Even in her adult career, she continued to be known for her landmark role as Dorothy. She later portrayed the stereotypical all-American girl in a series of roles, creating a model emulated by an entire generation.

Venus and Creativity

Venus' expression of artistry is also important in a creative context. This is the energy which allows us to experience and express our feelings. While the Moon represents feeling, Venus represents emotion—the expression of feeling. Venus also represents beauty, a quality which lies within each of us and which we all need to feel and express.

Venus in the Signs: Artistic and Creative Expressions

The sign in which Venus is placed offers input concerning the artistic gifts of the child. Venus in Leo is artistically dramatic and bold. Venus in Pisces is sensitive, flowing, musical, and transcendent. Venus in Capricorn flows in a more structured manner, with classical art forms often preferred. In Table 10, the correspondence between the sign Venus occupies and the child's artistic leanings are noted. These are only intended as basic guidelines to the analysis of creative artistry, and indications that are similar to those listed should certainly be included in your analysis of the possibilities of Venusian expression.

Venus Aspects

We also look to the planets that contact Venus by aspect to further define how this energy may be enhanced or inhibited. These aspects illustrate the support the Venusian energy receives or the obstacles which it may encounter. A strongly aspected

SIGN	ACTIVITIES
Aries	Jewelry-making, designing hats, hairdressing, glassblowing and glass-work, metal-etching, ceramics, woodburning, public speaking, drums, athletic dancing
Taurus	Singing and music, painting and drawing, flower gardening, making confections, jewelry-making, clay sculpting, pottery
Gemini	Writing, making models, puppetry, computer games (creating original games), caricature drawing, debate and oratory, broadcasting, violin, guitar, prestidigitation (magic tricks), wind instruments
Cancer	Cooking, gardening, watercolors, jewelry-making (especially with silver), pottery, doll-making, singing, water ballet, photography, knitting and sewing
Leo	Acting, circus performing, movie-making, jewelry-making (especially with gold), directing, persuasive speaking, creating games
Virgo	Writing, public speaking, sewing, sculpting, drafting, piano, voice, anatomical drawing, fine-line drawing and etching, calligraphy, making models and miniatures, crafts, percussion instruments
Libra	Acting, painting and drawing, making confections, fashion design, flower-arranging, music, writing poetry
Scorpio	Magic acts, dancing, painting, writing (especially mysteries), gardening (especially growing bulb flowers), piano, underwater photography, guitar, bass guitar, cello
Sagittarius	Writing and journalism, dancing, animal training (especially horses), broadcasting, public speaking, promoting others
Capricorn	Classical music, music composition, wood-working, gardening, comedy, cartooning, ice sculpting, ice skating and ice dancing, figure skating, pottery, crafts, creations with crystals
Aquarius	Music composition, astrology, synthesized music, ice skating, computer programming, anything to do with television and radio, innovative art forms, painting
Pisces	Dance, ballet, acting, singing, painting, photography, swimming, harp, guitar and ethnic instruments, mime, make-up and costume design, ventriloquism, animation, visionary art

Table 10. Venus in the Signs: Creative Focus.

Venus, regardless of the nature of the aspects, will indicate a desire to be more personally expressive or to meet the challenges of self-expression.

Venus and the Sun

The only major aspect is the conjunction. However, the Sun can also be semisextile to Venus, which is a much weaker connection and usually operates in a very unconscious manner during childhood. With the Sun conjunct Venus, the sense of self is expressed with grace and charm in a refined, artistic manner. With this aspect, the child may at times be uncertain of her creative potential since the need to please and to be liked can add hesitation ("does someone else approve?").

The Sun gives a dramatic power to artistic expression, while Venus makes beauty an important part of the self-concept. Even minor aspects between the Sun and Venus may indicate an interest in performing, with the dynamic vitality of the Sun boosting the artistic energy of Venus. This would be helpful in acting, public speaking, or modeling.

Venus and the Moon

Venus aspected by the Moon involves a deep need to be creative and to express inner feelings in a way which others will see and understand. The child should be offered ample creative projects, even at a young age. These aspects often confer talents in the more emotionally evocative art forms, especially music.

Venus conjunct the Moon—This child will be especially expressive and may project a powerful aura of creativity. Doing things which reach the emotions of others will be meaningful, and whatever the form of creative expression, he will likely put himself fully into the experience. There's also a lot invested in what he does, and the need for approval is very strong.

Venus sextile the Moon—With this aspect an ease of expression is present. A love of the arts can be present even at an early age, and exposing this child to as many forms of creativity as possible will enhance her sense of connection to the world. In addition to using the fine arts for self-expression, she may enjoy decorating, cooking, gardening, and flower-arranging.

Venus square the Moon—This child can have a strong need for approval and sense of inferiority or lack of perfection which can block creative flow. However, this child may still be very artistic and will be likely to crave experiences that feed that artistic sensibility. The square aspect is a motivator and a child with this aspect may be more artistically expressive since the desire to objectify the Venusian energy is very strong.

Venus trine the Moon—This aspect can show strong artistic leanings and talents, but the motivation to bring these into form may be lacking. This is a lazy aspect, indicating that he may enjoy doing the things that come easily, but he shies away from expressions which require effort or competitiveness.

Venus opposite the Moon—This child will be drawn to that which is beautiful and may have a strong need to express her emotions through artistry. While highly competitive situations may block her confidence in expression, encouragement from parents and teachers can provide a positive platform for developing talents. The conflict created by the opposition to Venus can in itself be the impetus for the child to explore creative outlets, if only to release some of the tension she feels inside!

Venus and Mercury

Mercury contacting Venus adds to the communicative nature of the creative flow. There may be talents in writing or speaking. Poetry and prose can be easy expressions, especially with the sextiles between Mercury and Venus.

Look to the elemental nature of the planets. If they are in air signs, writing beautiful words that communicate the idea of love may be easy, but any abstract forms of art may be easier. In fire signs, inspirational writing is more expressive. If there are different elements, blend those concepts to understand the underlying creative impetus. Encourage writing in all forms when Mercury-Venus aspects are present.

The child's handwriting may be artistic, with art forms such as calligraphy having appeal. Mercury is connected to the hands, so the hands themselves may be instruments of artistic expression. Crafts and needlework are often enjoyed. The speaking voice is often melodic. Encourage the child to read aloud to you. Later on, he might enjoy giving poetry readings or competing in speech contests in school. Singing may also be enjoyable, and could be something he will want to refine.

Venus conjunct Mercury—This aspect adds grace and style to verbal communication and writing skills and may indicate powerful artistic capabilities. If in earth signs, this may be seen as a child who enjoys sculpting, while in air signs, painting, etc. A melodious voice may become his trademark as well.

Venus sextile Mercury—This aspect can stimulate a desire to explore the arts and develop writing skills. This child may not be especially fond of working on the more difficult aspects of refining creativity, but doing things for pure enjoyment may be sufficient. He may not care so much about perfection as simply getting into the experience!

Venus square Mercury—This aspect can also indicate strong creative leanings, although a child may need extra encouragement or time to develop the abilities necessary to fully express those talents.

Venus trine Mercury—This child may have a definite preference for beautiful things and beautiful people. Harsh words and crass behaviors can be off-putting, and she is not likely to feel at all comfortable in situations she finds distasteful. This aspect can indicate creative talent that could be even further developed if properly stimulated. It is not likely that this child will want to push herself unless she can see the real value in it.

Venus opposite Mercury—With this aspect the creative impulse is powerful, and he may be especially adept in writing and communication. This can be a strong indicator of the potential to actualize creativity, since the opposition aspect requires objectification and expression in order to be satisfied.

Venus and Mars

Venus-Mars contacts give an assertive, direct quality to the creative flow. Drums and percussion instruments are strong expressions of Venus-Mars contacts. Athletic dancing might be enjoyable. More athletic forms of Venusian expression such as gymnastics or tap and other vigorous dancing could provide good outlets for the planetary energy. Mars also indicates cutting, and he may enjoy working with paper and scissors, carving, metal work, or jewelry-making.

Venus conjunct Mars—This aspect suggests strong energy directed toward creativity. There may be an exceptional talent in dance, and in the visual arts this child will be boldly expressive.

Venus sextile Mars—This aspect adds confidence to a child's creative expression. Regardless of the art forms chosen, she may be quick to progress toward the more refined elements of creativity rather easily.

Venus square Mars—This aspect illustrates inner frustration when expressing creativity. However, this aspect does not indicate a lack of talent, but more likely a problem directing it in the best possible way. Attention to grace, style, and flow will be helpful, whether he is singing, dancing, speaking, or working in the garden. Exercises like dance or martial arts can help him feel more connected between the emotional and physical qualities of expression. Otherwise he may feel like a klutz, with physical awkwardness leading to potentially embarrassing situations and more self-conscious behavior.

Venus trine Mars—This aspect can illustrate natural talents in the arts, but may also simply indicate an ease in self-expression, regardless of the form it takes. There can be some laziness, but because Mars expresses as action, it's unlikely that she will be exceptionally lazy. Still she may have a limit to the amount of hard work she is willing to do!

Venus opposite Mars—This aspect can add an edge to a child's personality, and may indicate a tendency to be competitive in artistic or creative endeavors. He will want to be first, the leader or the groundbreaker and may not like following in the footsteps of anybody else. Learning grace and flow can be helpful. For that reason, attention to body movement in expressions like dance, gymnastics, or martial arts can help him integrate the functions of the mind, heart, and body.

Venus and Jupiter

Venus-Jupiter aspects confer confidence, especially when they are harmonious and flowing. This child may attract the support of gifted teachers as part of her artistic expression, since these contacts are indicative of attracting support. This child may be easily inspired by a teacher or other mentor. There can be a love of travel and reading. Writing may be a strong talent, and so may public speaking. She can also be a positive supporter of others. This is a helpful connection to find in the chart of a cheerleader!

With the flowing aspects, it's easier for a child to know his limits, although he will have a desire to gain attention and will definitely appreciate praise when he does well. The dynamic aspects can indicate impatience with the process of developing creative refinement, and there can be a lack of focus or discipline unless other qualities in the chart indicate that potential.

Other Aspects to Venus

It has been my experience that some situations do not reach a child's awareness until she reaches or nears maturity. The accessibility and awareness of the energies and self-expression we define in the personal planets is greater during childhood than the connection to Saturn and the outer planets. While specific aspects do have their different indications, I have simply not observed a huge difference between a Venus-Saturn square and a Venus-Saturn opposition in terms of the way a child will perceive experiences associated with these energy expressions. The same is true of the flowing aspects. What is observable and seems to translate to real life awareness for a child is that there is a distinctive difference between harmonious contacts and frustrating contacts. For that reason, I define the remaining aspects from Venus to Saturn and the transpersonal planets in these simpler terms—flowing aspects or dynamic aspects.

Venus and Saturn

Venus-Saturn contacts bring discipline and structure to artistic expression. The flowing aspects can develop powerful abilities to discipline artistic efforts, thereby perfecting the skills necessary to become outstanding. The child may show special talents in the classical art forms with harmonious aspects between Venus and Saturn. There is also a strong sense of the business end of the arts, and he may understand early that things which are done well are more worthwhile.

Dynamic aspects between Venus and Saturn may stimulate the child to be excessively critical of her own efforts, thus restricting the creative flow and causing feelings of frustration. There can be a kind of procrastination present, with the child waiting until she feels that her efforts will meet with approval before expressing them or sharing what she has created. Creative talents may be overly structured and spontaneity can be lost or diluted. There can be a fear that she will disappoint someone whose endorsement carries great significance.

Venus and Uranus

Venus-Uranus aspects add a unique flair to a child's artistry. Tastes will be unusual, futuristic, and sometimes strange! The untried is fascinating. Applications of technological innovations to art may be strong (e.g., synthesized music, computer games, electronic art, desktop publishing). This child can be creatively innovative and sometimes prodigious in his artistic expression.

One factor which can be frustrating with Venus-Uranus contacts is the inability to focus and concentrate. Spontaneous inspiration may distract this child from completing the artistic project at hand. Part of the problem can also be that to this child, one form of expression is not quite right. A young boy comes to mind who has Venus quincunx Uranus in his chart. By age fifteen, he had "studied"—to use the term loosely!—piano, harp, oboe, violin, flute, and guitar. His mother, who described her son's room as "the attic of the local music store," was becoming rather upset—he had just requested a electronic keyboard and synthesizer for Christmas! The electronically enhanced keyboard seemed like the ultimate choice, however, since it can produce an endless variety of sounds. I encouraged her to buy it. Two years later, he was still working with electronic instruments, and was adapting his violin to run through his synthesizer! This was a perfect use of Venus quincunx Uranus.

Venus and Neptune

Venus-Neptune aspects bring sensitivity, mysticism, and vision to the creative expression. Venus-Neptune aspects are often most easily expressed through music, although painting, acting, and dance are also excellent outlets for this energy. With contacts between Venus and Neptune, the child can apply creative visualization very effectively. If the aspects are flowing, these visualizations will be even more easily realized.

Venus-Neptune connections are strong indicators of dramatic talents. There can be an outstanding ability to project a beautiful image. This lends itself to modeling or other situations in which a photogenic appearance is important. An appreciation for the beautiful and awe-inspiring is definitely present in the heart of this child.

The dynamic aspects between Venus and Neptune indicate a need to express the inner self creatively, yet something always seems to get lost in the translation. It may be difficult for parents or others to relate to what the child is trying to express artistically. With training, this confusing outflow can be more easily clarified.

The sensitive refinement of Venus-Neptune is usually attracted to the transcendent qualities in film-making, visual art, and in music. This child is a visionary artist.

Venus and Pluto

Venus-Pluto contacts bring intensity, power, and passion to artistic expression. There is a sensuality that could be expressed through painting (especially through the use of heavier mediums such as acrylics and oils). Transforming stone into statue is an excellent outlet for Venus-Pluto. However, earlier expressions can be seen in clay work or pottery-making. This child may also enjoy building sand castles, since digging into the sand and transforming sand and water into a work of art can be especially gratifying!

She can also create something new from something old. I have a client with a Venus-Pluto conjunct whose passion is collecting old lace, which she uses in her original clothing designs.

Sometimes a child with Venus-Pluto connections can inspire transformational change in others through his use of artistic expression. With dynamic aspects between Venus and Pluto, the child must learn how to express intensity without alienating his audience. The dynamic aspects can also indicate a mistrust of his artistic abilities and a strong tendency to destroy what he does not like or feels is below his standards. With any Venus-Pluto aspect, a child may want to keep something under wraps until he feels satisfied that it's ready for exposure. The child has to feel good about it, since exposing vulnerabilities can be difficult, and, after all, creative expression is a very personal thing!

Venus in the Houses and Creativity

With these basic ideas, we begin to see the primary factors which determine a child's creative abilities. Venus' placement by house tells us much about the child's creative artistry and will also show where she seeks approval and endorsement for her efforts.

Venus in the 1st House—This child will want to present a beautiful image to the world. This child's manner of dress, action, and speaking are likely to be refined.

Venus in the 2nd House—This child will want to make or do things which are appreciated and have a tangible value. "See what I made, Mommy?!" definitely requires a response, and may be accompanied by the need for some reward. Hugs and acknowledgment fall into the safe category!

Venus in the 3rd House—This child needs to express creative ideas and may have great pride in developing his handwriting. Writing and verbal communication can be inherent forms of his artistry.

Venus in the 4th House—This child needs approval by the family for her talents and creative endeavors.

Venus in the 5th House—This placement can be an indicator of a powerful need to dramatize creativity. He needs to do things which are not only enjoyable, but which give him a chance to show off.

Venus in the 6th House—This placement often indicates an interest in crafts and a love of working with and utilizing tools or instruments.

Venus in the 7th House—This child is more comfortable exercising creative skills and expression when somebody else is around to share the experience.

Venus in the 8th House—This child may be drawn to creative endeavors which are involved with restoration. This is also a good placement for individuals who can bring something out of an object. For example, using driftwood's natural shapes as a backdrop for painting the face of an owl, wolf, or even a seascape can be the kind of expression typical of Venus in the 8th House.

Venus in the 9th House—This child will love finely written and beautifully inspirational words. She may desire to develop communication skills like public speaking, and journalistic writing could be enjoyable. Encourage this child to keep a diary.

Venus in the 10th House—This child may want to develop an artistic career, or at least have some public exposure of his artistic talents. Approval from family is very important, and pleasing teachers may also be crucial to encouraging his talents. He may also be gifted directing the efforts of others.

Venus in the 11th House—This child may enjoy getting into creative endeavors which she can share with friends. Here, the idea of the neighborhood summer play in the backyard can take shape. Later, working with good friends to decorate a float for the homecoming parade or organizing a school dance could be great ways to express this energy.

Venus in the 12th House—This placement indicates a powerfully creative imagination. While this child may need extra encouragement to bring his talents into the open, there may be a wealth of inspiration, ideas, and images he can express through all sorts of creative endeavors. Photography, acting, or dance may be good ways to use this energy.

Mars and Creativity

Mars indicates the type of physical energy and drive the child uses to execute her talents. Mars in Virgo, for example, may be an excellent percussionist—the physical energy can be directed in precise ways with the hands. Mars in Virgo could also direct physical energy through meticulous hand movements in activities such as line drawings, hand-carved art, and needlework.

We also look to Mars to understand the child's basic physical energy level. If a child is interested in becoming a dancer but has Mars squaring Saturn and opposing Neptune, he may not have enough physical energy to endure the rigorous regimen of a dancer. Extreme supportive measures would have to be taken such as increased rest, heightened nutrition, and extensive training and conditioning.

Mars also indicates the ability to assert the self. The child who wants to perform in public would benefit from a strongly placed Mars, or from positive aspects between Mars and other planets in the chart.

Saturn Aspects: Structure and Inhibition

Aspects from personal planets to Saturn indicate the child's approach to discipline. The need for discipline in developing creative artistry is paramount. Without focus, there is little achievement or improvement in the quality of artistic output. This discipline can be encouraged and modeled by a child's parents and teachers. In fact, Saturn is representative of teachers.

Some children simply resist discipline. To offset this negativity, parents might try a motivational reward system. This sort of positive reinforcement brings more powerful gains than negative reinforcement.

To determine which types of rewards would appeal to the child, study the 2nd and 10th Houses, the Moon, and Venus. Rewarding the child with things which help her feel more secure (Moon) will benefit her and help her accept the need for discipline. The types of activities your child finds pleasurable will be shown by the sign placement of Venus (e.g., Venus in Pisces might enjoy an afternoon movie as a reward for her guitar practice). These reward systems will add feelings of self-worth and confidence.

Saturn does not have to bring only limitations and restrictions, it can also bring concentration, focus, and crystallization. The child whose chart indicates strong Saturn aspects may be the best candidate for some type of classical artistic expression, since he will appreciate form and structure.

The types of support the child needs will also be indicated by Saturn in the chart, with the flowing aspects indicating the most harmonious support system. When dynamic aspects are present, the child may feel too pressured by the parents or others to be more than she really is. Parents need to be careful of their expectations of their children when these types of aspects are present. Also, if parents find that teachers are showing inhibiting or excessively critical methods with a child, it's important to take action to change these circumstances.

Neptune and Creative Imagination

Neptune's placement in the chart indicates the areas where a child dreams most easily. The house position of Neptune can indicate the facets of a child's life where imagination flows and the inner realms can be connected to the outside world.

Neptune in the Houses and Creativity

Neptune in the 1st House—This child may enjoy dancing, acting, and singing.

Neptune in the 2nd House—This placement spurs a child's imagination about what he wants, and learning to use the imagination to make things can be a great idea. Designing clothes for Barbie could be fun, or making a special nest for the pet hamster out of old cardboard could be a great exercise. These are the kids who like to make things out of egg cartons.

Neptune in the 3rd House—This child will enjoy dramatic verbal expressions and may love reciting poetry, singing songs, or telling stories.

Neptune in the 4th House—This placement is perfect for a child who wants to spend time in the backyard playhouse or fort. Emulating the activities of the family stimulates creativity, and family holiday traditions can provide this child with an excellent forum for exercising talents.

Neptune in the 5th House—This placement suggests high levels of dramatic, performing, and artistic ability.

Neptune in the 6th House—This child needs to put imagination to work in more practical ways. This child might be the neighborhood bird rescuer or might enjoy a chance to do something nice for a sick friend. Developing drawing skills or getting into the creative flow playing a musical instrument could keep imagination flowing. She might also have fun with the video camera.

Neptune in the 7th House—This child will enjoy sharing imaginative ideas with others and may become a good persuasive speaker, dramatist, or photographer.

Neptune in the 8th House—This child may love mysterious tales, and needs to put the imagination to use exploring life's mysteries. Strangely enough, this is a good position for science, since letting the imagination go to work on how things or people tick will be right up his alley.

Neptune in the 9th House—This child will enjoy applying imagination to higher ideals. Whether she is enthralled with the stained glass windows in a cathedral or loves the pageantry of a parade, if there's inspiration involved, her imagination can go crazy.

Neptune in the 10th House—This placement suggests that a child needs to dream about what he will be when he grows up. Play-acting about jobs and work can be fun (playing teacher, firefighter, nurse, etc.). Start a collection of costume materials.

Neptune in the 11th House—This child will add energy to sharing dreams with friends and using imagination to make goals happen. Coupling applied energy to imagination will be necessary, though, since it's very easy for this child to just dream about what she hopes will happen. The motivation may have to come from elsewhere.

Neptune in the 12th House—This child needs plenty of outlets for his creative imagination. Encourage this child to share his dreams and to use them in story-telling, singing songs, or play-acting.

Pulling It All Together

Generally, children are not particularly interested in artistic expression until they reach school-age, although creativity and the imagination flow should be stimulated at early ages. Encourage the child to sing, dance, paint, draw, act silly, tell stories, make funny faces—whatever it takes to let her know that you enjoy her spontaneous creativity. This way, parents and teachers can gain some insight into the most power-ful talents the child may have, or at least into the talents the child is ready to develop.

Through analyzing the needs and potential talents symbolized by the 5th House, Venus, Mars, and the other planets, we can determine positive creative directions for the child and encourage him to explore and express these aspects of the self. Whether or not a child will become a professional artist or musician is not the issue. We are addressing each child's need to do something that feels creative and special to him.

You may be raising, teaching, or counseling a future Picasso, Pavarotti, or LeAnn Rimes, but it does not matter if the child is exceptionally talented—what he needs to feel is that there is something he does especially well, in his own special way. This will build confidence, a feeling of personal worth, and the potential for a joyful and abundant future.

9

The Spiritual Needs
of the Child

Children are born with their connection to the spiritual planes operating at a pure level. I sometimes think that life in the physical realm immediately challenges the spiritual essence. After all, we humans *are* spiritual beings in physical form! We spend our lifetimes trying to integrate this sense, with the challenge of being on earth testing our spirituality while at the same time strengthening it. The very nature of life has its origins in our spirituality. We usually link a sense of the spiritual with the concept of awareness. It is at the time when a child becomes more verbal that her awareness of the different levels of life begins to emerge.

As a child matures, his awareness expands. The developing child's world grows even more complex as he tries to balance the physical, emotional, intellectual, and spiritual aspects of life. By focusing on this balance during the childhood years, the child will acquire greater personal power. Maintaining balance and harmony between these systems is a constant challenge requiring different areas of emphasis at different ages.

We do not generally think in terms of a child's spiritual awareness, since the Higher Mind's functions are not fully developed until later in life. But children do have spiritual needs, and these needs are emphasized at different times along with the physical, emotional, and intellectual needs. In fact, I've always felt that children are more innately connected to the pure essence of spirituality, and that it is the programming of influential adults and the need to adapt to life on the physical plane that challenges this pure connection to the Source.

My own concept of the word *spiritual* involves an attunement to one's inner needs as directed by a Higher Source, as well as an awareness of the connection between the higher and lower parts of the Self. To be spiritually aware is to know the presence of the Divine. It matters not how we define that presence—we simply need to become aware of and connected to it. Intuition, which is knowledge received directly from the Higher Self, is a function of this connection between the spirit of the individual and the spirit of the One.

Children have a need to evolve spiritually, to know that they are connected with a power beyond themselves. This divine presence exists within the child, but is not always easy to identify. By encouraging a child to question the things that are difficult to understand and to express her creative impulses, parents and teachers actually strengthen the child's connection to and reassurance of her spirituality.

The energies in the astrological chart that are generally considered to have the greatest spiritual connotation are Jupiter and the outer planets: Uranus, Neptune, and Pluto. For me, however, the entire symbology of the chart is spiritual, since it indicates the needs that must be actualized in order for a person to become whole. By becoming one with the needs of the soul, we grow spiritually. If we are separated from any of our need levels—physical, mental, emotional, or spiritual—we cannot become whole.

Imbalance occurs when the whole spectrum of human needs is not considered. For example, the act of eating a meal does not simply entail the assimilation of food. It is a process of development on all levels, since physical hunger interferes with the ability to be filled emotionally, mentally, and spiritually. The same is true of spiritual hunger—if it is not filled, there will be something out of balance in the other need levels.

As we acquire a greater understanding of the need for integration and wholeness in our lives, we can see how to apply it in childhood. Children wonder about the changes in their lives. What causes them? Why do they happen? Explanations, of course, must be given at a level the child can comprehend. Even at age four, my son was concerned with identifying God: "What is God, Mommy? Where is God? How did God make the tomatoes on our table?"

Rather than simply answering "God can do anything because that's the way it is," I told him that God works inside us when we plant the tomato seeds. We tend the growing plants, work in harmony with the earth, sun, and water, and help the plants to grow healthy and strong.

The conversation really got interesting when he asked, "Well, if God is everywhere, does that mean that if we eat tomatoes we are eating God?" So next Mom had to find a way of explaining the parts of the Whole!

When parents are confronted with a child's spiritual questions, they are confronted with questions they must also answer for themselves. We begin to see the beautiful interaction between teaching and learning. If we are to apply spiritual principles to astrology, then we must develop a personal awareness of these principles on a spiritual level.

Spirituality Today Versus Yesterday

We are in the midst of powerful changes in human evolution. Personal and spiritual awareness have undergone tremendous changes in the last century. Family structures are radically different in our society, with the extended family now almost a thing of the past. There has been an alteration in the roles women play in society, with more options available to women for their creative outlets. On a global level, we now face the possible destruction of the very planet that sustains our lives. We are observing the extinction of different life forms and are more keenly aware of the relationship between humankind and the environment of Gaia, our planet. Yet we do not have to yield to this destructive potential.

Every change that occurs in the external environment is symbolic of changes in humankind's inner environment. If we watch the changes in the world around us, within our society, and within our families and relationships, we can see that the inner or spiritual needs of individuals are also taking on a different focus.

In my study of history, I have found far-reaching changes in societal structures. We live today in a patriarchal society, a male-dominated culture. This is neither good nor bad, but is simply the current state of affairs. In the past there have been many matrilineal societies, in which the women were the ruling force. But with the dawning of this new millennium, there is a dawning of a more complete quality of spirituality. Some say it is the return of the Goddess. I prefer to think of this time as the period when we are embracing all of life as symbolic of the soul's quest for perfection and understanding. A new mythology is emerging.

With the increased focus upon Christianity during the last several centuries, the principles of the Divine have been strongly correlated with a male deity. God is explained as a masculine principle. Even Eastern religions consider the male to be more spiritually advanced, with the result that women hold very limited power in these societies.

In Western society, the feminist movement has successfully challenged some of these views. Even within the Catholic Church, women are questioning why they cannot become priests. This is symbolic of changes going on within each of us. We are feeling an increasing need to reach a balance within ourselves, to allow the receptive aspect of our natures to blossom more fully. The old imbalance between the masculine and feminine is shifting. It is time for a blending of and harmony between these principles, so that men and women alike can be more free to experience and express themselves as whole beings, reflecting a deity which embodies both masculine and feminine strengths.

As psychology probes more deeply into human nature, we are understanding more and more the importance of allowing a child to grow into himself and fulfill his needs. We are realizing the damage that can be done if parents inhibit this natural development. More parents are now concerned with allowing their children to exercise their full potentials.

Parental roles are changing in our society. More women are working outside the home. Fathers are beginning to be more open and nurturing with their children. Women are becoming more assertive of their needs. With the alterations in family roles, the child's position is also evolving. In the past, a child was not given as much credibility, and approval was gained only by meeting her parents' sometimes rigid standards. Today it is becoming more important that the child be true to her own unique standards.

If we look to society as an indicator of humankind's spiritual evolution, we can observe the changing place of the church in society as an example. The primary role of the church has been to teach "right" living with guidelines for proper, moral behavior. God has been portrayed as the Divine Judge. Children have looked to these teachings as the fundamental principles for living.

But as society changes, so must the role of the church if it is to maintain any validity in the evolutionary process. At a time when fathers were stern family leaders, God was seen as stern and often angry. But now the idea of a God of Love is becoming more powerful, and fathers in our society are becoming freer to love and be loving. This is one example of how spiritual needs and change in a society are linked.

Now that individuals are seeking to know themselves and become whole beings, the concept of God is reaching a more universal definition. As children experience the changes within their parents, they also experience a new definition of their own inner needs.

And just as relationships between men and women are evolving, so are relationships between women and God evolving. Women are seeking to find a Oneness, a connection with the Divine. Hence, the emergence and embracing of the Goddess—the feminine principle of the Divine.

I have met many people who, without realization, have sought to find through their spiritual path what they failed to receive from their parents. Many of the seekers I have encountered have had difficult relationships with their parents, and often did not have one parent present in their lives. With these unfulfilled needs in the family, the logical place to look for fulfillment is through a spiritual path.

There is a danger, though, in transferring an emotional need to a spiritual one. Certainly, an individual can find ways to balance the self by seeking spiritual truths, but there can also be pitfalls. I have watched many young people transfer an emotional need onto a spiritual teacher or minister. The teacher then becomes the child's missing father or the spiritual counselor becomes Mother as the child tries to fill the gaping emotional void in his life. Therefore, emotional attachments to a teacher can overwhelm the genuine need to devote oneself to the truth of the teaching!

The child whose parents are self-aware individuals is truly blessed. As we evolve spiritually, we will find children seeking spiritual answers from a more balanced and secure perspective. Parents are a child's primary spiritual teachers and the lessons and attitudes instilled by the parents will remain a part of the child's matrix of Self throughout her lifetime. This gives the parents a challenging but rewarding responsibility: they must not only attend to their own needs for growth, but must also remain attentive to the child's deeper needs. I am seeing this type of relationship forming now in many families. Just as the structure of the family has evolved in the past, so it continues to change now.

Spiritual Principles Illustrated by the Planets

Each planet illustrates different spiritual principles. It is almost as though these energies serve as gateways to various facets of spiritual need and experience.

The Sun—The Sun is the divine spark in the human, the nurtured seed which blossoms into the willpower of the Self. The Sun is the flame of the heart. The Sun is spirit.

The Moon—The Moon principle is the soul which receives input from the Source. The soul is eternal.

Mercury—Mercury connects the human with the Universal Life Force through the mind. It illustrates the spiritual law, "What you think, you become."

Venus—Venus is the principle of love—not just a physical or emotional connection with another person, but a spiritual bonding and an endless flow of giving and receiving.

Mars—Mars is the principle of physical power, which is necessary for the human instrument to express the spiritual self. Mars is will.

Jupiter—Jupiter is the hunger to understand the Divine presence and is the application of the Law of Abundance. Through Jupiter we gain wisdom.

Saturn—Saturn is the Law of Karma, illustrating, "What you sow, so shall you reap." Through Saturn we mature, using the lessons of life as building blocks for security and stability. Saturn is form.

Uranus—Uranus is the principle of intuition, the connection from the Mind of the One to the mind of the individual. Through Uranus, we know.

Neptune—Neptune represents Divine Compassion, the surrender of the ego to the greater needs of the whole and the guidance of the Higher Self. Through Neptune we absorb vibration and reflect compassion. Neptune is forgiveness.

Pluto—Pluto eliminates the extraneous and brings transformation into our lives. Through Pluto, we are able to transmute difficulty into creative change. Pluto heals.

Jupiter As an Indicator of Spiritual Learning

While Jupiter's function on a psychological level may be the development of confidence and expression of generosity, it has a powerful function in relationship to spiritual development. Jupiter represents philosophy. It is through philosophical ideologies that we shape our basic attitudes toward life. Here, we build our moral attitudes. Here, we are inundated with platitudes!

Jupiter's sign and house placement can indicate of how a child relates to the principles and philosophies which are usually taught by churches or other religious communities. The sign placement suggests the filter through which a child can more easily be addressed when learning about right and wrong, as well as the concepts which will be most enduring in the child's ideals and belief systems. Jupiter's house placement shows where in a child's life his spiritual ideas are most likely to be real or accessible.

Jupiter in the Houses and Spirituality

Jupiter in the 1st House—This child responds best to spiritual lessons which allow her to understand that the way she presents herself to the world determines how others form judgments about her. Since the 1st House represents an individual's attitudes in general, Jupiter in the 1st House can be indicative of a jovial attitude—good humor, generosity of spirit, and an optimistic outlook. A spirituality that fuels the most positive elements of this type of expression will be most meaningful to this child.

Jupiter in the 2nd House—This child needs to understand the real nature of value systems. While this can indicate a strong sense of self-worth in an adult, for a child it indicates a potential to develop that sensibility and a need to understand the importance of a confident attitude about his values. Extending that concept, he may also need to learn how to handle practical values, since there is a tendency to take for granted the material things necessary for a truly abundant life. Learning to appreciate origins of personal and environmental resources can be a powerful lesson for this child.

Jupiter in the 3rd House—This child shows a sensitivity to the power of inspiring words and ideas. This child will respond positively to spiritual or religious instruction and training, but it is crucial that the ideals instilled and introduced help build a sense of hope. Anything that resounds negatively or is based upon fear is likely to be rejected by her—and rightfully so. Those fear-based concepts simply will not ring true to this child!

Jupiter in the 4th House—This child will most likely emulate the spiritual teachings of the family. Family values will have a powerful impact on his self-confidence and faith in others. He will be quite likely to gain tremendous enjoyment from family holiday celebrations and opportunities to gather with the "clan." There can be an emotional attachment to belief systems and ideals which is difficult to break, and that can be a problem if prejudicial attitudes are instilled.

Jupiter in the 5th House—This child needs to feel that life is a real opportunity. After all, the most significant creation we each explore is the creation of ourselves! Learning the value of creativity, love, and sharing is extremely meaningful to this child. She will benefit from learning that extending her talents to the world is one way to keep love flowing in her life.

Jupiter in the 6th House—This child responds best to teachings that have a sound basis in reality and can be useful everyday. If spiritual teachings are too abstract, he will simply not retain them. This child needs to get into the garden to experience the nature of life cycles, change, rebirth, and all the things nature can teach about the truth of life. He can also learn about acts of generosity and extending himself through caring for a pet—or even farm or zoo animals! Spirituality needs to be hands-on.

Jupiter in the 7th House—This child is especially responsive to a philosophy based upon sharing love and its importance in our lives. Learning the true meanings of justice and fair play can be very important, and if she witnesses unfair attitudes it's likely to prompt significant reactions on her part.

Jupiter in the 8th House—This child needs to learn respect for the essential changes which accompany life. Transitions from one stage to another and celebrations of those changes can help him understand that even belief systems transform! Nature can also be a good teacher for this child, since knowing that everything has its time of blossoming and strength will ring true to his ideals. Something as simple as watching the changing tides can be an excellent illustration of intangible values.

Jupiter in the 9th House—This child may be interested in religion and philosophy, and will love allegorical tales that drive home the meanings of universal Truths. Exploring other cultures can be an excellent way for her to learn the value of tolerance. She will have a strong appreciation for teachers who practice what they preach.

Jupiter in the 10th House—This child will seek strong spiritual leadership through parents and teachers. His enthusiasm for any value systems will be directly related to the type of response parents and other authorities provide during his formative years to subjects ranging from religious ideologies to political philosophies. It is crucial that he be given permission to explore ideals different from those of his origins in order to understand that one belief system is not necessarily better than others.

Jupiter in the 11th House—This child will appreciate the spiritual support gained through a community. She may enjoy experiences like Sunday school since sharing lessons with friends can feel especially self-confirming. Sports may be an excellent way to learn generosity of spirit and cooperative attitudes, and the higher ideals of sportsmanship can be especially powerful in her life.

Jupiter in the 12th House—This child will seek the truth through the most imaginative means possible. While parents may instill strong values and ideals, they may be surprised to learn that this child holds the ideals of his favorite Disney movie or Saturday morning cartoon show just as strongly. What he seeks to discover is a clear illustration of compassion and forgiveness, something that may be difficult to find in fairy tales, and just as rare in real life!

Affirmations for the Continually Evolving Soul

Astrological charts for children give us possibilities, showing us potentials which can be developed but which are not yet realized. Without self-awareness, the whole person is not complete. The process of developing self-awareness lasts one's entire lifetime, beginning with the moment of the first breath (and perhaps even while in the womb).

In aiding the child's spiritual maturation, we must feed physical, mental, and emotional needs. I think the spiritual knowledge children need most is how to uncover the truths of life.

Although tempting, it is dangerous to look at an astrological chart and judge a particular child to be a "highly evolved spiritual being." Nor should the opposite be assumed about a child who has difficulty adjusting to the physical plane because of emotional blocks and unresolved anger. She needs to sort these obstacles out before spiritual awareness can be significantly opened. A child may have a special connection with the higher realms of consciousness in the very early years, but cannot explain or express this connection to the outside world. As parents and teachers, we must give the child permission to have this awareness and acknowledge that it is okay. I have spoken with many children who tell me about their contacts with beings on other levels. They describe them as angels, fairies, or whatever words fit with their understanding. Even tiny children, about age two, will tell me about lights they see around another person or the light they see when they close their eyes. This is one level of spiritual awareness.

One thing we can do to help the child develop a stronger spiritual constitution is to use affirmations. Parents unknowingly give their children affirmations all the time: "You are such a brat!" or, "You are an angel."

Either concept can be difficult for the child. The child may not even know what a brat is, but the parent's attitude and tone of voice will certainly provide a strong hint! If the child believes himself to be a brat, he will work to become one.

The child whose mother calls him or her an "angel," may also face considerable confusion. "Well, if I am an angel," the child may think, "then everything I do is okay!" If we, as parents, will really listen to the way we speak to our children, we will begin to realize that we are, indeed, programming the child's consciousness.

Positive affirmations are positive ways to program a child's subconscious mind. Through the use of positive affirmations, we can help the child build a stronger connection with the Higher Self. Specific energy blockages indicated by planetary aspects in the chart can be transmuted to a more creative and positive expression by altering the child's attitude about how this energy operates within him. When considering the planetary aspects, we should find ways to work with these energies instead of against them!

With very small children, affirmations are most easily used in simple songs or chants. Use any tune you enjoy. Children usually don't care if you have a beautiful voice, they just like to sing along. Why not have your child singing words like, "I am the light and I am shining," instead of the latest Coca-Cola commercial? The influx of commercial advertising geared toward children during recent years has more than doubled. They're getting all kinds of affirmations, whether we want it or not. Parents and teachers have a large task today to create messages of their own to help shape the consciousness of a child.

When she was about three years old, my daughter would sing about what she saw around her. She sang lyrics such as "The birds are flying in the blue sky. I like the way they fly. I feel like a bird." Sometimes, when she would be feeling low, I would suggest to her that we make up a song about something especially lovely. This changed the focus of her mind energy and lifted her mood. This is an example of affirmations in action!

As a child matures, affirmations can be part of a morning or evening ritual. Your child may want to invent some of her own special affirmations. It is fun to share in this experience, and it offers the child a positive approach to making creative changes in her life.

Connections between personal energies and the outer planets seem to heighten spiritual sensitivity. But these same energies can also create havoc in the child's psychological make-up because they are not easy to rationally understand. It is these factors which can benefit the most by the use of positive affirmations and creative visualizations.

Saturn Aspects and Spiritual Values

I see Saturn as a feminine energy. It is the ruler of the sign Capricorn, yet traditional astrologers perceive Saturn as the Father. If we consider Saturn as the primary structure upon which our security is built, we can conceive of this energy as working through many levels of a child's experience. Not only is Saturn energy felt through parental structures, but through the basic foundations of society as well. Many of these foundations have their origins in religious teachings, since Saturn has a rather moral connotation. These morals are tied to the idea, "If you do something wrong, you will have to pay the price."

Saturn represents the Law of Karma, which enforces life's natural balance. When a child is taught to be personally responsible for his actions, he is learning how to properly deal with Saturn energy. Through this type of understanding, a child learns why he should behave in a particular manner.

If Saturn is aspected by a personal planet in the chart, the child will be forced to confront this particular quality of herself realistically and honestly. This does not mean negatively. However, we humans have difficulty with concepts such as "realistic" and "honest"! The limitation a child may feel through Saturn is usually present because the child needs to deal with a particular aspect of herself honestly. A child who has Venus squaring Saturn, for example, may feel that expressing love is a frightening proposition. She may perceive God as rather demanding, giving love only if she is "perfect." These children must learn to become more giving in order to receive, a spiritual lesson learned through an emotional release.

The child with challenging Saturn aspects in the chart will all too often resist the necessary confrontations in his life rather than working through them. The parents need to give these children ample opportunities to appreciate themselves and their particular gifts. It may be too easy to focus upon what the child does not have, rather than helping him see what he does have.

Affirmations: *I am safe and secure.*
I love to give to others.
I deserve everything I need.

Uranus Aspects and Original Thinking

A child with contacts between Uranus and the personal planets may be very original or eccentric. She may seem to march to the beat of an ever-changing drum. This is also true of children who have Uranus near the angles of the chart. These children need to learn how to trust their intuitive insights. They can benefit from exercises for quieting the mind, especially once the child is about five years of age.

Creative channels of expression must remain open for these children. Even with dynamic aspects between the personal planets and Uranus, the disruptive nature of the energy does not have to be the overriding influence if the child can learn to handle it.

The energy of Uranus is one aspect of the intuitive link between the human mind and the Higher Mind. When a child has increased Uranian energy, illustrated through Uranus' placement on the angles of the chart or in contact with the personal planets, he has a need to balance reason and intuition. Intuitive insights are usually powerful! These children may feel guided to do things their rational minds do not understand. With patient guidance from parents and teachers, the child can learn to trust these impulses. It is through this source that the child opens up to original concepts and ideas.

Affirmations: *I am special, I am me!*
I listen to the voice inside me for guidance.
I want to know the truth.
I am a good friend.

Neptune Aspects and the Inner Realms

With Neptune contacts, a child is drawn into the inner realms more easily. When personal planets are contacting Neptune, or when Neptune is near the Ascendant in the chart, the child may seem rather removed much of the time. She may also feel invisible, or that others just don't see or hear what she needs. Focusing on artistic expression often helps these children bring spiritual awareness into the personal realm.

The difficulty with Neptune and personal planet contacts lies in the desire to escape. The child has a special connection to Divine Love, and desires to bask in this radiance. There may be special a special awareness that the child does not understand, and which should be met by the parents with understanding and acceptance. To tell a child that something he perceives is wrong just because the parents don't see it that way is damaging to the child.

However, these children do need to learn how to balance physical reality with inner awareness. The spiritual need is to see the pure and perfect in each person and in all life. But this can also lead to overidealization, since the need for that perception may be so great as to overwhelm reality.

Neptune's realm is beyond normal reality. Children seem more easily connected to these intangible parts of the self in the early years. But as the rational mind begins its development, they seem to lose much or all of this awareness. It is difficult to maintain a balance when Neptune energies are strong. It is easy for this child to spend hours daydreaming in a world of inner visions. Rather than discourage this, we need to aid the child in focusing her visions and finding ways to direct them.

The process of creative visualization is a product of Neptunian energy. To do this, we create a desirable concept—a wish or a hope—within the mind. By focusing mental energy in this manner, we can crystallize this hope for ourselves and create a more positive reality.

The trick with creative visualization is learning what our real needs are. We must realize what our strengths and limitations may be in achieving what we desire from our lives. A child does not accept as many limitations as an adult—these are usually learned! However, a child can be encouraged to use the energy of his hopes and dreams to make his life more the way he wants it to be. What the child has to learn is how to balance his personal wants with personal responsibility. The Disney song, "When You Wish Upon a Star," has been a favorite among children for decades. It encourages a child to dream his dreams and make wishes, because they can come true. This song itself can be an affirmation for the child!

As parents and teachers, we need to aid the child with Neptunian vision to direct these wishes toward achieving peace and harmony on our planet. These children have the gifts necessary to help this process come to fruition.

Affirmations: *My guardian angel is my good friend.*
I can make my dreams come true.
I am love.

Pluto Aspects and Personal Empowerment

With personal planets contacting Pluto, the spiritual experience evolves around continual transformation. This can be most difficult for a child, who needs consistency and stability in order to feel comfortable. Drastic and sometimes difficult losses may accompany these contacts. These children must learn early about positive self-transformation, and must learn to appreciate themselves for who and what they are, and understand the limitations confronting themselves and others.

This child may feel especially attuned to the power of the Source, but will probably not understand how to use this power. These aspects require a great deal of maturity to manifest in their most positive light. The *Star Wars* films are wonderful examples of the uses of Plutonian energy. Each child will be confronted with her own power very early in life, but may not know how to direct it. Whether or not the child becomes a healer or a destroyer is strongly dependent upon how she deals with Plutonian energy. If a child suffers an extreme illness during childhood and is required to marshal all her resources to recover, she can become very familiar with the transformative qualities of Pluto.

We are, as a society, also confronted with this task. For example, nuclear power, which harnesses the physical properties of plutonium, can also poison or destroy our planet. We must realize that we have power equal to the splitting of the plutonian atom within us. This power comes from our connection with the Source of Life. Once again, the symbology of the external environment illustrates what we are learning spiritually. Just as important are the lessons of abuse and misuse of power. Child abuse continues to plague our world, and while children may not know how to organize their own power to rise up against this monster, as parents we can certainly work toward eradicating it. Plutonian connections sometimes indicate the potential for experiences of abuse of power, and if a child sees misuse and abuse of power as a normal part of life, what is he to think except that this is the way he is supposed to direct his own energy and power?!

Affirmations: *I am the Light and I am shining!*
My power comes from my Higher Self.
I am my own hero!

The Houses and Spirituality

Houses 4, 8, 9, and 12 have a stronger spiritual focus in our lives. Planets in these houses will prompt a child to seek answers about the deeper meanings of life and inner aspects of herself.

4th House—A child who has a powerful 4th House focus will need to develop a sense of rootedness, and will probably approach spirituality in an emotional manner. The parents will most likely be viewed as spiritual teachers.

8th House-With an 8th House focus, children are concerned with the mysterious and hidden aspects of life. Children with several planets in the 8th House may often be confronted with death. They are likely to feel forced to integrate an understanding of death and transformation into their consciousness rather early. This can be experienced through the loss of a pet but may also be through the loss of a family member or friend.

9th House—A strong 9th House focus gives a child a desire to understand the workings of spiritual laws. These children might enjoy the interactions they will have in religious activities at churches, temples, synagogues, ashrams, and other places of worship and spiritual growth.

12th House—A child with a 12th House focus may be deeply drawn into the Self. These children need time for privacy and reflection. He will also need to understand transpersonal human needs, and loves to feel that he can make a difference in the lives of other people.

Benediction

Basically, one's spiritual maturation is dependent upon the fulfillment of her other needs in childhood. Children seek to find Truth, and will initially trust what parents present to them is Truth. Hopefully, with humankind's increasing spiritual awareness, parents will present the Truth to their children more openly than in the past. When children come to parents with questions about otherworldly experiences, dreams, images, and illusions, the parent's response will condition the child's sense of this aspect of life. Offering the child permission to have these contacts and share them with the parents can make an important difference in her developing spiritual awareness.

Whether or not the parents offer permission, every human being must come in contact with the spiritual realm at some point. Some will be comfortable immersing themselves in this aspect of life, others will not. If a child is encouraged to question and explore these dimensions of life, his spiritual foundation will better prepare him to deal with the varied situations he will encounter in adulthood. After all, the ultimate goal is to make life itself the meditation.

10

The Child's Perceptions of the Parents

One helpful concept for when you're looking at an astrological chart is the realization that the chart itself represents the viewpoints and experiences of the individual involved. The energies of the chart are like a picture of a kind of internal universe specific to each person. It's necessary to remember that the chart indicates how and why an individual is experiencing something, but may not necessarily correspond with the perceptions of another individual. One key point is to use the chart to understand a child's *perception* of the parents. These perceptions are an important factor in the child's responses to the parents.

Our personal universe is perceived from within. If we are feeling balanced, centered, and happy, the world looks bright. Other people seem helpful and supportive. But if we suffer from emotional trauma, physical setbacks, or other problems, our perceptions become altered. The world can seem dark and cold, and other people may seem hostile and unfriendly.

This is especially true for children. When a child feels physically or emotionally low, her behavior and responses suffer. In relationships with others, children and adults alike will project their negative feelings and perceptions onto other people.

We have within ourselves many parts of the whole. At a very basic level, we have a feminine, receptive side (anima) and a masculine, assertive side (animus). For small children, these inner parts are difficult to perceive. They develop an understanding of themselves only through identification with significant others in their lives.

This anima/animus concept was presented by psychologist Carl Jung and has helped clarify how human relationships work. The impulses and needs driven by a child's feminine side will initially identify with the Mother archetype, while the masculine side will relate to the archetype of the Father. Therefore, when studying a child's astrological chart, we can delineate the feminine perceptions through the Moon (Mother) and Venus (women), and the masculine perceptions through the Sun (Father) and Mars (men).

Parental influences in general are more Saturnian, although many traditional astrologers would suggest this represents the Father. Over the years, my observations have proven to me that Saturn is parental, although not necessarily one parent over the other.

The child needs to experience herself through projecting her needs within her personal environment. In fact, the undeveloped aspects of the Self are usually projected onto others as a means of "seeing" these feelings or needs manifested in some way. Projection is a key factor in human psychology. In many instances, other people are reasonable targets for those projections, especially if their connections are bound by emotions or other commitments. As noted above, the inner feminine self of a child looks to Mother as the person who will reflect the nurturing feminine needs back to the child. There are particular things a child needs from the parents in order to attain a stronger sense of her own identity.

The Sun, which is the primary masculine energy in the chart, is also the sense of self. This sense of individuality may be strongly tied to the initial relationship with the father and, later, to interactions with other significant male figures. In early childhood development, the child's Sun does not express fully as an individual ego. Much of the power of the ego is projected onto the father by the child. The Sun powerfully affects the child's perceptions of Father; if the father is supportive and consistent, the child may feel that his own individuality is reliable and strong.

Mother often takes on the role as a child's primary parent. In this case, the projection of Father (Sun) energy may fall upon Mother, or may be transferred to other significant males. This idea will be explored in more depth as we examine aspects later in this chapter.

What the child perceives about the father comes from within. I have observed this when counseling families with several children. In one family, each child had the same Sun sign. All these children described the father in very similar terms. But in another family with four children aged several years apart and with different Sun signs, each child described the father quite differently.

The need for inner security is strongly associated with the Moon, which is the projection of the mother. Through the Moon, we find our sense of emotional fulfillment and the primary feminine aspects of the self. Relationships with the Mother and female figures are signified by the Moon. The specific type of nurturance a child needs is determined by the sign and house placement of the Moon. This need is then projected upon the mother. If the father is the nurturant parent to a child, Moon energies will be projected upon the father.

The other planets also reflect what a child needs from the parents:

Mercury—Mercury illustrates communication needs, the types of learning experiences best suited for the child, and the mental expression of the Self. Remember, Mercury is about expression of ideas and also about listening. This energy can indicate what a child wants to hear from her parents!

Venus—Venus, the expression of artistry and love, is also a feminine aspect of the Self. It is experienced through the manner in which the child feels love and expresses his sense of beauty.

Mars—Physical self-expression is signified by Mars, which also indicates the types of physical activity a child would like to share with the parents. Mars is one of the masculine principles in the chart. A child may learn about self-assertion from important males, but also learns about the way anger is expressed from all adults. Shaping Martian expression is one of the primary features of parenting.

Jupiter—Through Jupiter the child learns her philosophical and moral attitudes. These are first taught by the parents, then by society.

Saturn—Saturn indicates the child's response to and need for discipline, structure, and consistency. Saturn is also a factor associated with parents, discipline, and the structure of the family. Now that family structures are changing from the strict patriarchal model, fathers and mothers both are providing Saturnian influence. For this reason, I am reluctant to place Saturnian concepts in the category of the masculine parent alone. Also, sociologically, the structure and stability within the family unit has actually been carried by the women in society, and the deepest Saturnian influences may actually have been feminine all along!

Uranus, Neptune, and Pluto—The outer planets Uranus, Neptune, and Pluto are experienced at a deeper psychological level. These energies are involved with levels of awareness beyond the personality. Most children have little sense of these transpersonal energies unless they contact the personal planets, Jupiter, or Saturn. Thus, if the parents do not personify these higher principles, the child will not perceive them as readily until he has established a sense of Self outside the realm of parental influence.

The Child's Perceptions of Mother

Through the Reflected Light of the Moon . . .

The sign in which the Moon is placed will offer insights into how the child perceives the mother. It makes no difference whether the mother sees herself in this light or not—the child holds these particular perceptions of her because she is projecting her own inner needs for security onto her. As a child matures into adulthood, these perceptions determine how that individual will play the nurturing/mothering role.

Moon in the Signs and Perception of Mother

Moon in Aries—This child may perceive Mother as highly independent and strong-minded.

Moon in Taurus—This child may perceive Mother as stable, conservative, possessive, and earthy.

Moon in Gemini—This child perceives Mother as mentally active, talkative, changeable, and sometimes hard to pin down.

Moon in Cancer—This child perceives Mother as nurturing, protective, and sometimes smothering.

Moon in Leo—This child perceives Mother as powerful, strong-willed, and rather queenly or regal.

Moon in Virgo—This child sees Mother as fastidious and tidy, always concerned with the child's health and proper behavior. The way Mom does it is perfect!

Moon in Libra—This child sees Mother as interested in personal appearance and constantly interacting with someone. The Libra Moon child's mother may seem especially pretty to the child, symbolizing the ideal of true beauty.

Moon in Scorpio—This child may see Mom as quietly powerful, insightful, and sometimes ominous. Mother is usually viewed as highly spiritual, the projection of the Divine Goddess.

Moon in Sagittarius—This child perceives Mother as the teacher of spiritual truth. Mother may also seem very independent and sometimes unreliable.

Moon in Capricorn—This child sees Mother as having a strict set of rules for behavior. Mother represents control, organization, determination, and persistence.

Moon in Aquarius—This child may find Mother hard to reach and very unusual. Mom seems free-spirited, innovative, and highly intellectual.

Moon in Pisces—This child perceives Mother as personifying an ideal. Mom may be like an angel to the child, with a calming, mystical quality. Mom may also be difficult to figure out, since she does not always seem real.

Lunar Aspects and Mother

While the Moon sign is the underlying theme of the child's feminine self which is projected upon the mother, aspects from other planets to the Moon will alter these perceptions. With the softer, harmonious aspects, the child may handle the psychological traumas of her early life easily and with more support. Otherwise, the impact of emotionally difficult situations is usually dealt with only after the child is an adult in the throes of self-analysis. The dynamic, frustrating aspects are indicative of emotional discontent with what a child needs from Mother and what she is actually receiving!

Moon and Mercury—The Moon aspecting Mercury will open lines of communication between Mother and child. The child will perceive Mother as communicative. If the aspect is dynamic, the communication may often take the form of disagreements later on, especially during the teen years!

Moon and Venus—Moon to Venus signifies a sharing of artistic support between Mother and child. Beauty and Mother may be synonymous to this child. The difficult aspects may find the mother vicariously attempting to live her artistic fantasies through the child. If that is the case, the child can feel very frustrated by his attempts to express his own creativity while bound by the expectations and preferences of Mother.

Moon and Mars—When the Moon and Mars are connected in the child's chart, the child may see Mother as assertive, a woman ready to stand up for her own rights and beliefs. When dynamic aspects occur, the child's feelings of anger are often projected upon the mother. Sometimes these children have a basically angry temperament and need positive directions for that anger through the mother's example. If Mother has difficulty expressing anger, then the child will feel a strong inner frustration with his own angry feelings. It's as though Mom throws water on the fire.

Moon and Jupiter—With Moon and Jupiter connections, a child gains confidence through the relationship with the mother. However, Mother needs to be careful about permitting too many indulgences. Mom teaches optimism and encourages growth. This growth also involves the child's moral sense, which is likely to be modeled after Mother's.

Moon and Saturn—Moon to Saturn often brings a sense of separation or alienation from the mother. I have often seen these aspects in the charts of first-born children whose mothers were just learning about the responsibilities and restrictions that motherhood brings. These children often feel that they have to grow up too soon and take on major responsibilities earlier than their peers.

It is highly important that the mother not make the child feel that he must be perfect. She must allow him to have his virtues and shortcomings. These children may feel that the mother is not providing his fundamental needs, and may seek a substitute for the nurturing quality he feels is lacking. Sometimes, with difficult aspects, the child perceives Mother to be tremendously judgmental. He may feel guilty if he cannot meet the high standards Mother seems to require of him.

While any aspect between the Moon and Saturn can add a sense of restraint to the expression of emotional needs, the flowing aspects usually indicate that Mom shows a child how to take responsibility for her needs. The child may have a strong sense that Mom will always be there, and also may find it easier to respect the lessons she is teaching. With the dynamic aspects, the frustrations a child feels over not having needs met will be immediately be projected upon

Mother. While these aspects can indicate restriction or loss in regard to the relationship with Mother, they are not a reason to despair if you find them in the chart of your child. What you need to explore are the situations that could be emotionally difficult for a child. For example, if there is a crisis, move, or other significant change which could compromise a child's sense of emotional security, she will need greater reassurance that everything will be okay and that she is safe.

Difficult aspects between Moon and Saturn indicate that Mother may have to go the extra mile to reassure the child. It's also crucial for Mother to be aware of the manner in which she shows discipline, and to remember that if disciplinary measures are inappropriate for the situation, they will create emotional damage. Additionally, if Mother is failing to take full responsibility for her own job as a parent, the child will ultimately develop a kind of resentment that can result in emotional separation.

Moon and Uranus—Moon-Uranus children see Mother as unique. This uniqueness may be a plus for the child, or he may think, "My mom is weird." With dynamic aspects, the child often feels that the mother is too inconsistent in providing nurturance, protection, and support. One day, Mom may be balanced and approachable; the next day, she may seem unreachable. There may also be inconsistent messages from Mom about the child's independence.

The mother must make an effort to deal with the child consistently. Mom is viewed as being intuitive, and how the mother uses this intuitive flow will have a great effect upon the child's future use of her own intuitive perceptions. As the child reaches school-age, her mother may seem radically different from the other moms. If Mother has been secure in her sense of individuality, the child will not find this to be a problem. If Mom has been bizarre in her actions and disrespectful of herself, the child may have difficulty dealing with her feelings about her.

A key factor involved with Uranian aspects from the Moon is what the child learns about emotional distancing. If Mom seems "out there," then the child will develop a kind of emotional bubble which serves to maintain that distance. Eventually, this can have an effect on the way the child relates to others, and can be indicative of a pattern in which he seeks out relationships with those who are either inappropriate to fulfill needs or are unreachable themselves.

Moon and Neptune—Moon to Neptune perceives the mother as being rather vague, psychic, or difficult to reach. Mom may seem to be "out in the ozone" much of the time, or may be interested in spiritual aspects of life which the child has difficulty perceiving. With flowing aspects, this perception may be easily integrated and accepted.

These connections signify that Mother needs to personify a perfect ideal. If Mother fails in this, the child may be sorely disappointed and have difficulty relating to her feminine self and to other women later in life.

Mother may also be the perpetrator of a false illusion for the child. Sometimes the mother projects escapist tendencies (e.g., alcoholism). Often the child has difficulty identifying with Mother at all, and may believe that he was really left on the doorstep by a mysterious stranger.

Moon and Pluto—With the Moon aspecting Pluto, the child may think Mom has eyes in the back of her head. Mom is powerful, absorbing, and perceived as all-knowing. The child could sense that Mother holds the power of life and death. This can be a strong negative if the aspect is difficult and not confronted in a mature manner.

Mother may seem to be highly judgmental. She may also be expected to be Superwoman—able to cook dinner while leaping tall buildings with a single bound. This projection originates from the deep levels of the psyche, where the child feels that she (the child) must be more than human.

In some cases, Mother is so powerful that the child feels consumed by her and loses all sense of self. The child's emotions will be intense and often painful, and can easily be repressed. Mother may be experienced as heavy and emotionally intense, and may overwhelm the child with her own emotionality.

Mother can aid the child by striving to maintain open communications with him. She needs to give the child opportunities to exercise and own his own power, beginning in the early years. If mother usurps the child's sense of personal power, the child will experience difficulty later in life in achieving personal fulfillment and emotional openness. If Mom radiates the message "Don't feel" to the child, some serious problems can develop. Sometimes this occurs with Moon-Pluto contacts. The child believes, "Something's wrong with me because I feel this way," or, "If I tell Mom about this, she'll have my head on a platter."

I've seen difficult Moon-Pluto aspects in the charts of adults who have lost their mothers during childhood. This kind of scar can be especially difficult for a child to overcome, even with adequate support. What can happen is the instillation of guilt feelings. If circumstances of loss have arisen that can be emotionally devastating, then this child needs to learn first and foremost that she is not responsible for that loss. If she feels this kind of guilt, allowing room for real nurturance can be very difficult.

The other qualities projected onto and around Mother with Moon-Pluto aspects fall in the category of denial of need. While those "don't feel" messages can be delivered in all sorts of ways, sometimes Mother is not aware that she could be doing damage, and the child does not know to ask for anything else. Parents who observe these aspects in the chart of a child need to understand that the child may feel that Mother is trying too hard to be everything. So all you Moms out there, relax a little, and take the time to let the tenderness between yourself and your little one serve as a healing elixir.

The Child's Perceptions of Father

The child's perceptions of Father are strongly symbolized by the energy of the Sun in the astrological chart. The house placement of the Sun will indicate which elements of a child's personality will be most strongly influenced by the father and where a child will need recognition from Dad.

House Placement of the Sun and Perceptions of Father

Sun in the 1st House—This child needs consistent acknowledgment from Dad that he exists and is important. If this child feels that Father does not approve or acknowledge him, then the repercussions can range from acting-out behaviors to a loss in confidence. Dad is perceived as a strong link to the Self.

Sun in the 2nd House—This child will see Dad as the source of material security and may emulate his work or actions as a means to provide for herself during the later years. This child needs Dad's stamp of approval to feel worthy.

Sun in the 3rd House—This child needs Dad to provide the link in communication and may see him as knowledgeable. He may not feel that his ideas are worthwhile unless Dad acknowledges them.

Sun in the 4th House—This child sees Father as the strong security base in her life, even more than would be the normal perception. Father may also be perceived as the more nurturant parent.

Sun in the 5th House—This child needs Daddy to be a playmate and will gain great inspiration from the times he shares pleasurable activities with him. If this child is involved in anything special, Daddy needs to be there to give his stamp of approval or his absence will be sorely felt.

Sun in the 6th House—This child needs to see Father as a safety net, especially in times of trouble. He may need Daddy there on trips to the doctor's office, and when he is ill he will find Daddy's presence very comforting and necessary. The child sees him as the person who can fix anything.

Sun in the 7th House—This child sees Father as the pattern to emulate, especially within the context of community and social settings. Little girls with Sun in the 7th House ultimately look for a man who is just like Daddy to become their partner. Little boys learn about relationships from Daddy, and the way he treats Mommy will make a huge impression on this boy.

Sun in the 8th House—This child sees Father as all-knowing and ever-present, but may not trust him. She may feel that Daddy has tremendous power, and can have an underlying fear of what could happen if Dad found out about her transgressions. These children don't like to break the rules—at least not openly!

Sun in the 9th House—This child sees Father as the ultimate spiritual teacher. Dad's approach to spirituality and his basic philosophy will be strongly imprinted in the consciousness of this child.

Sun in the 10th House—This child will perceive Father as being very important. Dad's role within the family may command great respect, at least from this child, and he needs to experience positive leadership and guidance as a means of discovering his identity in the world.

Sun in the 11th House—This child is likely to be drawn to the idea of Father as a good friend, and may experience the greatest encouragement when Father gives his stamp of approval to the child's hopes and plans.

Sun in the 12th House—This child may overidealize Daddy, although the relationship can be close. If Dad's work or lifestyle makes him less available, then the child will be likely to create a "dream" Daddy in compensation.

Sun Aspects and Perceptual Viewpoints of Father

Aspects from the Sun to Jupiter, Saturn, and the outer planets will suggest particular alterations in the child's perceptions of Father. Of course, the sign qualities will reflect the characteristics involved in these perceptions.

Sun and Jupiter—With Sun-Jupiter contacts, Father is seen as the great provider, sometimes giving many material things to compensate for lost time. Father may be viewed as optimistic or enthusiastic. Sometimes, with dynamic aspects between the Sun and Jupiter, the child feels great expectations from Father. If this is the case, a child may continually "expand" the truth of her accomplishments in order to gain acceptance and praise from him.

Sun and Saturn—Sun-Saturn contacts are notorious in astrology for signifying a difficult relationship between Father and child. The restrictive, inhibiting, and separative influence of Saturn colliding with the dynamic willpower of the Sun does not generally make for compatibility and harmony!

The child may feel that Dad is just not there for him. Dad may be unavailable physically because of death, divorce, or a demanding job. Whatever the reasons, the child feels Dad's absence keenly. Consequently, the child may overreact by feeling that Dad is too critical or demanding. If the father is not present, the child may feel that he was abandoned. This can lead to intense feelings of guilt: "I was so bad that I made Daddy go away."

These types of feelings can lead to inhibited self-expression in the child, ultimately producing a less-balanced adult. This can result in a mistrust of all men and authority figures. These children need loving, patient, and accepting guidance from the father and other significant males in her life.

Sun and Uranus—Sun-Uranus contacts can produce perceptions of an exceptional father. They can also suggest that the child sees the father as too aloof and lead to feelings that Dad is unreliable or undependable. Dad may be rather eccentric. Sometimes, the child sees the father as a model so unique that he could never fit into it. He sees the father as beyond the limitations and structures of society, offering the child a different viewpoint of life from the norm. When given an opportunity to prove his own uniqueness to Father, the child needs positive reinforcement for his talents and abilities if he is to feel less isolated from society and confident in his individuality.

Sun and Neptune—Sun-Neptune contacts are especially difficult in childhood, since the evasive nature of Neptune makes it difficult for the child to see the "real" father. Dad can be overidealized; the real one may even have disappeared. I have often seen dynamic Sun-Neptune aspects in children whose fathers left when they were tiny. These aspects are also common in the charts of children of alcoholic or drug-dependent fathers, and this sense may also lead to the feeling projected by the child with the Sun in the 12th House.

Even the easier aspects are apt to create energies through which the child sees only an illusion of Father. This can produce problems for the child to see her Self since the role model is viewed through rose-colored glasses. The child may also expect the father to be rather saintly, and can be disappointed when she finds that this is not the case. These aspects call for honest relationships between parent and child.

Any child with Sun-Neptune contacts needs to have realistic and close contact with Father. While Father's sharing of his spirituality and creativity with this child can be positively reinforcing, he also needs to show his humanity to the child. Ultimately, it may also be helpful if this child has a male mentor who may be easier to identify with than Dad. This does not mean that another male needs to come into the child's life to usurp the role of the father, but that this could be a very positive compliment to the child's development.

This child needs a reason to have a male to idealize. That's quite a tall order for Father, but I know that many men are definitely up to the task!

Sun and Pluto—Sun-Pluto contacts are similar to Moon-Pluto perceptions. The child may perceive Dad as a superhero. You know the type: on the outside he looks like a regular guy, but inside he transforms into Superman. The child is likely to view Father as all-knowing, all-powerful and omniscient. This can block the child's ability to assert his or her own personal power. After all, how could he/she ever match up to something like that?

With Sun-Pluto contacts, especially the dynamic aspects, the child may perceive Father as ruthless. Sometimes these images are not even projected by the father to the child. They can come about through the child's fantasies and the impressions she has gleaned through observing life.

It is very easy for the child with Sun-Pluto contacts to sense that Dad does not want him to exist. Fathers of these children need to continually remind the child that he is genuinely loved and appreciated.

If, for any reason, this child experiences separation from Father, she may feel especially wounded. For a male child particularly, this can prove to be difficult, since it creates a basic lack of trust of himself. After all, a boy models himself after the father. If he has felt abandoned by Dad, then the resulting resentment can be especially deep. His tendency to project this resentment onto other men—teachers, stepfathers, or authorities—can reinforce his sense that he is somehow unworthy. For a female child, loss or separation from Father which is reinforced by the perceptions inherent in this aspect can create a wall of inhibition when it comes to men. She may feel that men cannot be trusted, period. Therefore, if your child's chart holds difficult aspects from Sun to Pluto, it is crucial that Father figures understand the potentially deep impact their actions and attitudes can have upon a child's perceptions.

Saturn and the Parents

Another concept children have about their father and mother can be analyzed by examining Saturn in the chart. Saturn brings structure, form, and solidity. Saturn energy feels judgmental and limiting much of the time, especially in childhood. Many children are anything but delighted at the prospect of being responsible—that's what adults are supposed to be, not kids!

The placement of Saturn not only symbolizes the parents, but also authority in society. The father is usually the one who teaches the child the lessons of authority, but Mother also is instrumental in this role. If Mother has given authoritarian roles in the family over to Father, then Saturn needs to be read as a Father influence in a child's life. The sign and house placement of Saturn in the chart, along with its aspects, indicates the child's responses to discipline, responsibility, and structure. In these areas, the influence of the father is likely to be very strong, although it can indicate parental influence in general. For the most part, what Saturn symbolizes is how the child needs to be stabilized and what she requires to feel safe and secure.

Saturn in the Signs and Perceptions of Parents

Saturn in Aries—Saturn in Aries indicates the need for self-respect. This child may see parents as courageous and independent, and will appreciate parents who give him a chance to make a few mistakes without undue restrictions.

Saturn in Taurus—Saturn in Taurus signifies a need for consistent, stable lessons and teachers. The child will need to see parents as providing reasonable, loving restraint, and she will appreciate sound material and environmental stability.

Saturn in Gemini—Saturn in Gemini signifies the need for open communication with parents, and this child will feel more secure if he knows that his voice is being heard. He may also need to learn tolerance for the diversity of life, and parents whose attitudes reflect this will provide a greater sense of security to this child.

Saturn in Cancer—Saturn in Cancer suggests a powerful need for family ties and this child is likely to think of the parental structure as representing an ideal. The child needs to see the parents as true providers of emotional security and a clear sense of home.

Saturn in Leo—Saturn in Leo indicates a need for parents who hold a respected place in the community or overall family structure. This child needs to see how parents handle their own individuality, since this child is striving to claim her own autonomy. It's important that the child not feel pushed into prominent roles in society unless there is adequate support, since she will take the burden of fame or recognition very seriously.

Saturn in Virgo—This child needs to learn the value of applied effort. He will look to the parents to determine the value of work and service.

Saturn in Libra—This child seeks confirmation of equality and the importance of consideration for others. If the child learns that she stands above others, the tendency to categorize people by class or social status will be difficult to undo.

Saturn in Scorpio—This child needs permission to explore life's deeper questions without feeling that this will undermine his acceptance by the family.

Saturn in Sagittarius—This child insists on finding Truth, and if parents teach stilted lessons about universal principles, then the child will be likely to lose respect for the parents once she discovers other ways of looking at life. Acceptance and integration of cultural diversity helps to stabilize this child.

Saturn in Capricorn—This child responds best to a parental situation which displays consistent and well-defined roles. This does not mean that traditional concepts are the only ones which will make sense to the child. As long as family structure and parental messages remain intact, the child will feel like he stands on solid ground.

Saturn in Aquarius—This child may grow up in situations that defy traditional concepts learning to accept and feel that this is normal and right for her. However, regardless of the family values the child learns, she will be likely to feel most stable when she has plenty of room to explore individuality within a framework of personal responsibility. She needs parents who are comfortable standing up for humanitarian ideals.

Saturn in Pisces—This child needs to experience strong support for spirituality and human compassion from parents. He will feel much more secure in a world in which there seems to be a natural flow, and may resent extreme restraints. Wishy-washy attitudes from parents is not the answer; more appropriately, this child needs to learn that it's safe to reach out to the world.

Saturn in the Houses

Saturn's position in the Houses in the astrological chart signifies the facets of a child's life which require consistency and in which the child will respond to well-defined structure.

Saturn in the 1st House—This placement cries out for confirmation of the Self and represents a child who needs to be positively acknowledged by parents and teachers.

Saturn in the 2nd House—This child needs to be taught the value of things, the importance of valuing oneself, and the right use of resources. This child needs to see the parents represent an attitude of respect toward resources and the environment.

Saturn in the 3rd House—This placement represents a need for some structure in the learning experience. Parental encouragement regarding education is absolutely necessary. If this child feels that the parents place little value on learning, she will be very likely to adopt that attitude.

Saturn in the 4th House—This placement symbolizes a child's need for a sound home environment and sense of family continuity. If his parents show respect for family, it will be especially confirming for him.

Saturn in the 5th House—This placement represents the need for confirmation that creativity is important to parents. The child may also need to learn how to apply herself to the task of developing her creativity.

Saturn in the 6th House—This placement during childhood can be seen as lessons learned about health. The child needs to learn from parents what part personal responsibility plays in maintaining health, but he also will be looking for ways to approach duties and everyday tasks. Being part of the family's household chores and maintenance is important. This does not mean, however, that this child is to become the housekeeper in the family!

Saturn in the 7th House—This placement represents the need to learn how to honor promises. She will look to the parents to see how they deal with commitments.

Saturn in the 8th House—This placement represents a need to learn how to handle inevitable changes. The child will seek confirmation from parents that change is safe, and he needs to learn how to identify his responsibilities to others. He also needs to know that his curiosity about sex, death, and other deep questions will be met with honest, straightforward information. If parents present inhibitions or fears in this area, then he may spend a lifetime overcoming them.

Saturn in the 9th House—This child seeks security through establishing a strong sense of moral values. If this child learns intolerance for other belief systems from the parents, she is likely to become dogmatic in her opinions.

Saturn in the 10th House—This placement generates a strong desire to be respected. The child needs to be able to respect parents, since if he is going to know how to handle being in positions of respect, he will require a positive model to follow. Excessive rules from parents will be inhibiting, but well-defined expectations can be helpful.

Saturn in the 11th House—This placement represents the need for goals and objectives, and if this child is taught the importance of clarifying her aims then she is already on a solid path to success. The importance of confirmation from friends and community is also part of this child's basic security framework.

Saturn in the 12th House—This placement indicates that a child needs to feel comfortable with life's intangible elements. He may have some trouble handling fears, but if parents show him how to determine when something is worth caution or if it's just a product of imagination, then trust of the inner self will grow.

Finally . . .

Although we cannot always determine how the parents view themselves in relationship to a child, we can gain insights into how the child is likely to view the parents. This slant can aid parents by helping them understand the child's personal needs in relation to their own. Parents also provide a psychological reflection, much like a mirror, for the child to see herself. Some children will have more difficulty than others in accepting these reflections. Children will also project certain qualities and attitudes upon the parents.

This process of mirroring can go back and forth indefinitely until the parents offer the child opportunities to see the reflection of his own true self. As conscious interaction occurs more and more between parents and children, more powerful transformational changes can be made in the child's life. By doing this, we can begin to bridge the gaps between parent and child.

Developmental
Crises in Childhood

One of the outstanding features of astrology is the study of cycles, which are analyzed using the basic natal chart as a blueprint. At certain times, which are indicated by the cyclical transits and progressions to the natal chart, different aspects of the Self will be emphasized. This process of basic human development is logical and easily mapped.

When a child does not meet the established criteria for normal development, parents often become concerned and look for the underlying causes of slowed or accelerated development. There are often interesting correlations in the chart for these alterations. Specific astrological cycles can be helpful to parents and counselors of children in understanding psychological, social, and creative development.

Saturn and Uranus Cycles

Saturn represents the process of time itself. At this point in human evolution, we conceive of time as linear involving the past, present, and future. This is a rather simple system, and is easy for the logical mind to grasp. But there are also other conceptualizations of time, one of which is cyclical. These time cycles mark periods of review, giving us opportunities for increased awareness of ourselves and our purpose. Saturn and Uranus cycles are two such markers which indicate significant periods of growth.

Uranus is the awakener, offering new possibilities by breaking up the structures Saturn so carefully builds. Uranus embodies the process of personal freedom, and its cycles mark this unfolding. When Uranus contacts personal planets or angles in a child's chart, there are frequently disruptive changes, or the child may be showing more rebellion or stronger needs for change.

The transits of Saturn to planets and sensitive points in the natal chart mark periods of increased responsibility, more focused awareness and, usually, increased limitations. Saturn's return cycle takes about twenty-eight years from the time of birth until it cycles, by transit, back to its natal position. The precise length of this cycle varies from person to person, and must be calculated. The maturational processes a person undergoes during this first Saturn return cycle are the basis for her responses throughout the rest of his or her life.

The first major contact of Saturn to its natal position occurs at age six or seven. Astrologically speaking, this is the time Saturn first squares its natal position by transit. Physically, the child is losing baby teeth and developing permanent teeth (Saturn rules teeth). In Western society, the child enters primary school full-time around age six or seven, and is no longer under the explicit tutelage of the parents. Society begins shaping the child more directly. He must respond more readily to discipline and structure or suffer the consequences. Peer pressure begins to develop.

Another factor of marked importance at this age deals with the psyche. This child feels responsible for everything. Parents may not realize the far-reaching impact these types of feelings have for the child. If the parents divorce at this time, the child may feel responsible for the divorce, responsible for the care of the custodial parent, and responsible for the resulting turmoil and unhappiness. She may never say a word, but may internalize these feelings of guilt. Whatever changes are occurring in the outside world may well be "my fault" or "my glory," depending upon the circumstances. Parents and teachers who are aware of this process can help the child by making it clear that she is not the cause.

The child can be given additional responsibilities during this first Saturn square, but also needs to receive rewards or recognition for fulfilling them. This aids in the child's approach to meeting new challenges and taking on new tasks. At this time, Uranus usually forms a semisextile aspect (thirty degrees) to its natal position, moving the child's awareness into a new concept of freedom. Parents can begin to teach the lessons of harmonizing freedom and responsibility at this age. Additionally, the child's perceptions of the world are increased during this cycle.

The second major contact Saturn makes to its natal position in the chart is the opposition at about age fourteen. This is the period of puberty: the hormones are awakening, the physical body is once again growing rapidly, and the child is becoming an adolescent. At this age, Uranus forms a sextile aspect (sixty degrees) to its natal position.

The task at age fourteen is to balance personal responsibility (Saturn) with freedom (Uranus). This is also a marked identity crisis as the child begins to see himself as markedly different from his parents. The confrontation indicated by the opposition often leads to open conflict with the parents and with authority in general.

It's important to remember that the opposition, depicted by a straight line, also represents a bridge, indicating that this is the time to close the gap between parent and child. Parents can focus on the special and unique aspects of the child emphasized by the Uranus sextile and allow her increased freedom as she accepts increased responsibility. But if the parental and/or societal structure is too rigid during this cycle, the child's rebellion is likely to be pronounced.

The last major contacts of Saturn and Uranus to the natal planets during childhood are at age twenty-one. At this age Saturn is once again making a square to its natal position; the child is leaving another nest. In Western society, this age marks the beginning of legal adulthood. Uranus is also contacting natal Uranus by square about age twenty-one, further prompting the need to be recognized as a fully-functional individual. Major life changes are prompting the young adult to become his own person, build his own foundations and test his wings. Many young adults complete their college educations about this time, and must begin to relate to the real world. The real world at age seven was still protective. At this age, it sometimes feels adversarial.

Saturn and Uranus can also make contacts to any other planet or sensitive position in the chart, and it is during these times that a child may feel especially tested in some way. Frequently when parents consult me about particular issues or problems with children there will be well-defined Saturn or Uranus cycles at work.

Moon Cycles

One of the first cycles I ask parents to be aware of is the natural cycle of the Moon. Small babies seem to be especially fretful and sensitive during the three days around a Full Moon. This is especially true of babies born at the time of the Full Moon (when the Sun and Moon are in opposition in the chart). The child's emotional sensitivity is often increased at this time. Although I have not completed a scientific study of this concept, I have talked with hundreds of mothers whose experiences have confirmed this. As the baby grows, this sensitivity seems to decrease somewhat.

Another period of increased sensitivity occurs each month when the Moon returns to the sign it was in at birth. This is especially noticeable during infancy. During these two to three days each month, the child may be very emotionally expressive and is likely to cling to Mother. A baby is more reluctant to let Mommy out of her sight at this time. To find this, determine your child's Moon sign, then look to an astrological calendar for the days when the Moon is in that sign.

Once a child is able to communicate, this can be a good period to have discussions with him about his feelings; he will be able to express feelings more freely during this time. If there have been hurts or disappointments, they may be easier to understand fully and examine during this cycle.

The days when the Moon is traveling through the child's 12th House by transit is another significant period. The 12th House transit of the Moon pulls the child more deeply inside herself. Small babies are sometimes more physically vulnerable at this time, and should be guarded against excessive exposure to any environmental extremes (e.g., very cold or hot temperatures). Young children may be somewhat apprehensive, and may have very vivid dreams during this two-to-four-day transiting period. Parents who are aware of this can more easily deal with the child's fears, which may well be imaginary. Teens may withdraw more readily during this time, and may seem hard to reach. It is important for parents to realize that their children may need this period for reflection and privacy.

Over the course of the cycle of the Moon, every planet is contacted and each house in the chart is sensitized. As planets are contacted by the Moon, their energies become more focused in relation to the child's needs. This is a very simple cycle to observe, even for a novice. A current astrological calendar or ephemeris will indicate the daily placement of the Moon by sign.

The Progressed Moon

The secondary progressed Moon is calculated using precise mathematical formulas. These calculations should be made by a professional astrologer or calculated using reliable astrological computer software in order to be fully useful. Once you have the progressions calculated, you can use the secondary progressed motion of the Moon to determine important periods of change in the child's life. The secondary progressed Moon (based upon the "day-for-a-year" formula) indicates when aspects in the child's life will be emotionally heightened. (See the bibliography for more information about secondary progressions.)

If the position of the Moon at birth falls in the early degrees of a sign (for example, two degrees Aries), it will be about two and one-half years before the progressed Moon changes signs (moving into Taurus). This transition would mark one of the first significant changes in the child's emotional security base. If the Moon at birth is in the middle degrees of a sign (e.g., fifteen degrees Aries), the Progressed Moon would move into the next sign (Taurus) at about the age of eighteen months.

What I have observed in these early changes of the Moon by sign is a different emotional focus in the child's life. Sometimes the family may move, forcing the child to adapt to new surroundings. At other times there may be changes in the family such as a divorce, new siblings, marriages, or Mom's return to work outside the home.

The external event is not as important as the fact that the child is experiencing a new emotional level of himself when the progressed Moon moves into the next sign. At first this new level of experience is likely to feel strange, confusing, or otherwise disconcerting. The child needs additional support and understanding from the parents at this time. If he does not receive added care and concern from the parents during these transitions, a gradual undermining of his emotional security is likely to result.

As the progressed Moon continues its motion through the chart, different aspects of the Self will be activated. It takes twenty-seven to twenty-nine years for the progressed Moon to travel completely around the chart and return to its natal position. This process of maturing is slow, deliberate, and repetitive. It allows the child to learn early that change can be made without negative results, and that it is the only way she can constantly develop her different levels of needs. As you may note, secondary progressed Moon timing is an interesting accompaniment to the cycles of Saturn through its return cycle. As the progressed Moon makes a series of aspects to the natal Moon, a gradual unfolding of the individual's emotional and spiritual evolution is symbolically pictured. The cycles of the progressed Moon indicate the strengthening of the individual's emotional sensitivity and awareness of her needs and feelings.

When the progressed Moon makes aspects to any planet in a child's natal chart, that period will indicate changes in the child's perceptions and can indicate when a child is ready for different experiences. This could, of course, entail a whole new book. Since progressed cycles fall into the intermediate to advanced levels of study, I will not go in depth here. However, if you are heading there in your study of astrology, keep in mind that the progressed Moon contacts are always indicators of change. The nature of the aspect will indicate if the change will be easier (flowing aspects) or more challenging (dynamic aspects) for the child.

While a child may not fully understand why certain things are happening, if parents and teachers can address the underlying issues, he will be able to handle the changes with greater grace and acceptance. By becoming aware of when these progressed Moon changes are occurring, the parents and guides of the child can be ready to help him over these new emotional hurdles.

Jupiter Transits

Jupiter typifies expansion, optimism, and increased confidence. It takes Jupiter about twelve years to return to its natal position by transit. During the course of Jupiter's transit through the chart, the child gains an expanded awareness of the planetary energies and environments (houses) indicated by the exact natal placement of Jupiter. Jupiter's contacts to its natal position represent decisive periods. For example, if Jupiter is transiting in conjunction to a child's Venus, she may feel more urgency in expressing artistry and will desire to enhance skills or may even attract more recognition for them.

During Jupiter's cycle toward its planetary return at age twelve, there is a significant growth process at work. The first square from Jupiter to its natal position occurs about age three. This phase coincides with open interaction with other children. A wider exploration of the personal environment ensues, with the child heading off toward new horizons at the first opportunity.

The young child is also challenged to expand the mind. He wants to hear stories, communicates more readily, and is generally a bit rebellious. This rebelliousness may be partially due to a need to go beyond established limits; Jupiter contacts often tempt us to push these limits until they break! If this cycle coincides with the progressed Moon changing signs, the rebellion may be even more marked. Tethering the child may not be the best answer, but it is understandable why many parents choose to find some reasonable method of restricting a child's movement during this active phase. It's probably best to provide support and guidance during these cycles, allowing the child the freedom necessary for exploration and growth within safe parameters or environments.

Jupiter opposes its natal position at about age six. This coincides with the tone of the first Saturn square and also Uranus will be transiting in semisextile to its natal position. Fortunately, Jupiter reinforces a need for expansion and stimulates an eagerness to learn. Saturn is there to keep some positive boundaries through its square to the natal position of Saturn. Uranus stimulates experimentation.

At this age the mind is ripe for more abstract forms of learning such as mathematics and reading. Prior to this, such abstract concepts might have infringed upon the creative, imaginative processes. The very young child (under age six) especially needs to keep the creative flow going, since she seems to respond to life in a right-brained manner.

The next Jupiter square occurs at age nine. Because Jupiter is about expansion, many children begin to look a little chunky at this age. Once again, the child is raring to get beyond his limitations. He may be a bit snippy and seem too big for his britches. This time can be most effectively used if the child can be given ample challenges for the mind and be urged to develop a willingness to give in exchange for what he wants to receive.

During the first Jupiter return at age twelve, the child becomes more confident. Mental functioning is strong, and her communicative abilities are nearing an adult level. At this age the child is usually a joy, and begins to seek companionship from the parents. This is a wonderful time to travel, study, and learn with a child.

The next periods of Jupiter squares, oppositions, and conjunctions occur at roughly ages fifteen (square), eighteen (opposition), twenty-one (square) and twenty-four (conjunction). Correlating the Jupiterian concept of needing to go beyond limits with the Saturn and Uranus cycles gives us a clearer understanding of the developmental stages of childhood.

Other Planetary Transits

By following the transits of planets to the child's natal chart, parents can more readily understand the frustrations and the growth confronting him. Transits from Mars are easily noticed in the early years of development, indicating times when physical energy and tempers run high.

When Mars makes dynamic contacts to the Sun, Moon, Mercury, or Mars, a child will seem more volatile. If Mars is making a dynamic aspect by transit to Saturn, the child may feel excessively frustrated and seem harder to handle. With dynamic transits from Mars to Uranus, the child may act boisterous and tend to take too many risks. Noting these particular times can help parents when planning special activities with a child. If you are planning a trip to Grandma's house during the time Mars is opposing the child's Uranus, Grandma may wonder how you ever deal with such a rambunctious child—and she'll probably be glad to see you leave!

I also encourage parents to watch Mars transits for times when children seem more accident-prone. Especially challenging are the dynamic aspects when Mars transits natal Mars, Saturn, Uranus, and Pluto. When Mars transits natal Mars, the child feels the need to test her strength and courage, and may instigate squabbles with friends or push herself too far too fast. Mars contacting Saturn may bring a clash with a resistant force, and the child should be guarded against exceeding her limitations.

Mars-Uranus periods mark times when the child is willing to take dangerous risks (e.g., jumping off the house to see how it feels to land). With dynamic aspects between Mars and Neptune, the child is often unaware of potential dangers. Mars-Pluto dynamic transits sometimes bring him into contact with circumstances beyond his control, which could result in accidents.

To understand these transits, use the key concepts of the planetary energies involved. During transits of Mercury, the child shows interest in communicating and sharing ideas. Venus transits are times when artistic energies can be more easily encouraged.

When working with a child's chart, remember that the expression of the energy is still maturing. The child's response to the energy will depend heavily upon the type of support received from the parents and family.

The Continuing Process of Human Development

Our development does not end with childhood. We continue to grow, change, meet challenges, and gain more self-awareness each day of our lives. But it is the delicate beginnings of childhood that will often determine how we will act and react as adults. The universe gives us many opportunities to find ourselves. If we fall short during one challenge, we will certainly have other opportunities!

In my career as a professional astrological counselor, I encourage my clients to focus upon the tasks before them and develop at whatever level their experience, confidence, and awareness allow. The beginnings of wholeness are rooted in our childhood. This sense of wholeness is a continual process, filled with joy, wisdom, and an ever-increasing understanding of ourselves and the universe in which we live. Self-acceptance increases and self-awareness becomes more refined.

As you grow and prosper in your life through interactions with the young children on our planet, seek to recover the true child within yourself. Heal that child by loving, teaching, and growing with your own children. Through love and understanding, we can become whole and powerful beings together.

Appendix

All of the natal chart information has been calculated using the Koch House system. My preference for this house system has been established for the last fifteen years, although some astrologers use other house systems (such as Placidus or Porphyry).

The data sources are listed according to the Lois Rodden rating scale. In as many cases as possible, I've used charts with data from official sources like a birth certificate (this is "AA" data). The least reliable data source I have used is printed biographical material (this is noted as "B" data). For all the charts used as examples within the text, the data is top-drawer "AA" data. Each chart in the appendix has its data and data source rating noted next to it for those of you who wish to do further calculations or have these as a good source for your own reference.

Muhammad Ali
January 17, 1942
Louisville, KY
6:35 P.M. CST
38N15   85W46
Tropical
Koch
"AA"

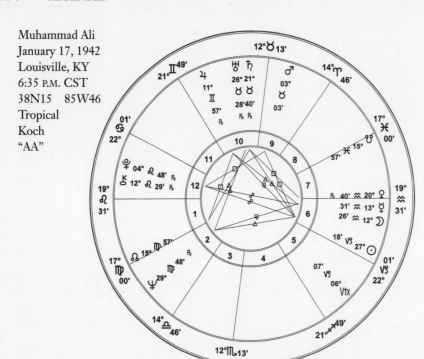

Arthur Ashe
July 10, 1943
Richmond, VA
12:55 P.M. EWT
37N33   77W28
Tropical
Koch
"AA"

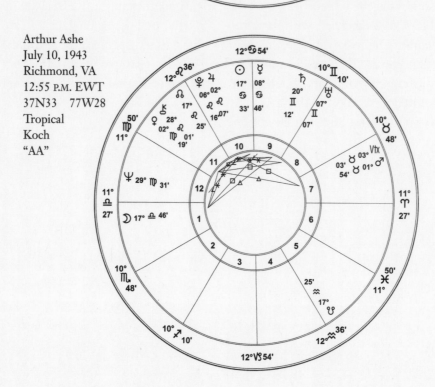

Dennis Rodman
May 13, 1961
Trenton, NJ
12:10 A.M. EDT
40N13   74W45
Tropical
Koch
"AA"

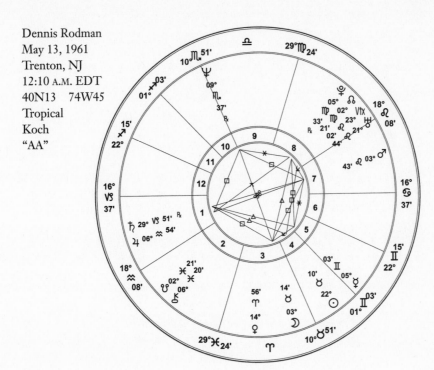

John Travolta
February 18, 1954
Englewood, NJ
2:53 P.M. EST
40N54   73W58
Tropical
Koch
"AA"

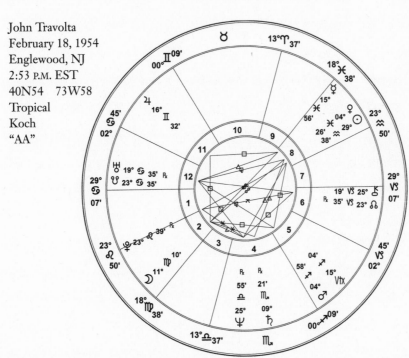

Robin Williams
July 21, 1951
Milwaukee, WI
1:34 P.M. EST
40N54   73W58
Tropical
Koch
"AA"

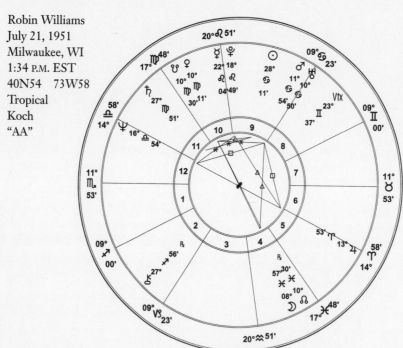

Venus Williams
June 17, 1980
Lynwood, CA
2:12 P.M. PDT
33N56   118W13
Tropical
Koch
"AA"

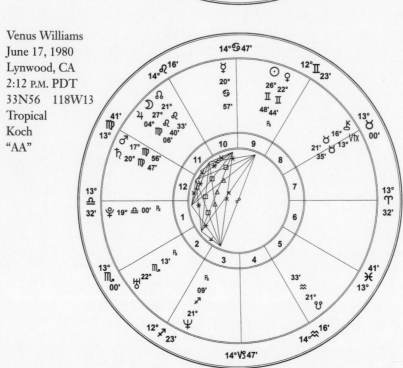

Julie Andrews
October 1, 1935
Walton-on-Thames,
  England
6:00 A.M. GMD
51N24   00W25
Tropical
Koch
"B"

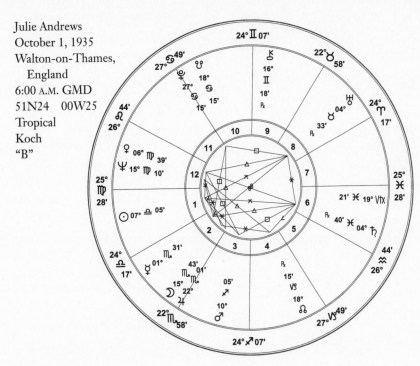

Drew Barrymore
February 22, 1975
Culver City, CA
11:51 A.M. PST
34N01   118W24
Tropical
Koch
"AA"

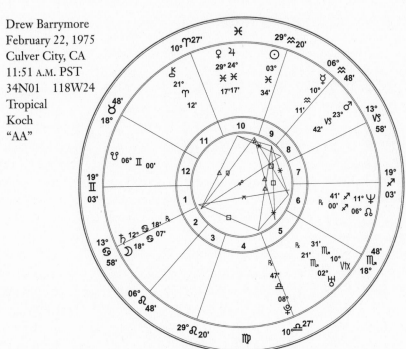

Albert Brooks
July 22, 1947
Los Angeles, CA
3:00 A.M. PST
34N03   118W15
Tropical
Koch
"AA"

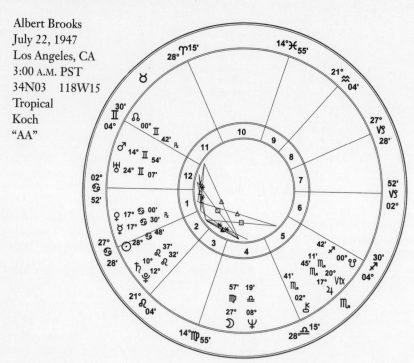

Sally Field
November 6, 1946
Pasadena, CA
4:23 A.M. PST
34N09   118W09
Tropical
Koch
"AA"

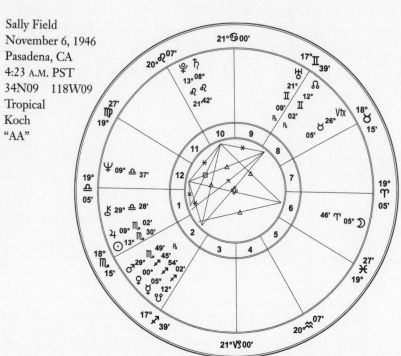

Jodie Foster
November 19, 1962
Los Angeles, CA
8:14 A.M. PST
34N03   118W15
Tropical
Koch
"AA"

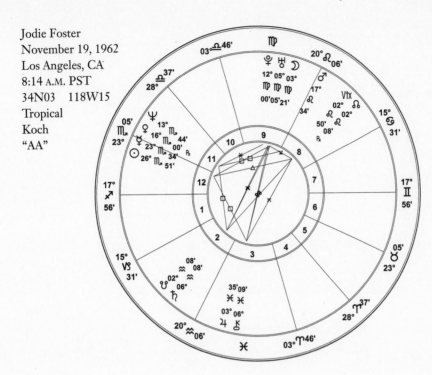

Michael J. Fox
June 9, 1961
Edmonton, Canada
12:15 A.M. MST
53N33   113W28
Tropical
Koch
"AA"

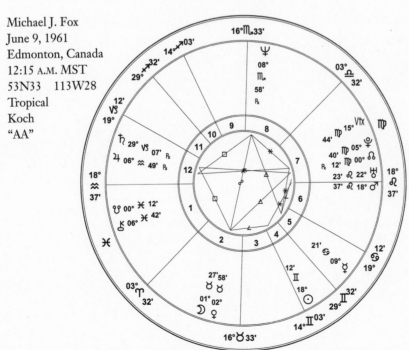

Bill Gates
October 28, 1955
Seattle, WA
10:00 P.M. PST
47N36   122W20
Tropical
Koch
"A"

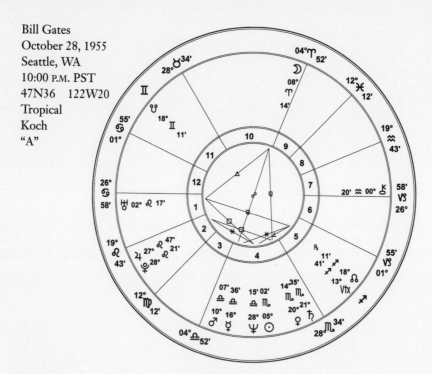

Steffi Graf
June 14, 1969
Mannheim, Germany
4:40 A.M. CET
49N29   08E29
Tropical
Koch
"AA"

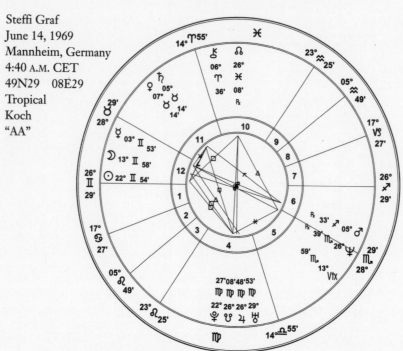

Dorothy Hamill
July 26, 1956
Chicago, IL
9:18 P.M. CDT
41N51   87W39
Tropical
Koch
"AA"

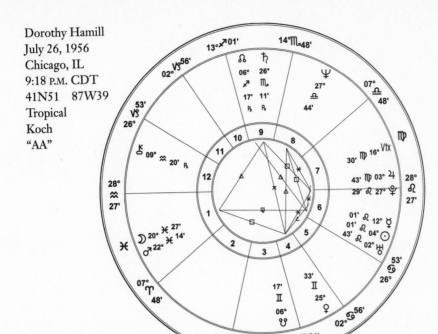

Scott Hamilton
August 28, 1958
Toledo, OH
9:00 A.M. EST
41N39   83W33
Tropical
Koch
"AA"

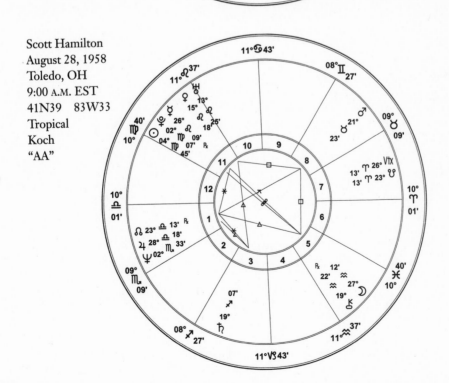

Goldie Hawn
November 21, 1945
Washington, DC
9:20 A.M. EST
38N54   77W02
Tropical
Koch
"AA"

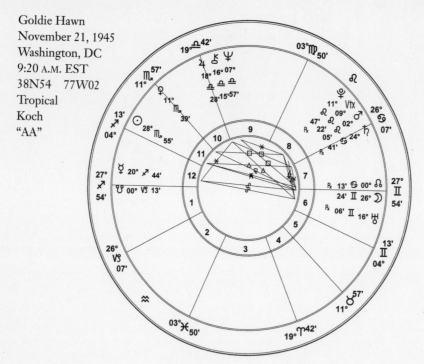

Florence Griffith Joyner
December 21, 1959
Los Angeles, CA
12:11 A.M. PST
34N03   118W15
Tropical
Koch
"AA"

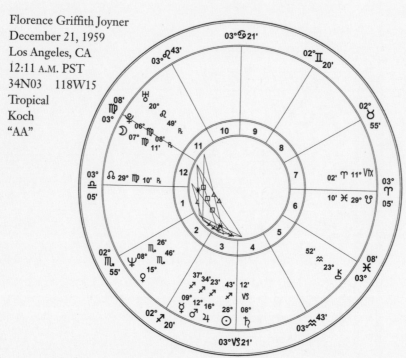

John Lennon
October 9, 1940
Liverpool, England
6:30 P.M. GMD
53N25   02W55
Tropical
Koch
"A"

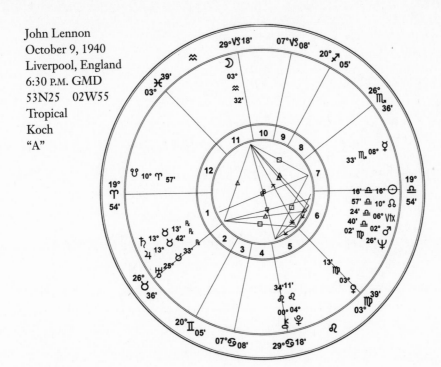

Alanis Morissette
June 1, 1974
Ottawa, Canada
9:39 A.M. EDT
45N25   75W42
Tropical
Koch
"AA"

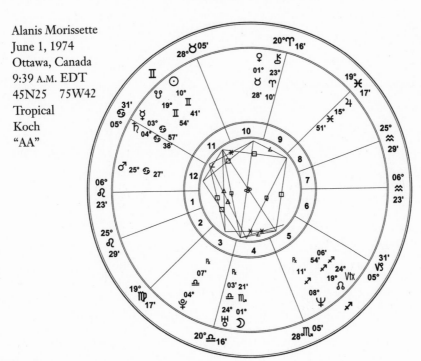

Tatum O'Neal
November 5, 1963
Los Angeles, CA
3:38 A.M. PST
34N03   118W15
Tropical
Koch
"AA"

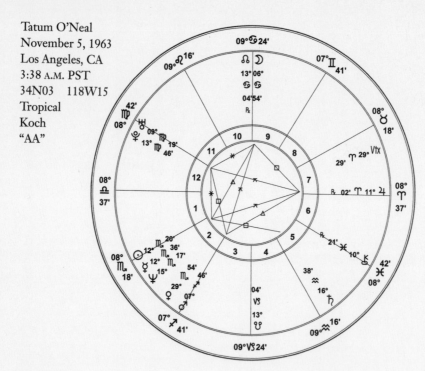

Elvis Presley
January 8, 1935
Tupelo, MS
4:35 A.M. CST
34N15   88W42
Tropical
Koch
"AA"

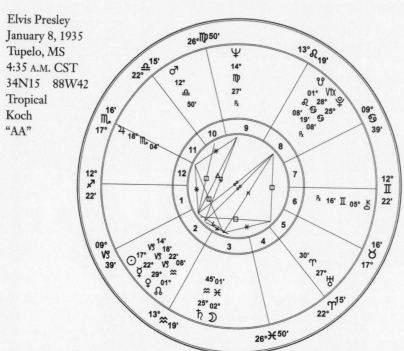

Christopher Parkening
December 14, 1947
Los Angeles, CA
3:26 A.M. PST
34N03   118W15
Tropical
Koch
"AA"

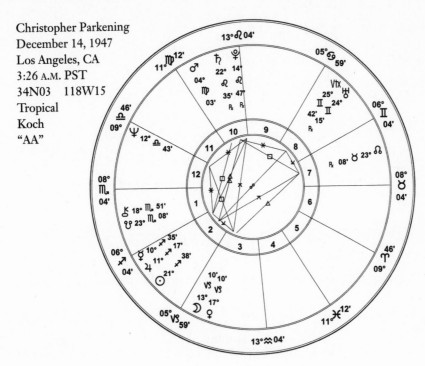

River Phoenix
August 23, 1970
Madras, OR
12:03 P.M. PDT
44N38   121W08
Tropical
Koch
"AA"

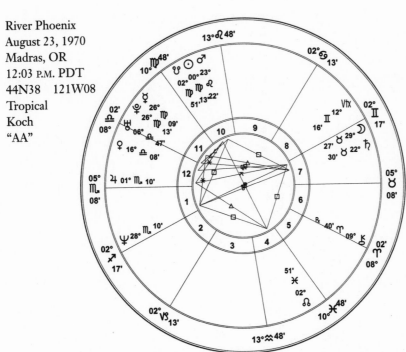

Helen Keller
June 27, 1880
Tuscumbia, AL
4:02 P.M. LMT
34N44   87W42
Tropical
Koch
"AA"

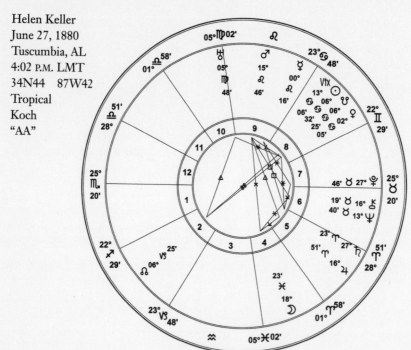

Bernadette Peters
February 28, 1948
Ozone Park, NY
10:45 P.M. EST
40N41   73W51
Tropical
Koch
"AA"

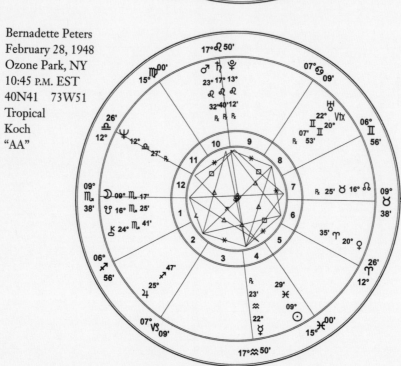

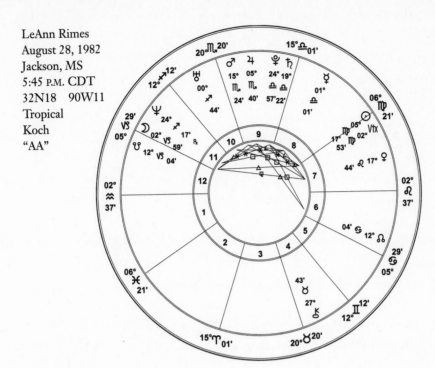

LeAnn Rimes
August 28, 1982
Jackson, MS
5:45 P.M. CDT
32N18 90W11
Tropical
Koch
"AA"

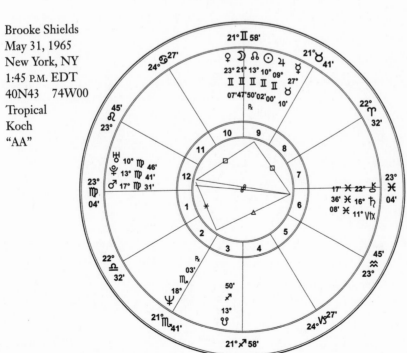

Brooke Shields
May 31, 1965
New York, NY
1:45 P.M. EDT
40N43 74W00
Tropical
Koch
"AA"

Elizabeth Taylor
February 27, 1932
London, England
2:00 A.M. GMT
51N30   00W10
Tropical
Koch
"A"

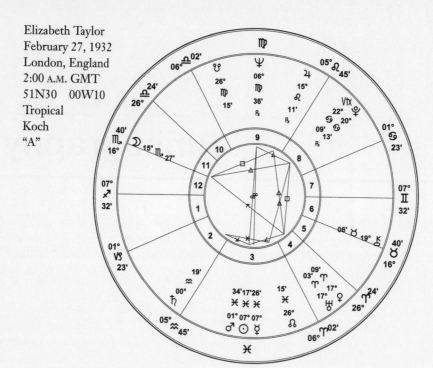

Eleanor Roosevelt
October 11, 1884
New York, NY
11:00 A.M. EST
40N43   74W00
Tropical
Koch
"AA"

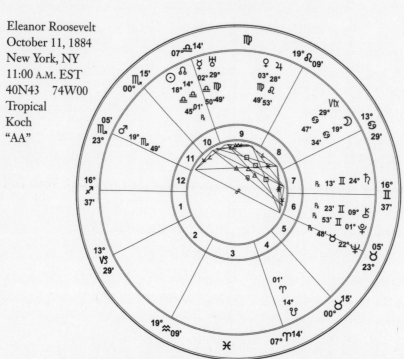

Bibliography

Abrams, Jeremiah. *Reclaiming the Inner Child*. Los Angeles: Jeremy P. Tarcher, Inc., 1990.

Arroyo, Stephen. *Astrology, Karma and Transformation*. Davis, CA: CRCS Publications, 1978.

———. *Astrology, Psychology and the Four Elements*. Davis, CA: CRCS Publications, 1975.

Cunningham, Donna. *An Astrological Guide to Self-Awareness*. Reno, NV: CRCS Publications, 1978.

Green, Jeff. *Pluto: The Evolutionary Journey of the Soul, Volume I*. St. Paul, MN: Llewellyn Publications, 1986.

Greene, Liz. *The Astrology of Fate*. York Beach, ME: Samuel Weiser, Inc., 1984.

———. *Saturn*. New York: Samuel Weiser, Inc., 1976.

Greene, Liz and Howard Sasportas. *The Development of the Personality*. York Beach, ME: Samuel Weiser, Inc., 1987.

Hand, Robert. *Horoscope Symbols*. Rockport, MA: Para Research, 1981.

———. *Planets in Youth*. Rockport, MA: Para Research, 1977.

Hickey, Isabel. *Astrology: A Cosmic Science*. Watertown, MA: Altieri Press, 1970.

Jung, C. G. *On the Nature of the Psyche*. Princeton, NJ: Princeton University Press, 1960.

Lewi, Grant. *Heaven Knows What*. St. Paul, MN: Llewellyn Publications, 1969.

Miller, Alice. *The Drama of the Gifted Child*. New York: Basic Books, Inc., 1981.

Oken, Alan. *As Above, So Below*. New York: Bantam Books, 1973.

Pearce, Joseph Chilton. *Magical Child*. New York: E. P. Dutton, 1977.

Rodden, Lois. *AstroDatabank*. Manchester, MA: AstroDatabank Company, 1999.

Rudhyar, Dane. *The Astrological Houses*. Garden City, NY: Doubleday and Company, 1972.

————. *Astrological Signs: The Pulse of Life*. Garden City, NY: Doubleday and Company, 1963.

Sakoian, Frances and Louis Acker. *Astrologer's Handbook*. New York: Harper and Row, 1976.

Sargent, Lois Haines. *How to Handle Your Human Relations*. Washington, DC: American Federation of Astrologers, 1970.

Teal, Celeste. *Predicting Events with Astrology*. St. Paul, MN: Llewellyn Publications, 1999.

Tyl, Noel. *The Horoscope as Identity*. St. Paul, MN: Llewellyn Publications, 1974.

Whitfield, Charles L. *Healing the Child Within*. Deerfield Beach, FL: Heath Communications, Inc., 1989.

Index

REACH FOR THE MOON

Llewellyn publishes hundreds of books on your favorite subjects!
To get these exciting books, including the ones on the following pages,
check your local bookstore or order them directly from Llewellyn.

Order by Phone
- Call toll-free within the U.S. and Canada, 1-800-THE MOON
- In Minnesota, call (651) 291-1970
- We accept VISA, MasterCard, and American Express

Order by Mail
- Send the full price of your order (MN residents add 7% sales tax) in U.S. funds, plus postage & handling to:

> **Llewellyn Worldwide**
> **P.O. Box 64383, Dept. 1-56718-649-1**
> **St. Paul, MN 55164–0383, U.S.A.**

Postage & Handling
(For the U.S., Canada, and Mexico)
- $4.00 for orders $15.00 and under
- $5.00 for orders over $15.00
- No charge for orders over $100.00

We ship UPS in the continental United States. We ship standard mail to P. O. boxes. Orders shipped to Alaska, Hawaii, the Virgin Islands, and Puerto Rico are sent first-class mail. Orders shipped to Canada and Mexico are sent surface mail.

International orders: Airmail—add freight equal to price of each book to the total price of order, plus $5.00 for each non-book item (audio tapes, etc.).

Surface mail—Add $1.00 per item.

Allow 2 weeks for delivery on all orders.
Postage and handling rates subject to change.

Discounts
We offer a 20% discount to group leaders or agents. You must order a minimum of 5 copies of the same book to get our special quantity price.

Free Catalog
Get a free copy of our color catalog, *New Worlds of Mind and Spirit*. Subscribe for just $10.00 in the United States and Canada ($30.00 overseas, airmail). Many bookstores carry *New Worlds*—ask for it!

Visit our website at www.llewellyn.com for more information.

For Readers of

Astrology & Your Child

only

FREE Natal Chart Offer

Thank you for purchasing *Astrology & Your Child*. There are a number of ways to construct a chart wheel. The easiest way, of course, is by computer, and that's why we are giving you this one-time offer of a free natal chart. This extremely accurate chart will provide you with a great deal of information about yourself. Once you receive a chart from us, *Astrology & Your Child* will provide everything you need to know to interpret your child's potential.

Also, by ordering your free chart, you will be enrolled in Llewellyn's Birthday Club! From now on, you can get any of Llewellyn's astrology reports for 25% off when you order within one month of your birthday! Just write "Birthday Club" on your order form or mention it when ordering by phone. As if that wasn't enough, we will mail you a FREE copy of *What Astrology Can Do for You*! Go for it!

Complete this form with your accurate birth data and mail it to us today. Enjoy your adventure in self-discovery through astrology!

Do not photocopy this form. Only this original will be accepted.

Please print

Full Name: _____

Mailing Address: _____

City, State, Zip: _____

Birth time:_____ a.m. p.m. (please circle)

Month:_____ Day:_____ Year:_____

Birthplace (city, county, state, country):

_____

_____

Check your birth certificate for the most accurate information.

Complete and mail this form to: Llewellyn Publications, Special Chart Offer, P.O. Box 64383, Dept. 1-56718-649-1, St. Paul, MN 55164.

Allow 4-6 weeks for delivery.